DOMESTIC FRONTIERS

KEY
• Town or city
■ Town or city that had an American mission station

RUSSIA

AUSTRIA–HUNGARY

Odessa•

Braila•
Tulcea■

ROMANIA

Belgrade•

SERBIA

Bucharest•

Vidin•
Lom■

Svishtov•
Rusé•

Silistra■

Black Sea

100 miles

BULGARIA

Shumen■
■Turnovo

Gabrovo• •Tryavna
Shipka•■•Kazanluk
■Stara Zagora

Sofia•

Samokov■

■Plovdiv

Veles•

MACEDONIA

Bansko•

THRACE

■Edirne

Istanbul■

Bosporus

Thessaloniki■

ALBANIA

Bitola■

TURKEY

Bursa•

OTTOMAN EMPIRE

•Izmir

Athens•

Argos•

GREECE

Mediterranean Sea

BLACKMER MAPS

The Ottoman Balkans, 1831–1908, showing major towns, American mission stations, and other locations mentioned in the text. blackmer maps.

DOMESTIC FRONTIERS

Gender, Reform, and American Interventions
in the
Ottoman Balkans and the Near East

BARBARA REEVES-ELLINGTON

UNIVERSITY OF MASSACHUSETTS PRESS
Amherst and Boston

ISBN 978-1-55849-981-2 (paper); 980-5 (hardcover)

Designed by Sally Nichols
Set in ArnhemFine and MrsEaves
Printed and bound by Thomson-Shore, Inc.

Library of Congress Cataloging-in-Publication Data

Reeves-Ellington, Barbara, 1949–
Domestic frontiers : gender, reform, and American interventions
in the Ottoman Balkans and the Near East / Barbara Reeves-Ellington.
pages cm
Includes bibliographical references and index.
ISBN 978-1-55849-981-2 (paper : alkaline paper) — ISBN 978-1-55849-980-5 (hardcover :
alkaline paper) 1. Women missionaries—Balkan Peninsula—History. 2. Women missionaries—
Turkey—History. 3. Missions, American—Balkan Peninsula—History. 4. Missions,
American—Turkey—History. 5. Protestant churches—Missions—History. 6. Sex role—Religious
aspects—Christianity—History. 7. Home—Political aspects—Balkan Peninsula—History.
8. Home—Political aspects—Turkey—History. 9. Balkan Peninsula—Race relations—History.
10. Turkey—Race relations—History. I. Title.
BV2410.R44 2013
266'.02373056—dc23
2012031200

British Library Cataloguing-in-Publication Data
A catalogue record for this book is available from the British Library.

TO THE
MEMORY OF MY DEAR MOTHER,
MARJORIE JOAN REEVES,
ALL-LOVING,
ALL-GIVING

Contents

Illustrations

Acknowledgments

The Balkans first impinged on my imagination when my brave mother took her children on vacation to Yugoslavia one summer long ago. As a young teenager I was immediately enthralled by the sights, sounds, and smells of an environment so very different from my own. The fascination stayed with me as I explored southeast European regional studies at the University of London School of Slavonic and East European Studies and spent a summer semester at the University of Sofia, Bulgaria. Somewhat belatedly, I thank the late Vivian de Sola Pinto, Muriel Heppell, and Leslie Collins for introducing me to Bulgarian language and literature, medieval Balkan history, and Ottoman history, respectively, and my old friend and colleague Gordon Burnett for the shared years of study of things Bulgarian. For care and sustenance in Sofia, my heartfelt thanks to the dearly departed Stanka Petkova; and for a life-time of help navigating the contours of Bulgarian culture, a deep debt of gratitude to my good friend Krustina Petkova.

Only much later at the State University of New York Binghamton did I connect Balkan history and U.S. history. In Kathryn Kish Sklar's core colloquium on U.S. women's history, I was reading Jane Hunter's *The Gospel of Gentility*, about the lives and work of American women missionaries in China, when an idle question crossed my mind: *I wonder if there were missionaries in the Balkans?* Two research seminars with Kitty Sklar and Tom Dublin persuaded me that I had a topic. A course with the late Donald Quataert and conversations with Rifa'at Abou-El-Haj brought me new perspectives on the Ottoman Balkans. I thank Kitty and Tom for their enduring faith in me, and my good friend and colleague Connie Shemo for the shared years of study of women missionaries.

Funding for the research for this book was provided by the Fulbright Program, the Hilandar Research Library at the Ohio State University, and the Committee on Teaching and Faculty Development at Siena College. For facilitating my research year in Bulgaria, where I had the good fortune to work with Nadya Danova of the Institute of Balkan Studies, Bulgarian Academy of Sciences, I thank the Bulgarian Fulbright Commission, particularly Julia Stefanova and Ekaterina-Maria Radoslavova.

Funding for the valuable time to write was provided by reassigned time awards and a generous sabbatical year from Siena. I have the great fortune to work in a wonderfully collegial department within the greater Siena community. For their support and encouragement, I thank Ralph Blasting, dean of the School of Liberal Arts, Jim Harrison, chair of the History Department, and all my colleagues in the department, Karl Barbir, Fr. Daniel Dwyer, O.F.M., and Nii Nartey, but, in particular, the members of the department writing group, Tim Cooper, Jennifer Dorsey, Bruce Eelman, Karen Mahar, Wendy Pojmann, and Scott Taylor, and the gender research group, particularly Vera Eccarius-Kelly, Margaret Hannay, and Laurie Naranch.

Many fellow participants in conferences, seminars, and workshops around the world have contributed to engaging conversations over the years. For a stimulating workshop on U.S.–East European cultural exchanges at the East-West American Studies Conference in May 2002 at the Johann Wolfgang Goethe–Universität in Frankfurt, I thank organizers Christa Buschendorf and Astrid Franke (who also generously provided the funding to attend). For inspiring discussions on the broader significance of the concept of conversion, I thank my fellow participants in the seminar "Converting Cultures: Religion, Ideology, and Transformations of Modernity," organized by Kevin Reinhart and Dennis Washburn at the Leslie Humanities Center, Dartmouth College, in the fall of 2002, particularly Ertan Aydın, Marc David Baer, Laura Jenkins, and Nancy Stalker. My very warm thanks go to all the participants in the "Competing Kingdoms: Women, Mission, Nation, and American Empire" conference at the University of Oxford in April 2006; I learned so much from all of you. In November 2008, I first sketched out a paper on the Constantinople Home at the Teaching American History workshop organized by

Thomas Dublin at the State University of New York, and I am indebted to the participants, particularly Phyllis Amenda, for their comments.

Several friends and colleagues have offered valuable critiques and shared ideas over the years, including Nikolay Aretov, Brian Bademan, Pepka Boyadzhieva, Galya Chakurova, Nadya Danova, Krassimira Daskalova, Mehmet Ali Doğan, Carolyn Goffman, Susan Gray, Noriko Ishii, Eliza Kent, Rui Kohiyama, Tanya Kotzeva, Christine Lindner, Melanie McAlister, Keta Mircheva, Laura Murphy, Nadir Özbek, Dana Robert, Timothy Roberts, Rhonda Semple, Alexander Shurbanov, Daniela Shurbanova, Kornelia Slavova, Wendy Urban-Mead, and Julietta Velichkova-Borin.

A special word of thanks goes to the people who perform the impossible on a daily basis in archives and libraries. My first debt of gratitude is to the librarians in the Standish Library at Siena College, particularly Patricia Markley in the interlibrary loan office. I spent a delightful month at the Hilandar Research Library at the Ohio State University thanks to Predrag Matejic, M. A. (Pasha) Johnson, Helene Senecal, and their colleagues. At the United Methodist Church Archives, Madison, New Jersey, Mark Shenise is always helpful. Patricia Albright at Mount Holyoke College has welcomed me several times. The offices of Robert College of Istanbul in New York offered a very comfortable environment in which to peruse the Records of the American College for Girls, and for a very pleasant week there I thank Lynne Prevot. The staff of the Houghton Library at Harvard University and at the National Archives in Britain have been unfailingly generous. I also want to recognize Martha Smalley at the Yale Divinity School Library and Sophie Papageorgiou at the Gennadius Library in Athens.

In Sofia, I owe a great debt of gratitude to Maria Lovdjieva, former curator of the Slaveykov Museum and Archive, and also to Liliana Yanakeva, Violeta Brandiyska, and Anya Dzheneva at the Bulgarian Historical Archive, Saints Cyril and Metodi National Library. Special thanks go to Atanas Stamatov at the University of Mining and Geology, who introduced me to the collections and procedures at the National Library in Sofia. In Plovdiv, I wish to acknowledge the assistance of Veneta Ganeva, Special Collections, Ivan Vazov National Library, and Anna Ilieva, Khristo G. Danov Museum. In Stara Zagora, I thank Neycho Kunev, Svetla Dimitrova, and Sofia Ivanova of the Historical Museum; Kalinka Atanasova and Radoslav Bonev of the State

Archive; Snezhana Marinova at the Zakhariy Knyazheski Library; and Slava Draganova at the Rodina Library.

At the University of Massachusetts Press, I have had the good fortune to work with the wise Clark Dougan, my acquisitions editor, the ever resourceful copyeditor Mary Bellino, managing editor Carol Betsch, designer Sally Nichols, and the strong editorial and publishing teams that brought this book to the light of day. My gratitude to all of them. It was also a pleasure to work once again with indexer Jan Williams. My special thanks to the now not-so-anonymous readers of my manuscript, Mary Renda and Heather Sharkey, for their generous and perceptive reviews.

Material from the Papers of the American Board of Commissioners for Foreign Missions appears by permission of Wider Church Ministries of the United Church of Christ. Material from American College for Girls Records appears by permission of the Trustees of Robert College of Istanbul, New York. Material from the personal papers of alumnae of Mount Holyoke Female Seminary appears by permission of Mount Holyoke College Archives and Special Collections. Material from the Clarke Family Papers appears by permission of the Hilandar Research Library, Ohio State University. Material from the Methodist Episcopal Church Missionary Society appears courtesy of the United Methodist Church Archives.

Chapter 3 includes in revised form and with new interpretations some material that appeared in "Embracing Domesticity: Women, Mission, and Nation Building in Ottoman Europe, 1832–1872," in *Competing Kingdoms: Women, Mission, Nation, and the American Protestant Empire, 1812–1960,* published by Duke University Press.

A Note on Terminology

In an area of the world that embraced several different religious, cultural, and linguistic groups, the naming of geographical areas is complex. Different groups used different names for the same places, and their names for geographical areas did not necessarily correspond with their names for the political entities that incorporated those areas. Political transformations in the post-Ottoman world added to the complexity. Territorial losses and subsequent name changes challenged national identities and could obliterate history. The American Board of Commissioners for Foreign Missions used names for the places where they lived and worked that differed from Ottoman and Bulgarian names for those places. They also altered the names of their missions as a consequence of missionary reorganizations and political changes. I explain here my choice of names. In all cases, my aim is simplicity and consistency.

In the nineteenth century, Americans followed British usage and used the term "Near East" to describe the geographical area that stretched from the Adriatic to the eastern Mediterranean. The American Board referred to the general area covered by its missions in this region as their Near East Mission. Again following British usage, Americans referred to the political entity that was the Ottoman Empire as Turkey. They referred to the region west of the Bosporus as European Turkey, or Turkey in Europe, and to the region east of the Bosporus as Asiatic Turkey, or Turkey in Asia. To complicate matters, they divided their Near East Mission into separate organizations: the Western, Central, and Eastern Turkey Missions. The Western Turkey Mission incorporated Istanbul, the cities of Bursa and Izmir, and the European provinces of the Ottoman Empire. The missionaries subsequently split their Western

Turkey Mission; the European provinces of the Ottoman Empire became the European Turkey Mission in 1871 and, later, the Balkan Mission. I use the term "Near East" when speaking about the region as a whole and follow the changes the missionaries imposed on their naming of their missions.

The Ottomans referred to their European provinces as Rumeli (the name comes from *Rum millet,* meaning the community of the Romans, actually the Byzantine Greek Christians). The area represented by Rumeli shrank over the nineteenth century as a consequence of territorial losses and administrative restructuring. As a result, it did not always correspond to the area designated by missionaries as European Turkey. By the 1850s, the urban educated Bulgarian Orthodox Christians who lived there called it Bulgaria. Rumeli and European Turkey covered areas that are now part of Turkey, Bulgaria, Greece, Serbia, Macedonia, and Albania, states that are commonly referred to collectively as the Balkans. So as not to favor any contemporary political configurations or cause confusion, I refer to the area as the Ottoman Balkans. "The Balkans" is a term that modern readers can recognize as a geographic location; the designation "Ottoman" indicates the nineteenth-century context.

Missionaries initially referred to the cities where they established their missions by the names that had existed since ancient Greek and Roman times—for example, Constantinople, Adrianopolis, Philippopolis—thereby obliterating Ottoman and medieval Bulgarian history. Ottomans and Bulgarians had their own names for these places. I have used current (2012) designations for the names of all cities; for example, Istanbul (not Constantinople or Tsarigrad), Izmir (not Smyrna), Edirne (not Adrianopolis or Odrin), Plovdiv (not Philippopolis or Filibe), Stara Zagora (not Eski Zağra or Zheleznik), Rusé (not Ruschuk). When citing sources, I retained the names used by contemporaries.

I have transliterated all personal names unless sources provide their owners' preferred renditions in English. (This has led to some inconsistency.) I have transliterated the Cyrillic alphabet according to the conventions of the United States Board on Geographic Names for Russian, with modifications for differences in Bulgarian and without diacritics. Ottoman Turkish terms and names are given in their modern Turkish spelling. Unless otherwise stated, I am responsible for all translations. As I do not read Ottoman Turkish, I have used published or archival translations of Ottoman documents in English, French, and Bulgarian.

DOMESTIC FRONTIERS

The Home as the Focus of Women's Civilizing Mission

In October 1876, officers of the Boston-based Woman's Board of Missions of the Congregational Church celebrated the completion of the Constantinople Home, their ambitious new center for women missionaries in Istanbul.[1] The officers deemed the city an important location for their work; it was, in their view, "second to none in the foreign field."[2] Perched along the cliffs above the Bosporus, the Home was prominently sited in Üsküdar, a quarter in the Ottoman capital. Its location was no accident. As Nathaniel G. Clark, foreign secretary of the American Board of Commissioners for Foreign Missions, remarked in a speech he gave in London, American women were dedicated to the social and spiritual uplift of women throughout the Ottoman Empire. The Constantinople Home was erected in "the very center of Mohammedan power," where it "looked down on the mosque of St. Sophia, and on the palaces and seraglios of sultans."[3] Clark seemed to suggest that the Home signified a superior culture to the symbols of Islamic religious and temporal power. Officers of the Woman's Board and the American Board, with which they were affiliated, expected the Home to be a major site for the religious and cultural conversion of women to an American brand of Protestantism. Their new building was a potent symbol of the expansive nature of the American Christian home, with American Christian women at its helm.

The Constantinople Home represented a powerful projection of American Protestant ideas about women and the broader civilizing mission of the United States in the nineteenth century. Descriptions of the Home resounded with the entwined discourses of American domesticity and Protestant superiority, which celebrated female moral authority at home and in society, denigrated non-Protestant religions, framed American perceptions of other cultures, and legitimized women's contributions to American cultural expansion.[4] The Home testified to the conviction of American evangelical Protestants, women and men, that their mission to transform the religious and cultural life of the Ottoman Empire through its women would prevail.

Domestic Frontiers tells a story of that mission. The book reconstructs a series of encounters in Istanbul and towns across the Ottoman Balkans to show how ideas about women, religion, and home traversed national boundaries from 1831, when American Board missionaries first arrived in Istanbul, to 1908, when some women missionaries in Istanbul split with the Woman's Board of Missions, who yielded their institution in the city to an independent board of trustees. It highlights the ways in which Protestant missionaries exported American domestic ideals, shows how those ideals were negotiated by missionaries and individuals in the communities in which they worked, and examines the changes that took place in the mission, the local environment, and the United States as these ideals were variously interpreted.

The language of domesticity was an enduring yet extremely flexible device for women and men within the missionary enterprise who used it to serve their own purposes. American Board policy makers first employed it to justify sending women abroad as the wives of missionaries. Woman's Board officers used it almost defensively as they walked a fine line between observing the necessary deference to the American Board and branching out along a separate path to manage their own work for women around the world. Male missionaries adopted it in an effort to maintain their own authority, insist on women's subservience, and justify the need to promote female education as a mission strategy for the conversion of souls. Missionary wives retooled it to accept their domestic duties, extend their work outside the home, and fulfill their own visions of home and reform. Several prominent single women missionaries drew on it to question male assumptions about their ambitions and behavior and challenge the patriarchal mission culture that male missionaries worked hard to foster. Strains of domestic discourse echoed constantly within the mission and were refracted in ways most missionaries least expected.

Missionaries also successfully promoted American domestic ideals across the Ottoman Empire, but women and men in Ottoman communities redeployed them in surprising ways. For Orthodox Christians within the empire, the message of American domesticity held considerable appeal precisely because it bundled ideas about religion, race, and gender relations into a project of modern nation building at a time of massive social and political upheaval in Ottoman domains. Urban, educated Orthodox Christians adopted the language of domesticity to bolster an emergent Orthodox Christian nationalism that countered Protestant influences and thwarted Ottoman efforts to shape a universal Ottoman citizenship.

The Ottoman capital of Istanbul and its European hinterland in the Balkans offer a unique location in which to explore the expansion of American evangelical culture for four reasons. First, religion was a strong pillar of politics and identity in New England and the Ottoman Empire, and Christian-Muslim relations resonated with Americans in the nineteenth century as they do in the twenty-first. Istanbul was built on the Byzantine capital of Constantinople, the center of the Eastern Christian world. Missionaries portrayed these European domains as an important part of the lands of the Bible and ancient Greece and Rome, the cradles of European civilization and Christianity, where St. Paul himself had preached. American missionaries imagined that they were following in the footsteps of St. Paul to bring the promises of modern forms of Christianity, civilization, and family life to Eastern Orthodox Christians who, in their view, had become degenerate while in contact with Islam. Precisely because American missionaries sought to convert people who were already Christians, their project was cultural. Conversion to Protestantism would be accomplished through educational programs that offered social and material advantages as well as spiritual transformation. The missionaries believed that a revitalized Christian church in the East would present a strong challenge to the primacy of Islam in the region.

My research opens up a new window on American encounters in the Ottoman world and reveals the intricacies of Protestant-Orthodox relations in a region where American missionaries dominated the missionary enterprise in the nineteenth century.

Second, the Balkans was a veritable laboratory of reform when American missionaries arrived there in the mid-nineteenth century. The Ottoman government was beset by internal disruptions and external interference by the European imperial powers. In an effort to modernize the empire and safeguard it against internal sectarian impulses and foreign intervention, in 1839 Ottoman statesmen inaugurated an extensive reform program, known as the Tanzimat, to restructure the empire socially, politically, and administratively.[5] The population in the Balkans became a focus of Ottoman experiments. With its emphasis on progress, improvement, and civilization, the language of the Tanzimat created a favorable environment for the reception of American messages of reform, particularly domestic reform. In the absence of imperial and community reforms that dealt with the status of women, missionaries exploited an opportunity opened up by Ottoman omission and Orthodox neglect to target women through educational programs specifically addressed to them. This setting provides a fruitful environment in which to examine gender relations, domestic ideals, and the interplay of the various reform impulses that came from the Ottoman state and the missionary enterprise.

Third, in the nineteenth century Ottoman rule was associated with expressions of increasing nationalism, including armed rebellion, among the empire's Christian populations.[6] By midcentury, missionaries had turned their attention to ethnic Bulgarians, who remained a prominent group of Orthodox Christians in the Ottoman Balkans. In urban locations, their identity as part of a larger group of Orthodox Christians slowly disintegrated under the pressure of nationalism. The efforts of missionaries to secure results for their ventures by supporting peaceful Bulgarian nation-building movements complicate the notion of cultural imperialism that provides the interpretive framework for so many missionary studies. By encouraging Bulgarians in their quests for educational and ecclesiastical reform, missionaries contributed to social and religious fragmentation within the Ottoman Empire.[7] As a region of great diversity of religious, cultural, and linguistic communities situated at a geostrategic crossroads between Europe and Asia, the area presents an opportunity to add complexity to discussions of identity, race, and the missionary enterprise that offer new insights on the consequences of American interventions in nation-building projects.

Finally, in the Ottoman Empire American cultural expansion proceeded initially under the protection of British imperial power. Because of its geopolitical and strategic significance, the Ottoman Empire was the site of serious rivalries among the European imperial powers, chiefly Russia, France, Austro-Hungary, and Britain. Perceiving the Ottoman Empire as weak, the European empires jockeyed for influence, seeking to extend their power in the region at Ottoman expense and, ultimately, to partition it among themselves without waging war, a situation they referred to as "the eastern question." Each sought to intervene in Ottoman affairs by claiming to represent its Christian communities—Orthodox, Catholic, or Protestant. In this context, where religion became a site of confrontation, American missionaries were content to be identified with British imperial power, comfortable in the knowledge that they operated within a Pax Britannica.[8] This circumstance presents an opportunity to begin to explore the inroads of American influence even in the absence of American state power in Ottoman domains.

The idea of domestic frontiers offers an analytical framework for exploring these varied aspects of missionary encounters in the Ottoman Balkans. In this analysis, the term *frontier* incorporates the ideas of place, process, and possibilities. How far could the language of domesticity travel geographically and still retain the central features of its New England Protestant origins? How much could it change in the hands of missionaries who traveled to the Ottoman Empire and in the hands of the men and women they encountered there? The term *frontier* also provides a framework to explore the ways in which all parties engaged in cross-cultural encounters met, exchanged views, and sparked change.[9] Rather than contributing to an ongoing debate that emphasizes the dichotomous dimensions of missionary activities by pondering whether missionaries were imperialists or humanitarians, the framework makes possible a more contextualized narrative of missionary encounters by emphasizing players in the local environment.

The scholarly debate that began in the 1970s about whether or not missionaries were cultural imperialists continues to evolve.[10] It has shifted from an understanding of missionary encounters as a unidirectional exercise of power to the detriment of its target audience (a view influenced by focused readings of the missionary archive within national historiographical frameworks) to a more nuanced understanding of American encounters as interactions that created opportunities for new social configurations (a view shaped by readings in foreign-language archives alongside the missionary archive and in global context).[11] This is not to deny that missionaries believed in the superiority of their culture and aggressively pursued activities that were intended to transform other cultures. It is, rather, to look more carefully at the processes through which they projected American power across the globe, how that power was negotiated by individuals and communities caught up in the encounters, what changes occurred in the local environment, and how the changes reverberated in the United States.

A transnational approach to the analysis of religion at the intersection of women's history and American foreign relations has contributed greatly to the study of American cultural expansion.[12] Yet the promise of the transnational turn at this particular intersection remains unfulfilled. Historians have traced the spread of American cultural and religious ideals abroad, but they have barely begun to exploit the sources that could elaborate the redeployment of those ideals outside American networks. In an attempt to bring the metropole and the periphery into one analytical field on a broader global stage, scholars have struggled to strike a balance so as not to privilege the missionary archive at the cost of local perspectives.[13]

Previous emphases on the American side of missionary stories is in large part due to the sheer mass of material in missionary archives, the occasional sparseness of non-U.S. sources, and the concomitant difficulty of gaining access to non-U.S. archives, for political, financial, or linguistic reasons. Scholars who take up the challenge of the new transnational history are examining ways in which a focus on the local environment and local sources can shed greater contextual light on the activities and textual productions of American missionaries and the people among whom they worked. It is not enough to paint the local environment simply as a backdrop to the missionary enterprise. Historians must examine local perspectives that reveal intricate interchanges in the host environment.[14] This book seeks to do just that.

The archives of the American Board are crucial to the story I tell here, but they contain great silences. The voices of women are rare before the formation of the Woman's Board in 1869, and the voices of converts and other actors are almost entirely absent. A focus on local players in Ottoman communities shows that cultural conflict could be creative and expands understandings of what can constitute archives for the study of missionary history.[15]

The activities of American missionaries in the Ottoman Empire are a neglected area of American foreign relations; untapped reservoirs of evidence illuminate the wide-ranging activities of missionaries, the vehicles they used to circulate American ideals in local communities, and the ways in which local actors parlayed those ideals. My sources—Ottoman, Bulgarian, Russian, French, and English—tell a compelling tale of American intervention in the affairs of the Ottoman state and illuminate the complex responses of Ottoman subjects to American intrusions into their everyday lives. This multilingual source base encompasses a rich array of state documents, diplomatic papers, municipal reports, newspaper accounts, memoirs, and personal correspondence that reflect the extensive changes in the local environment. By employing a transnational approach informed by multiple archival resources, I hope to contribute to the scholarly movements to internationalize U.S. history and broaden the debate about the substance, extent, and impact of the American Protestant empire.

Linguistic complexities mean that studies of American missionaries in the Ottoman Empire tend to deal with one particular group of Eastern Christians. For example, in recent books that illuminate the "foundational encounters" of missionaries in the Near and Middle East, Ussama Makdisi, Heather Sharkey, and Hans-Lukas Kieser studied Maronite, Coptic, and Armenian Orthodox Christians, respectively.[16] My account examines encounters of missionaries with ethnic Bulgarian Orthodox Christians in the Balkans and the towns of western Anatolia. For them, Istanbul was not merely the administrative center of the empire. The city contained the largest population of Bulgarians of any town in the empire and was the center of Bulgarian cultural and political life.[17]

Bringing Istanbul and its European hinterland into a single analytical frame, I provide a perspective on the missionary enterprise from the western reaches of the Ottoman Empire. This study broadens the scholarship on American missionaries in the Near East and highlights a significant area of the American missionary map that has long been neglected by historians of American empire. By using gender as a category of analysis, I have identified the language of American domesticity as a major nineteenth-century export to this part of the world. My study reveals the ways in which actors in the local environment adapted it to meet their own needs and demonstrates the tenacity of local cultures to deflect change that they could not use to their advantage.

Established in 1810, the American Board was the first American missionary society to organize the sending of ordained ministers and their wives abroad.[18] The missionaries were part of a larger Anglo-American Protestant endeavor to evangelize the unconverted at home and abroad. As Rufus Anderson, the influential, long-serving foreign secretary of the American Board, remarked, quoting Matthew 13:38, "the field is the world."[19] Ostensibly interdenominational, the board drew its support mostly from Congregationalists and Presbyterians in New England and New York who believed that they occupied an exceptional place in history as a people covenanted with God to save "the heathen." Shaped by a strong regional culture, American Board missionaries grafted their New England values onto a national American identity that they then embraced to sponsor a project of global dimensions.

American Board missionaries first arrived in the Ottoman Empire in 1819 on their way to Jerusalem, and they began to settle in Istanbul in 1831. The Ottoman capital became the headquarters of their Near East Mission in 1854, and their expansion into the Ottoman Balkans began after the Crimean War (1853–1856). In their work among Bulgarians, they were the senior partner in a joint enterprise with the Missionary Society of the Methodist Episcopal Church. For these missionaries, the project of conversion was explicitly connected to a restructuring of gender relations. The Christian home was a central component of mission policy.[20] It is also the driving force at the center of this narrative.

The evangelical New England cultural formation of the modern Christian home postulated marriage between a man and a woman who shared a companionate relationship. In this marriage, the husband enjoyed Christian headship, and the educated Christian wife and mother, while subordinate to her husband, exercised her moral authority to shape the character of the family, the community, and the greater national body. In this view of family life, evangelical Christians elevated the work of women to a national, indeed a global task. They believed that the United States was at the pinnacle of civilization as a white Protestant republic and that the Protestant American home should serve as the model for the spread of Christianity and civilization across the American continent and around the world. Women were at the center of this civilizing project, which justified and encouraged their participation in the missionary enterprise.

Evangelical Protestant ideas about home exerted a powerful influence on Anglo-American society in New England and the Midwest as the language of domesticity contributed to the elaboration of a female sphere of action in the service of moral and social reform across the nineteenth century.[21] Americans fashioned out of domesticity an imperial discourse that connected home to the nation, linked the "civilizing" work of the home to the task of national expansion and empire building, and determined who would be included within, and who excluded from, the national polity.[22] In the United States, missionaries used domestic discourse to construct racial distinctions that marked their proselytes as outsiders, but converts could rearticulate domestic discourse to create transnational spaces where they belonged.[23]

Each of the following chapters builds on these insights to reveal the contributions of an American imperial discourse based on the home to mission policies, ethnic Orthodox nationalisms, and Ottoman domestic reforms. They demonstrate the extraordinary pliability of the Christian home and the ways in which missionaries rearticulated domestic discourse to shape their projects to meet local needs while excluding converts from full membership of the Protestant community. They also trace the ways in which Bulgarian Orthodox Christians redeployed domestic ideals to build their own platforms for national reform, mount challenges to mission projects, and contest Ottoman restructuring. Ultimately, Ottoman statesmen embraced female education as a way to deflect Protestant successes among Christian communities in the empire.

Mission policy became a victim of the surprising malleability of the Christian home within the missionary enterprise. Domestic discourse contained within it the inherent contradictions of American society and missionary society that celebrated women's contributions to society while rendering women subservient to men. As a result of their experiences in Ottoman cities, women missionaries—married and single—rearticulated domestic discourse to challenge the gendered and racial hierarchy of missionary society. Against the wishes of their male colleagues, women missionaries in Istanbul, Stara Zagora, and Samokov attempted to shape institutions that enabled them to enjoy female companionship and establish their authority in home life and professional work. Contrary to the expectations of their mission board, however, the women of the Constantinople Home, together with their students, transformed the institution into a multicultural, multilingual institution, where women of all religions were welcome. Experiences in Istanbul in particular influenced an emergent strand of feminist internationalism that reverberated across the Near East and the United States in the late nineteenth century.[24]

I also explore the ways in which American missionaries used domestic discourse in an attempt to transform gender relations in Orthodox Christian communities and bring them into the Protestant fold. Through their schools and publications, missionaries were an important conduit of ideas that infused nationalist movements with Protestant values at a time of increasing ethnic segmentation across Ottoman domains. They contributed to boosting ethnic and religious nationalisms and undermined the attempts of Ottoman statesmen to limit increasing sectarianism within the empire.

Ethnic Bulgarian Orthodox Christians easily rearticulated American domestic ideals to develop a new strain of Orthodox nationalism. They grafted American ideas onto a gendered language of moral reform through which they reenergized national movements to organize female education and promote the idea that the Orthodox home was the fulcrum of national progress. They adapted American models for schools, family life, and civic associations. At the same time, they used the cultural formation of the Christian home to build on their perception of themselves as Christians and to differentiate themselves from other ethnic and religious groups within the empire. The nationalistic strains of American domesticity became an anticolonial tool that thwarted American and Ottoman attempts to bring Bulgarians into a broader community.

While Bulgarian Orthodox Christians grappled with their emerging national identity, Bulgarian converts to Protestantism struggled to be accepted into the idea of the larger Bulgarian nation. Converts were also denied full access to the Anglo-American community. In their interactions with Bulgarians, American missionaries introduced their own understanding of a global racial hierarchy, which separated them from their own converts within the Protestant fold. The assumptions that missionaries held about cultural difference prevented them from embracing Bulgarian converts as equals. Caught between Bulgarian Orthodox and American Protestant societies, converts were forced to contemplate the constructed levels of difference that located them at the margins of the communities within which they operated. American-Bulgarian encounters raised questions about what it meant to be civilized and fit for self-government in the Balkans in the mid-nineteenth century before the large migrations of southern Europeans to the United States.[25]

Working across national histories, this book also closes a gap between prominent Turkish historians, such as Selim Deringil, who argue that missionaries challenged the legitimacy of Ottoman state power, and Bulgarian historians, such as Tatyana Nestorova, who claim that missionaries had little impact in the Balkans. According to Deringil, of all the challenges that the Ottoman state experienced in the nineteenth century, none was more troubling than the activities of American missionaries.[26] Ottoman officials believed that missionaries sought to undermine Ottoman power by fomenting revolution among the empire's Christian populations. Historians who have explored missionary activities from the Bulgarian perspective have found their activities less consequential. Some have noted the contributions that missionaries made to higher education for men and praised their translations of the Bible.[27] Others have accused the missionaries of laying the groundwork for some future (nebulous and unexamined) economic imperialism.[28] Yet others have surveyed the work of missionaries and argued that their activities did not amount to a great deal. In Nestorova's view, the missionaries "did much in Bulgaria but accomplished little."[29]

How can scholars of mission reconcile the contention that missionaries were subversive agents with the conclusion that their efforts did not amount to much? One way is to broaden the analytical field: Deringil focused his study on the Ottoman state and Ottoman sources; Nestorova's structural approach relied heavily on missionary statistics. Another is to look for areas of neglect to try to bridge the analytical gaps. Most historians of Protestant-Orthodox encounters have viewed them from the teleological perspective of the post-Ottoman state and have consequently neglected the Ottoman context. They have excluded women—American and Bulgarian—from their analyses, even though women always represented at least half of all American missionaries and gender was at the heart of the missionary enterprise. Finally, Nestorova pointed to the failure of missionaries to convert large numbers of Orthodox Christians to Protestantism to support her contention that the missionaries were marginal figures who wielded little influence among Bulgarians.

The focus on a narrow definition of conversion and small numbers of converts has persuaded historians to ignore Bulgarian converts. Historians have also overlooked some of the prominent Bulgarians who did not convert but nonetheless worked alongside missionaries as teachers, translators, and mediators and found new ideas useful to their own causes. During the Cold War, when materialist, nationalist perspectives dominated the writing of Bulgarian history, such connections could hardly be made visible.[30] In the post–Cold War world, however, the descendants of early Bulgarian converts to Protestantism looking to establish contacts to a wider world are beginning to recover their history and discover their broader connections to the United States.[31] The missionary impact cannot be assessed based solely on bald numbers of converts, however. If conversion is understood more broadly to refer to changes in personal outlook or community action, a more compelling tale of American missionary influence emerges.[32]

It was not enough for missionaries to transport their visions of home to the Ottoman Empire for them to take root in new soil. They had to adapt them to the local environment and to their circumstances. Their visions challenged and were challenged by individuals within missionary circles and the people among whom missionaries worked. Expansion of the Protestant faith and New England culture was constrained by tensions within the mission. The domestic ideals that missionaries carried with them were reinterpreted by men and women, missionaries and converts, who sought to establish their own authority in missionary society. Responses from the local environment were also diverse. Some Orthodox Christians, men and women, embraced evangelical Protestantism and found in their new faith a new spirituality, a new locus of personal identity, and a newfound moral authority. Others discovered in the religious and social messages of Protestant reform new understandings of social organization that they reconfigured to bolster Eastern Orthodoxy and demand reform within the Orthodox community. A gendered analysis of American Protestant–Bulgarian Orthodox encounters against a global canvas that includes all the characters in the plot extends our understanding of the reach and implications of American cultural expansion in the nineteenth century.

In each of the chapters that follow, rather than offer a continuous chronological narrative, I examine a single encounter that throws light on the larger environment in which missionary engagements took place and the issues at stake within the mission and in Ottoman society. Each chapter explores adaptations of domestic discourse within a particular context and shows how the language of domesticity subtly changed over time to provoke major shifts in mission policy that reverberated in Boston and New York as well as Istanbul and other cities across the Ottoman Balkans. In some chapters, the concerns of missionaries take precedence; in others, the Bulgarian Orthodox community features more prominently.

A change in domestic arrangements for missionary Mary Van Lennep in 1843 provides the context for chapter 1, "Missionary Families and the Contested Concept of Home." I show how the ideal of the Christian home evolved in mission policy and how missionaries used the language of domesticity to shape, support, and subvert policy. In Ottoman towns, missionaries found that the borders of home became porous, stretching to accommodate mission goals, local needs, and personal visions. The chapter explores changes in the meaning of home to show how missionaries adapted to their local environment and appropriated the language of home to both fortify and challenge the gendered structures of missionary society and Ottoman society. Changes in women's education in the United States resulted in challenges to the ideal of the Christian home from graduates of Mount Holyoke Female Seminary.

I address these shifts in women's education and point out the moments that make the trajectory of missionary thinking about women and home both continuous and disruptive.

A violent attack on a mission home in the town of Stara Zagora in 1867 provides the encounter for chapter 2, "Education, Conversion, and Bulgarian Orthodox Nationalism" in which I examine the conversion to Protestantism of a young Bulgarian mission-school graduate named Maria Gencheva. Her conversion led to the attack and a legal battle in an Ottoman court, in which American missionaries were defended by a British consul. The court case persuaded prominent Bulgarians to question the political motives of American missionaries and cast doubt on the patriotism of Bulgarian converts to Protestantism. In an effort to deflect the inroads missionaries had made in Bulgarian communities, leading members of the town of Stara Zagora adapted the language of American domesticity to launch a nationwide campaign against mission schools. I examine the positive and negative moments in the encounter, and show why, despite areas of common ground, both sides became increasingly entrenched in their positions.

In chapter 3, "The Mission Press and Bulgarian Domestic Reform," the serialization of *Pisma za mayki,* a Bulgarian translation of missionary Martha Jane Riggs's *Letters to Mothers,* beginning in 1864, provides an opportunity to review the contributions of the mission press to Ottoman Bulgarian print culture, analyze domestic discourse in mission publications, and trace that discourse through Bulgarian newspapers. Here I explain the shared interests that united missionaries and some prominent educated urban Bulgarian women and men, chief among them Anastasiya Tosheva, Evgeniya Kissimova, and Petko Slaveykov. Missionaries targeted Bulgarian women through their monthly mission magazine, *Zornitsa (Day Star),* which enjoyed wide distribution in the Ottoman Balkans. Its editor, Methodist missionary Albert Long, expected it to attract Bulgarian women to Protestantism. Instead, it encouraged readers like Tosheva and Kissimova to develop their own domestic platform to advance the cause of female education and Bulgarian national progress. In the process, they shaped a new identity as modern Orthodox women, began to develop an understanding of their position within a global civilizational hierarchy, and constructed a dual political allegiance to the Ottoman state and the Bulgarian nation. Domestic discourse became linked to a civilizing mission with nation-building goals within the larger Ottoman polity.

Although gender is the key analytical category in this book, the different perspectives and experiences of some missionaries contribute to more complex interrogations of gender in relation to race, ethnicity, and class. In chapter 4, "Unconventional Couples—Gender, Race, and Power in Mission Politics," I examine a crisis in missionary circles in 1876 occasioned by the uncommon views of three single women, two of whom—Esther Maltbie and Anna Mumford—were graduates of Oberlin College, a midwestern college that, since its founding in the 1830s, had embraced radical notions of gender and racial equality. The two graduates set up house together. The third woman, Elizabeth Bevan, married a Bulgarian convert to Protestantism, Ivan Tonjoroff, and was ostracized by the larger mission community because she married across a cultural divide that missionaries increasingly perceived as racial, thus defying the mission's racial hierarchy. The egalitarian vision of Christian community that the three women shared challenged the gendered and racial hierarchical structure of missionary society but failed to change it. I explore the construction of race within missionary circles and the moments when the cultural formation of the Christian home offered the promise of equality and then failed to live up to its potential.

The construction of the Constantinople Home in Istanbul in 1876 led to a novel interpretation of American domesticity that embraced female headship. In chapter 5, "The Constantinople Home," I argue that experiences in the Ottoman capital allowed single women missionaries at the Home to develop a nonsectarian, feminist consciousness through which they challenged the authority of the men of the Near East Mission who supervised their work. Led by long-serving president Mary Mills Patrick, the women worked to develop an international, ecumenical women's institution, renamed the American College for Girls in Constantinople, and ultimately provoked a split with the Woman's Board in 1908. I view this as one of the pivotal moments in mission history that contributed to the demise of the women's missionary movement in the United States. Events in Istanbul led to far-reaching changes in the mission that brought Muslims into American educational institutions and shifted American cultural intervention in the Near East away from American Protestant missionaries toward powerful individuals in the commercial world of New York. I trace the moments in Boston and Istanbul that led to this major shift.

These encounters illuminate the connections between domestic social change and international relations from 1831 to 1908 by tracing important changes in women's education and in interpretations of American domesticity in the Near East and the United States. Women missionaries, Bulgarian converts, and Orthodox Christians challenged the hierarchical structures of missionary society that were based on evangelical American perceptions of the meaning of home. The encounters reveal that the meaning of home was neither static nor monolithic. American domesticity was a sufficiently pliable concept to allow missionaries and converts to disrupt conventional understandings of the gendered and racial ordering of American society. New expressions of domesticity wrought extensive change in Boston as well as in Istanbul. Domestic frontiers were both spatially distant and metaphorically close to home.

CHAPTER 1
Missionary Families and the Contested Concept of Home

Once she had settled into her new home in Izmir toward the end of 1843, Mary Van Lennep wrote to her mother in Hartford, Connecticut, to describe her new environment in the major Ottoman sea port south of Istanbul:

> Our house is quite a warm one for this place, and the little parlor in which I am writing is heated by a cheerful grate. The two little tables on either side the fire-place are ornamented by the gifts of my friends. The work-box which Mrs. E. gave me is a treasure. One large window lights the room, looking on the street, and white muslin curtains, with a pretty green and purple fringe, hang very gracefully over it. Our little room I am sure you would call quite cheerful. It has an American look. Our desire is to have things neat, plain and in taste, so that we can be comfortable, and have it pleasant for our friends.[1]

Like any daughter far from home, Van Lennep wanted to assure her mother that she was happy and secure in her new surroundings. Cheerful, cozy, well lit, and full of mementos from friends in Hartford, her "little parlor" had "an American look." It was almost like home. She expected to radiate from there the beneficial influences of Anglo-American Protestant culture and entertain her acquaintances. Little did she know that she was not to enjoy her pleasant surroundings for long. Her influence was required elsewhere, and only two months after she described her home in Izmir to her mother, she wrote again to report that she and her husband were to be transferred to Istanbul. There, she would have to adjust to a new idea of home.

As a result of changes in strategy at the American Board of Commissioners for Foreign Missions, the Van Lenneps had a new assignment in the Ottoman capital. Mary's husband, Henry, was to preach among Armenians; she was to supervise a boarding school for Armenian girls. Her new home would be in the school, a proposition that filled her with dismay. "Sometimes my heart died within me," she wrote despondently, "to be at the head of a seminary, and to have no home but in a boarding school." She shrank from the sacrifices this move would entail. Her vision of home must extend to incorporate a family of people she did not yet know. It must also stretch to duties she did not relish. "I do not like the idea of becoming the head of a boarding school and superintending all its concerns," she confessed. "I love a quiet way of living too well to make the idea of becoming a matron very pleasant."[2] The changes that would transform her home and family life were unwelcome.

Mary Van Lennep was born in Hartford in 1821 to the Reverend Joel Hawes and his wife, Louise. Growing up, she enjoyed the comfortable surroundings of a well-appointed New England home and had the best education her environment could provide. She attended Catharine Beecher's female seminary in that town and was trained as a teacher. Her father was minister of the First Congregational Church and a prominent member of the American Board. Brought up in a family committed to evangelical Protestantism, she supported the cause of Christian missions, but was not necessarily well prepared to be the wife of an American Board missionary. The job she must contemplate did not suit her temperament. After thoughtful prayer and reflection, however, she acknowledged that the change was God's work and committed herself to the project. She anticipated adapting her home life to a boarding school as her duties demanded. Her domestic frontiers expanded.

Van Lennep's letters emphasize the importance of the domestic realm for women missionaries who took their visions of New England homes with them to the Near East. Neat, tidy, snug, and warm, home was a place where women nurtured family and welcomed friends but kept outsiders at bay. Her letters also highlight the flexibility inherent in the idea of home that shaped American Board policy. Women's visions did not easily accommodate to the theory of home that shaped board policy, but policy responded to mission needs, and missionaries had to adapt to the realities imposed by their changing circumstances. The missionary home extended to take in all sorts of outsiders and additional duties, even if its residents did not embrace them. As Van Lennep explained to her mother, by incorporating a missionary home within a female boarding school the American Board "want[ed] the influence of a Christian family to be exerted over those who are to become the wives and mothers of the Armenian nation."[3] The duties of home life had national—and international—dimensions.

The cultural formation of the Christian home with the educated Christian woman at its heart justified the participation of women in the missionary enterprise and evolved as a significant element of mission theory in the nineteenth century.[4] The shifting locations of women in New England culture in the decades before the American Civil War helped shape new ideas of home and extend the realm of domestic duties. As missionary wives learned, however, the idea of home had to evolve to adapt to circumstances. An examination of the discursive practices and daily experiences of missionaries alongside a review of evolving American Board policy reveals the initial contradictions inherent in the concept of the missionary home and the ways in which missionaries in the Near East adjusted their visions to changes in the United States and in their local environment. Missionaries used a language of domesticity to show their commitment to policy or justify the ways in which they circumvented it. In effect, missionaries supported, subverted, and manipulated the idea of the domestic realm to promote Protestantism, expand the frontiers of American culture, and bolster their personal ambitions. The different constituencies of the American Board appropriated the language of home both to fortify and to challenge the gendered structures of missionary society. The cultural formation of the Christian home was sufficiently pliable to incorporate and validate their different projects.

The American Board Policy of the Christian Home

The nineteenth-century Protestant ideal of a husband and wife as a cohesive missionary unit marked a sharp distinction from the eighteenth-century model of a lone male missionary operating on the rude frontiers of colonial American society. Jonathan Edwards's account of the life of missionary David Brainerd, first published in 1749, shaped an earlier public perception of missionaries that remained popular in the decades prior to the Civil War.[5] Brainerd became the iconic representative of the self-sacrificing mission-ary—always gendered male—working in a harsh wilderness environment. In contrast, the first foreign mission of the American Board (to India in 1812) included women: two single men, Gordon Hall and Luther Rice, were accompanied by three couples—Adoniram and Nancy (Ann Hasseltine) Jud-son, Samuel and Harriet (Atwood) Newell, and Samuel and Roxana (Peck) Nott. By the mid-nineteenth century, a series of memorials to the wives of missionaries shaped a new image of the self-sacrificing female missionary in foreign lands.[6] The missionary was still officially male—only an ordained minister could aspire to the title—but his wife became an assistant mission-ary. The educated Christian wife and mother anchored family life within the missionary home and soon became a central tenet of mission policy.

This new construct of the missionary family emerged from the conflu-ence of several factors as evangelical Protestants gained ascendancy in New England political culture in the early American republic.[7] Religious reviv-als, the beginnings of industrialization, westward population movements, and increasing European immigration all helped to forge new understand-ings of the contributions that women could make to American society within their families and communities. At the same time, the early nineteenth-cen-tury Anglo-American global missionary endeavor called women to greater participation in the public realm. In the process, a reformed and revitalized New England theology led to demands for greater educational opportuni-ties for women and inspired women to new levels of religious self-assertion.

In an era of evangelical revivals in which women figured prominently as participants, evangelical preachers and writers began to promote what they claimed to be women's superior piety and capacity for self-sacrifice, which they recognized as a positive influence for cultural and religious stability.

Women's increasing prominence in congregations and religious organizations influenced ministers to dismantle austere Puritan ideals and replace them with a sentimental, reform-oriented religiosity.[8] As the strict Calvinist interpretation of predestination gave way to the idea of free-will conversions, evangelical Christian mothers accepted the burden of ensuring the conversion of their children to safeguard their salvation in Christ. As early as 1815, women in the northeastern United States began to form maternal associations that would help them educate themselves for this responsibility. They published magazines through which they shaped and promoted ideas about domesticity and reached tens of thousands of women across the country.[9]

The duty of childhood instruction increasingly fell to mothers at a time when industrialization removed fathers from the household as they gradually exchanged independent family workshops and offices for jobs in mills and factories. Husbands remained the heads of households; wives were subservient within the family hierarchy, but women exerted moral influence. This important social change was reflected in the publication of many advice manuals, books, and periodicals throughout the eastern United States between 1820 and 1860 that promoted changing perceptions of women's contributions.[10] As instructive books for children featured mothers in the role of teachers, fathers receded into the background, and patriarchal households yielded to "the empire of the mother," as a "vast army of mothers" sought to do its duty[11]

The childrearing work of women took on national significance as westward population movements and increasing European migrations of non-Protestant populations threatened to destabilize close-knit New England communities and undermine the authority of institutions such as the family and the church in an era of disestablishment. Catharine Beecher, daughter of the well-known Congregationalist minister Lyman Beecher, was one of several prominent women writers who declared that the home was the place where American mothers would nurture piety, encourage self-reliance, and shape the American character. The Christian home became the driving force of the extension of evangelical Christianity and Anglo-American culture throughout the expanding American nation. Beecher carved out a central place for women in national life by promoting an expansive vision of evangelical motherhood. In her mind, the maternal imperium would extend beyond the borders of the United States. In Beecher's much-cited words, Providence had ordained that the United States had "the grand, the responsible privilege, of exhibiting to the world, the beneficent influences of Christianity, when carried into every social, civil, and political institution."[12]

This vision of sprawling domesticity evolved as Americans encountered nonwhite Protestants across the American continent: the idea of the home became linked to the idea of the nation.[13] The task of the educated mother was to extend the benefits of Anglo-American Protestant home life and culture to all inhabitants of the North American continent while protecting the residents of the home and nation against the noxious foreign influences they encountered during the national expansion. Domestic discourse justified the extension of U.S. power, shaped debates about who could be included and who must be excluded from the American polity, and contributed to the structuring of a gendered and racial hierarchy in American society.

The meeting of British and American missionaries with non-Christian societies around the globe also informed the ideal of the Christian home.[14] The overwhelmingly negative descriptions that male missionaries provided of women in India, China, the Hawaiian islands, and the Near East in the early nineteenth century served in their view to emphasize the distinctions between Christian and non-Christian societies. These early Protestant missionaries argued that women were despised and degraded in non-Christian societies. Uneducated, they failed to earn the respect of their menfolk and could neither instruct their children nor shape the moral fiber of their families. Consequently, they could not raise useful members of society. Such descriptions convinced evangelical Protestants that Protestantism was responsible for the respected position that American women enjoyed in the United States. They served to justify the need for American women to participate in the missionary endeavor to bring the promise of salvation and education to the millions of women around the world who had not yet heard the message of Christianity.

The cultural formation of the Christian home, then, was shaped by an antebellum evangelical Protestantism worldview and infused with strains of Manifest Destiny and Orientalism.[15] Women's work remained chiefly in the domestic sphere, but it was connected to the world outside the home. The ideal of maternal power posited the focal point of maternal influence in the home but did not confine it there. The Christian home became a launching pad for social change. Radiating out from the family circle, the ideals of domesticity and moral reform carried women into the community and across the nation into projects that formed the bedrock culture of evangelical community construction. The rhetoric of maternal influence associated with the evangelical Protestant virtues of benevolence and usefulness guided the lives of evangelical women who joined the social reform movements of antebellum America, from sewing circles to mission societies, maternal associations to temperance unions, abolition to women's rights, moral reform to global renovation.[16] American women missionaries took this model of home with them around the world.

The codification of the Christian home in American Board policy came as American women were beginning to move into the public sphere on a platform of social reform. At the same time, the board had acquired a quarter century of experience in foreign missions. The experiences of missionary wives in Hawaii showed that women's extensive domestic duties frequently prevented them from aspiring to ambitions outside the home.[17] In 1836 the American Board secretary, Rufus Anderson, summed up his view of the Christian home as a guiding principle of missionary work.

Anderson sought to clarify the expectations that the American Board had of missionary wives in an introductory essay to a memorial of Mary Mercy Ellis, the recently deceased wife of a British missionary with the London Missionary Society.[18] He enshrined the Christian home as a major focus of mission policy and the missionary wife as the anchor of the missionary endeavor. Anderson specified three areas where a wife was expected to contribute to mission: she was to protect and nurture her husband, serve as a role model to local mothers, and teach local girls and women. Although she should assume duties in all three areas, her household remained her primary responsibility.

In Anderson's view, missionaries needed wives in the same sense that church ministers needed wives. Using euphemisms that could not be misconstrued, Anderson argued that missionaries possessed "the same nature" as ministers and should not remain single.[19] Anderson's reasoning had less to do with assistance with parish or mission duties and more to do with sexuality and creature comforts. According to Anderson, wives offered protection for the "powerful law of nature" that produced "the family state." The experiences of the London Missionary Society in the South Sea Islands and South Africa had shown that single men could not resist succumbing to temptations of the flesh in societies that did not share evangelical Protestant views about sex, marriage, and religion.[20]

In connection with marriage, Anderson also injected a criticism of the Catholic Church, arguing that the married state offered a better model than the "monastic principles of the Romish church." A wife would supply a missionary's "personal wants," including his food, clothing, and company, so that he would not waste his time trying to provide these himself. Nurtured, advised, and protected by a wife from sexual relations with native women, a missionary would be "more of a man, a better Christian, a more contented, zealous, faithful, useful missionary." Wives were needed to keep husbands on the straight and narrow path of Christian monogamy, morality, and mission.

Anderson acknowledged that domestic chores would take up most of women's time and sap their strength. Insisting that missionary wives were responsible first and foremost for domestic work, he located the authority for his policy in the Bible. "The care of her household is the duty, to which all others must be subservient," he wrote. "This is the scriptural view of her peculiar responsibilities under all possible circumstances."

Despite his emphasis on domestic responsibilities, Anderson's second conceptual point about the Christian home was related to the idea that women in non-Christian countries were degraded slaves who could not hope to improve their status in life without appropriate models. Anderson recognized that character was formed in all homes, even the homes of the heathen; yet the homes of the heathen were "dreadfully disordered." Anderson admonished missionary wives to be models of Christian virtue at the center of Christian families. They would provide "living illustrations" to women in non-Christian—and non-Protestant—societies who would learn "everything that goes to constitute the virtuous, useful, praiseworthy wife and mother." Anderson proposed that, by modeling simple Christian lives within Christian homes, missionary wives would accomplish a major part of the work expected of them to help elevate the social status of non-Christian women.

Scholars have emphasized Anderson's second point in elaborating the importance of women's contributions to the work of missions.[21] Yet Anderson devoted only half a page to the idea of modeling the Christian home to women around the world. The longest section of his essay dealing with the work of wives emphasized their contributions as teachers. Education took up the bulk of his message. Anderson's travels in the Mediterranean at the conclusion of the Greek War of Independence had persuaded him that missionary wives were needed to teach women and children.[22] In his clarification of a missionary wife's duties, he strongly recommended that wives be properly trained in pedagogy in the United States before they left on missionary assignments. In his view, the American Board had missed opportunities because wives were not adequately prepared to work as teachers. Wives could have exerted far greater influence than had been achieved if, as a group, they had been appropriately prepared, more interested, and better acquainted with suitable textbooks before leaving home. He believed that if missionary wives with children of their own established infant schools, they could "shorten the work of missions by one or two generations." There could be no doubt, he wrote, of the importance of "commencing the religious education of heathen children everywhere at a very early age, before the mind is pre-occupied and perverse habits are formed." In his view, this was a job for married women, not single women, and they should take up this task "notwithstanding the pressure of domestic cares."[23]

Anderson's statement prescribed the gendered contours of missionary operations, but his policy was inherently contradictory. The Bible confirmed that the task of a missionary wife was primarily the care of her husband and household. She must also engage with the women among whom she lived if she was to model the ideal home. And she must educate young children in infant schools to accelerate the work of the American Board. Or, as Mary Van Lennep discovered, she must extend the frontiers of her home into a school. Thus American Board policy was rife with tensions and open to interpretation and manipulation.

One additional piece of policy affected the intimate corners of the domestic realm. At a time when it might take months for missionary couples to reach their final destination, Anderson was concerned to protect young women from the dangers of childbirth in inhospitable locations. Early missionary memoirs are littered with accounts of maternal and infant death. American Board manuals for missionary candidates insisted that wedding ceremonies take place close to the day of departure for the mission station. The manuals euphemistically stated that "for obvious and weighty reasons, marriage should be one of the last preparatory measures." Anderson wanted to avoid the possibility of a wife becoming pregnant before she left Boston. The advice was to postpone marriage—and therefore sex—until the last possible moment. The manual pointed out that "great personal inconvenience and evils" had occurred when missionaries ignored this rule.[24]

Marriage on the eve of embarkation was a precaution against childbirth on the high seas or in surroundings where midwives, medical assistance, or friendly help were absent and the lives of a young missionary wife and her child might be endangered. Most missionary candidates followed the American Board's recommendation; the wedding dates and sailing dates of missionary couples heading for Istanbul confirm their compliance.[25] Nonetheless, because the journeys were long wives were frequently pregnant by the time they reached the city where they were to establish their new homes. Poor health afflicted many of them. The reality of household duties, providing for husbands, and childrearing responsibilities rapidly impinged on their daily existence. Regardless of mission board policy, in practice the internal dynamics of the home took precedence in women's lives, particularly during their childbearing years.

The Mission Home

The interpretations of three prominent members of the first generation of missionaries to the Near East Mission demonstrate the contested nature of the cultural formation of the Christian home. William Goodell, Harrison Dwight, and Elias Riggs all commented on the nature of the domestic realm of missionary couples and its possible extensions. Their observations shed light on the ways in which individual couples tried to negotiate mission policy to limit or expand their domestic frontiers.

William Goodell stressed the importance of his wife's domestic sphere. In response to a request from the American Board for his views on the qualifications required of a missionary's wife, Goodell confirmed that her work was likely to be mundane. The highest qualifications were those that best enabled her to do the work of a wife and mother. Whether she "looketh well to the ways of her household" was the main question. "Poetry and eloquence in America may sing a rapturous song and tell a thrilling story about her future labors," he wrote, "but she will find, after all, that her most important duties are those which are too common to be celebrated in song, and too humble to procure renown."[26] Goodell challenged the idea that missionary work was a life of romance and adventure. He also shattered the notion that wives could make substantial contributions to the missionary endeavor.

In contrast, Goodell's colleague Harrison Dwight affirmed a contested vision of the home. He was supportive of women's vocational ambitions. Like Anderson's policy statement, however, his response expressed contradictions. In his view, the home remained a wife's primary domain, but she should aspire to loftier goals. Although her "principal, direct efforts will be made in her own household," her task was greater than simply being "the purveyor of her husband's table, and the superintendent of his wardrobe."[27] She might even supervise schools, although Dwight thought that this should be the exception rather than the rule. In his view, a wife's education should prepare her to exert an influence "in whatever way the providence of God may direct." He thought that wives should be open to the opportunities that their environment might offer.

Elias Riggs provided one prominent example of a missionary who was ambivalent about board policy and supportive of his wife's missionary work. He and Martha Jane Riggs formed a partnership devoted to educational work. They had their own understandings about the importance of education in missionary work and criticized Anderson's new policy in the 1840s that removed funding for all schools that did not prepare a native ministry. Anderson increasingly admonished missionaries to focus on evangelizing, and this strategy established a clear hierarchy of work within the mission.[28] Preaching was the paramount activity of all male missionaries, taking precedence over translation and teaching. Throughout his long missionary career, Riggs maneuvered to focus his own energies on translation work. He rarely preached in public outside mission circles. The fact that he felt compelled to mention, in Martha Jane's obituary in 1888, that they accomplished their educational work together notwithstanding his devotion to preaching and her commitment to her household suggests that missionaries recognized a need to report a commitment to the dictates of board policy regardless of the work they actually performed.[29]

However board policy evolved, and whatever visions of home missionary families cherished, wives were forced to come to terms with the real worlds in which they lived. In the 1830s and 1840s, wives understood the sacrifice they were making when they left the only home they knew in the United States to make a new home in a foreign environment and take up missionary work. Elizabeth Dwight shrank from the task with a sense of "*utter inability and unworthiness.*" She hoped "that *life even* might not seem *too dear a sacrifice*" and that she might live long enough for the world to "*feel our influence.*"[30] Mary Van Lennep contemplated parting from her parents "in an agony of tears" while reading a memoir of "Mrs. Smith's Life" (mostly likely a reference to Sarah Huntington Smith of the American Board mission to Syria); yet she later hoped to find in her heart "a more ardent desire to be wholly devoted to Jesus."[31] Henrietta Jackson Hamlin could hardly console herself with the parting words of her father that she should not expect a long life. It was, he said, the idea of "comparative usefulness, rather than length of days" that she should embrace.[32] Her wedding ring bore the inscription "Luke 18: 29–30" to remind her of the words of Jesus to his disciples, who gave up everything to follow him: "And he said unto them, Verily I say unto you, There is no man that hath left house, or parents, or brethren, or wife, or children, for the kingdom of God's sake, who shall not receive manifold more in this present time, and in the world to come life everlasting." Hamlin believed that her reward was to be eternal life.

Facing a real fear of the unknown, young women made decisions to marry missionaries based on a deep sense of faith, a desire to do their duty, and an ambition to achieve something of lasting value. The tension between sacrifice and usefulness shaped their lives. Regardless of Anderson's views on the Christian home, the work that was nearest to the hearts of missionary wives—the care and nurture of their own children for their personal salvation and for the work of spreading the Gospel—remained the focus of their exertions. Missionary wives believed that their most important domestic duty was to instruct their children in the teachings of Protestant Christianity, inculcate in them their New England home culture, and raise future generations of missionaries. In the absence of local American schools, mothers also had to act as their children's schoolteachers. These tasks took most of their time and were of far greater importance to them than modeling the Protestant home to women in the local environment. Mothers worked and prayed daily for the salvation of their own children and to protect their home from what they perceived to be baneful external stimuli.

American mothers in the Near East lost no time in informing their families, friends, and supporters back home how much more difficult this task was away from the positive influences of New England. Writing in response to a "Mrs. H." whose letter had been published in *The Mother's Magazine,* Elizabeth Dwight asked her reader to imagine how much more difficult the work of mothers was in Istanbul: "And now, dear madam, if the weight of maternal responsibility almost crushes mothers in America, blest with every facility for enlightening the minds of their children, and purifying their own hearts, and surrounded with all the means of grace, what think you a Christian mother in this land of spiritual darkness must feel?"[33] Replete with tropes of darkness and contamination, missionary correspondence conforms to a pattern of evangelical Orientalism that denigrated non-Christian societies, privileged Anglo-American culture, and justified the work of missionaries. By putting themselves to work in foreign cultures that they hoped to transform, missionaries exposed themselves—and their more vulnerable children—to the possibility of transformation. Fear of contamination by outside influences is a common theme in the letters of women missionaries.[34]

In Istanbul, Dwight was concerned that her Christian home was being undermined by the customs of the eastern churches. She reported that in their play the mission children imitated the processions of Orthodox Christians who carried icons; when asked what they were doing, the children replied that they had "got a picture, and are playing *worship idols.*" Dwight shared her concern that her children were growing up in an environment where the wrong type of Christianity predominated. Describing to readers of *The Mother's Magazine* a grim picture of idolatry brought into her home, she emphasized the importance of maternal influence on her children. She insisted that "a *mother* must be the model, and almost the only model of virtue and religion her children will have."[35]

The wives of missionaries also lived in fear that they might die before their children converted. This concern lay heavily on Elizabeth Dwight's heart. Shortly before her death, she bemoaned the culpability of mothers for the eternal ruination of souls that were not "brought into the fold while under the influence of parental restraint, and while within the reach of the means of grace."[36] Published after her death, these words reflect the tragedy and irony of the missionary mothers' dilemma. Their anxiety could not have been eased by articles they read that bemoaned the lack of missionaries and suggested that there must be "a defect somewhere" in "the early training of children."[37] Acutely aware of the fragility of their own lives and the possibility that they would not have time to assure their children's conversion, and concerned that they might fall short in their duty, missionary wives enlisted the aid of important elements of their home culture to help them, and chief among them were maternal associations.

Recognizing the "arduous duties of a Christian mother," women in the eastern United States organized associations, gathering regularly to devise the best ways to bring up their children "in the nurture and admonition of the Lord."[38] Evangelical American women espoused the concept of Christian nurture before it became an issue of serious debate among Congregationalist ministers in New England.[39] Their maternal associations were a public demonstration of their commitment to Christian nurture and the significance of their work. As representative examples of antebellum New England culture, maternal associations served as one of the earliest extensions of the work of the home into the public sphere of the Near East.

In August 1835 Elizabeth Dwight, Abigail Goodell, and Mary Shauffler organized a maternal association in Istanbul and patterned it on the constitutions of maternal associations founded in New York and New England in the 1810s and 1820s.[40] Initially the women of the Izmir station—Eliza Schneider and Martha Temple—enrolled as distant members of the Istanbul circle of mothers, but they organized their own association as more missionary families arrived in Izmir.[41] The women met on Wednesdays, as did women in the United States, and prayed for divine assistance in the task of bringing their children to Christ. They connected, through prayer, with missionary women in other towns in the Near East and with women across the United States as they prayed at the same time each week in their different locations for their children's salvation and the conversion of the world. Maternal associations in the United States donated funds through *The Mother's Magazine* to be sent to the missionary wives in Istanbul and other towns in Western Asia.[42]

Advice manuals offer another prominent example of the extension of American domestic culture into the Ottoman world. When Martha Jane and Elias Riggs moved to Izmir in 1838, Martha Jane discovered a new vocation in writing. Following the format and content of antebellum American advice manuals and magazines, she composed a 260-page book, initially published in Greek in 1842 as *Encheiridion tes metros, etoi, Epistolai pros adelphen peri anatrophes teknon* (*The Mother's Manual, or Letters to a Sister about the Instruction of Children*) and subsequently translated into Bulgarian, Armenian, and Ottoman Turkish. Its Bulgarian title, *Pisma za mayki, ili rukovodstvo za mayki v dobroto otkhranvanie na detsata im* translates as *Letters to Mothers, or a Mother's Manual on the Good Nurturing of Their Children.*[43] The book was broadly disseminated through missionary distribution channels. The title of the work and its intended audience reflect the importance to Riggs of reaching out to women in other cultures with the news about the power of maternal influence. Riggs advocated female education and emphasized the contributions that educated Christian women could make to their society by assuming responsibility for the religious, moral, and intellectual training of their children. More than any other missionary wife, Riggs was responsible for promoting to Orthodox Christians in the Ottoman empire the cultural ideal of the educated Christian mother at the center of the Christian home and the singular importance of Christian nurture. Nowhere in mission publications were American evangelical gender ideals so well articulated as in her writings.

The Christian home offered another enduring contribution to relations between Boston and Istanbul. When Martha Jane and Elias Riggs celebrated their fiftieth wedding anniversary in Istanbul in 1882, the photograph commemorating the occasion shows a family of twenty-one individuals across three generations that connected the Riggses, the Dwights, and the Trowbridges through marriage as well as mission. Several of the children and grandchildren of these families worked as missionaries in Istanbul,

Martha Jane and Elias Riggs with their extended family in Istanbul (Constantinople) on the occasion of their fiftieth wedding anniversary, September 18, 1882. Courtesy Rev. Katherine A. Rice, great-great-granddaughter of Martha Jane and Elias Riggs.

eastern Anatolia, and Syria or served the missionary cause in the United States. From 1830 to 1908 and beyond, missionary families shaped connections between the United States and the Near East.

Although married women missionaries exerted their greatest efforts within the domestic circle, the reality of the mission home was that its fluctuating, porous borders could accommodate shifting visions and populations. As Mary Van Lennep learned, the home frequently incorporated a school or was organized within a school. The family often expanded to include students, servants, single missionaries, temporary visitors, and even long-term guests.[44] Sometimes absence laid bare the heart of the mission home. Indeed, it was the unusual mission home that modeled the ideal of the Christian home.

Elizabeth Dwight feared contamination of her home from the outside, yet she and other wives brought local children into their homes to educate them and to get help with household chores. The introduction of outside influences had to be balanced against the need for help. Most of the early mission schools in the Near East began as home schools that trained domestic help and taught basic literacy. In the early 1830s Abigail Goodell began teaching Greek girls in her home in Istanbul, as did Eliza Schneider and Martha Temple in Izmir. In a more ambitious project, Martha Jane and Elias Riggs began an elementary school for girls in Argos, Greece, in 1834. Within three years, they added a secondary level and organized a teacher-training course; by 1838 more than one hundred students attended the school.[45] The elementary schools that missionary wives operated provided the foundation for the expansion of mission education for girls throughout the Near East and the Ottoman Balkans.[46] The fact that day classes operated within the homes of missionaries, or that their homes were located in larger structures that could incorporate classrooms, indicates that the idea of home was flexible enough to incorporate the exigencies of the missionary enterprise in the local environment.

Missionary wives also took young converts to Protestantism into their homes, usually girls who attended mission schools. An assumption of cultural superiority inclined women missionaries to the view that they were better models as wives and mothers than the girls' birth mothers.[47] They also feared that the girls would revert to their traditional religious customs if they returned home to live. If they stayed in the mission home, they could maintain Protestant practices, experience the Christian home at first hand, and be trained to become the future wives of native pastors and teachers. Whether wives took students into their homes or made their homes in rooms within schools, the purpose was the same: to offer a model of educated Christian womanhood at the center of a Christian home. The job of their students was to learn from them and ultimately emulate them.

Boarding schools represented a difficult proposition, however, because space constraints and the task of supervising boarders imposed additional strains on missionary wives. In addition to living in cramped quarters, wives had to organize meals, lodging, and laundry for the students and provide basic medical services. Wherever missionaries established boarding schools, their wives took on these responsibilities as an extension of their domestic work and at the expense of their vision of home. Like Mary van Lennep,

Henrietta Jackson Hamlin was dismayed when she learned that she was responsible for the provision of boarding services for twenty-seven boys and an assistant teacher in the boys' school that her husband founded. According to Cyrus Hamlin, his wife's duties encompassed "labors foreign to her literary tastes and habits," yet the work became "her great object in life."[48] In this case, however, Henrietta's responsibilities represented not so much an extension of her home duties as an assumption of work related to her husband's professional responsibilities. When women were obliged to accept these altered definitions of the work of home, their health and their vision of home frequently suffered. Mary Van Lennep was a frail young woman from a genteel background who suffered from poor health. Supervising a boarding school was a task too onerous for her. Even without the additional work, she was vulnerable; she died less than a year after moving to Istanbul.

One American Board missionary, Charles Morse, provided a description that illustrates just how cramped living arrangements could be in the mission home. The Morses lived in the building of the Bulgarian girls' school in Stara Zagora for two and a half years, which he described as "a severe trial." During that time, Eliza Morse had "only one ordinary square room in which were 2 beds, a large and a small, a bureau, a trunk and in winter a stove."[49] The Morses' one room served as parlor, dining room, and bedroom. Charles found it particularly troubling that Eliza had to teach her own children in the same room where she taught Bulgarian girls. The purpose of her domestic sacrifice remained the same for her in the 1860s as it was for Mary Van Lennep in the 1840s—to model the Christian home for Orthodox Christians and train particularly promising graduates to become the wives of native pastors and teachers.

Boarding of visitors became another extension of the work of the mission home, which was expected to offer hospitality to visiting dignitaries and missionaries. The duties once again fell chiefly within a wife's domain. Mission homes in Istanbul and Izmir, both major port cities, were frequently full of guests. Dignitaries expected their vision of home away from home to be fulfilled when visiting missionaries abroad. Newly minted missionaries who arrived in major sea ports en route to more distant destinations expected to see a well-rooted mission home and learn from its inhabitants. In Izmir in the 1840s and early 1850s, all new arrivals stayed with the Riggses. "Mrs

Riggs keeps house," wrote Seraphina Everett, and "the rest of us boarded."[50] Martha Riggs became the chief missionary welcoming agent and caregiver in Izmir, performing a major service for the American Board by housing and feeding missionaries who passed through the town until they became settled in their own homes. Among the tasks that prevented them from more meaningful missionary work in the 1860s and 1870s, Ursula Clarke Marsh in Plovdiv and Zoe Noyes Locke in Samokov mentioned "duties as hostess," and "entertaining guests sometimes for weeks."[51] The missionary residence often looked more like a boarding house than a model of the Christian home.

Indeed, another service that missionary wives provided was boarding single men and women missionaries. Because the Christian home was deemed to be a positive influence on everyone who lived in it, and because it was considered inappropriate to leave unmarried missionaries unsupervised, the American Board required single men and women to live with married couples. Constrictions of space might make the experience unpleasant for everyone concerned. On the positive side, a female boarder would mean help with domestic chores. But a male boarder would mean nothing but additional work for the missionary wife.

Single and widowed men were encouraged to marry, and they usually chose not to remain single for long. None knew better than men whose wives had died how essential wives were to their comfort and effectiveness in the missionary enterprise. When Emily Meekins Arms died after childbirth in Plovdiv in 1861, just eighteen months after leaving Boston, her husband, William, requested permission to return to the United States to find another wife. In his letter to Rufus Anderson he wrote, "My usefulness as a missionary and my happiness both temporal and spiritual would be greatly increased by such a step."[52] He needed a wife not only to look after the baby and himself, but also to prevent his being a nuisance as a lodger with another missionary family. Men were keenly aware that they needed to find a new wife, particularly if they had children. "There is a dread of trying to find a companion, and especially with a feeling of haste," another widower, Jasper Ball, wrote from Edirne as he pondered who among his acquaintances might be a suitable mate and who would be willing to take on a ready-made family.[53]

Death meant the reconfiguration of more than one missionary home, and

the narratives of the deaths of women missionaries and their children make
for difficult reading. When Elizabeth Dwight died, she left three boys under
the age of seven. Seraphina Haynes Everett, who assumed Mary Van Lennep's responsibilities at the girls' boarding school, also left three children
when she died. Henrietta Hamlin left five daughters between the ages of one
and ten; Harriet Lovell, the second Mrs. Hamlin, died leaving two more children; and the third Mrs. Hamlin took over a home and seven children. The
deaths of Susan and William Merriam left their child a homeless orphan.
Although Martha Jane and Elias Riggs lived long lives, two of their eight
children died in childhood and two as young adults.

Men's absences from the home also challenged the ideal of the Christian home. One of the key elements of modeling the Christian family was to
demonstrate the idea of togetherness in companionate marriage. The task
became difficult when husbands were frequently absent, as the missionaries were. Sometimes they spent weeks, and even months, touring the countryside around their mission stations. Wives complained. Loneliness was a
constant refrain in mission correspondence. According to Zoe Locke, most
of the missionary wives found their husbands' long touring absences "the
most trying part of their lives," particularly when children were small.[54] Isabella Clarke's letters express her misery when she was left alone for long
periods, yet her obituary, written by missionary Henry Haskell, makes no
note of the solitude and suggests that Isabella was perfectly happy when
her husband set off on his travels, mentioning her "cheerful willingness to
allow her husband to leave her for weeks at a time."[55]

Here is a blatant discrepancy between the reality of home life and the
discursive practices of male missionaries who wrote the obituaries of missionary wives. Haskell used the language of domesticity to eulogize Isabella
Clarke by demonstrating that she was a model of domestic perfection. In
fact, her husband's absence not only made her miserable but prevented her
from doing her job. The long absences of male missionaries meant that the
mission home reflected not the ideal Christian home but the typical Ottoman home. In towns and villages across the Ottoman Empire, seasonal
migratory labor was the norm and men frequently worked far from home,
leaving their wives alone to cope with the household.[56] Unlike Ottoman

Isabella and James Clarke with their children James, Willie, and Lizzie, ca. 1870. Courtesy Hilandar Research Library, Ohio State University.

women who had extended families and communities to rely on, missionary wives had only other missionary couples to come to their aid if they needed assistance. Except for Istanbul, where several missionary families resided, mission stations in the Balkans consisted of only two families. The life of a missionary wife was often a lonely one.

Second-Generation Missionary Wives

Although the internal dynamics of the mission home determined how a missionary wife would spend the larger part of her time and energy, wives who had personal ambitions in the work of moral reform eventually found a way to fulfill their vocations. This was particularly true of the second generation of missionary women in the Near East. Some wives, like Isabella Clarke and Margaret Haskell, had no particular desire to become a missionary but simply chose to marry a man who was a missionary candidate. Others, such as Zoe Noyes Locke and Fannie Bond, had distinct ambitions for their missionary careers. The shift in attitudes and opportunities was made possible in the United States by changes in higher education for women demanded by men and women reformers as well as members of a prominent midcentury women's rights movement.

The first generation of women missionaries was well educated, yet no mid-nineteenth-century educational establishment did more to prepare women for the missionary movement than Mount Holyoke Female Seminary and its daughter colleges. Mount Holyoke was founded by Mary Lyon in South Hadley, Massachusetts, in 1837.[57] Committed to the Christian home, evangelical reform, and global conversion, Lyon developed a philosophy based on traditional religious and societal values that had the practical advantage of confirming the home as the central sphere of influence for women while enabling them to seek new avenues of opportunity outside domestic boundaries. Mount Holyoke graduates expected to contribute to missionary work beyond the domestic realm. More than 80 percent of young women who graduated from the institution between 1838 and 1850 taught for several years before marrying, and their median age at marriage was twenty-six, rather than twenty-one in the general public.[58] These women had experiences before they left the United States that gave them greater maturity than some of the first-generation wives and created different expectations in them and in their families.

Letters of recommendation for Mount Holyoke graduates reflect the expectations of the young women who hoped to become the wives of missionaries. The American Board screened all applications from candidates for missionary work very carefully. As part of the process the board required testimonials for spouses and fiancées. By the 1850s, the professional quali-fications of potential spouses dominate. Letters introducing Mount Holy-oke graduates to the American Board frequently emphasized the women's intellectual capacity. In a recommendation for Eliza Winter, Mount Holyoke instructor Mary Chopin wrote that her former student showed "more than ordinary perception and reasoning power and in every branch of study pur-sued ranked as a scholar among the *first*." Winter's fiancé, Charles Morse, commented on her work as a teacher, insisting on her scholarly achieve-ments. "Her intellectual and moral qualities predominate," he wrote. Writ-ing to explain why she would not attend her first class reunion at Mount Holyoke, Eliza Winter informed her classmates that she was shortly to be married and was "under appointment as a Missionary of the American Board."[59] She used the word "missionary," not "assistant missionary" or "mis-sionary wife," which were the terms that Rufus Anderson used. Her choice of this word indicates that she expected to contribute to mission but not simply as a helpmeet.

Margaret Hallock Byington's father, himself a missionary, wrote that nei-ther he nor his daughter attached much importance to her domestic talents. Among the "more important things" he listed her three years of study at Mount Holyoke and two years of teaching. In his view, she possessed "a man-liness and womanliness" rarely found in one person and would apply herself to solving problems and removing obstacles rather than complaining about them.[60] Moses Day, uncle of Susan (Diamond) Merriam, described her as "a young lady of no common worth" and possessed of a "high moral and Chris-tian character" who had given "unqualified satisfaction" as a schoolteacher.[61] Letters on behalf of Emily (Meekins) Arms praised her character and her experience as a teacher in Sunday school and public schools.[62]

Letters for Mount Holyoke graduates emphasized intellectual strengths, previous useful experience, and an ability to cope with difficulty. Once a mis-sionary wife was at work, a rare personal letter might indicate that profes-sional interests took precedence over the domestic realm. One such example is provided by Mount Holyoke graduate Clara (Kate) Pond Williams:

> I'm not much of a housekeeper and I often think with sorrow
> upon the small credit that I must reflect upon my early training.

Eliza (Winter) Morse with son Charlie, ca. 1860s. Courtesy Hilandar Research Library, Ohio State University.

I should have done far better at it when I was eighteen than I do now. But then—what is the use of giving al[l] one's energies to bread & butter ** clean dishes ** clean cupboards—clean windows & floors—clean dish towels & the like? Use or no use I can't do it & I am fast becoming orientalized—shut my eyes to what I can't well help and let Yakob [a servant] reign supreme in his department returning now & then to make a suggestion about towels. I must say I feel rather shaky when I think of the young ladies fresh from America with all their nice American notions. I am afraid we shall shake them terribly with our outré ways.[63]

In her defense, Williams accounts for her loss of orderly American domestication by explaining that she had become "orientalized." She indicates that the domestic sphere belonged to her male servant and that if his ways were not American ways, she could adjust. She suggests that she has better uses for her time than the household, and she hints not too subtly that young American women arriving in the Near East will be just as rapidly corrupted. Yet despite previous experiences and personal expectations, the domestic realm continued to dominate the discursive practices of women missionaries. The general contours of society, particularly missionary society, had not changed sufficiently to allow most Mount Holyoke graduates greater flexibility of action.

The experiences of two women who left the United States to work in the Near East Mission in 1868 highlight the different ways in which wives used the language of domesticity and moral reform to carve out space for their work and describe their activities. Fannie Bond and Zoe Noyes Locke were considerably older than the normal age of marriage when they embarked from Boston: Bond was twenty-eight years old; Locke was thirty-five. Both women taught before they married. Their ages are indicative of considerable experience before marriage, which perhaps translated into greater maturity as they adjusted to their situation in the Ottoman interior.

Fannie Bond described a vision of home in which gender equality seemed a reality. She waxed eloquent about her work, painting a picture of a most unusual mission home in which both spouses adjusted to allow the other

Margaret Byington with daughter Carrie, ca. 1860s. Courtesy Hilandar Research Library, Ohio State University.

time and space to fulfill their own ambitions. Bond decided that one way to alleviate the burden of domestic work was to hire additional servants. Mission homes typically had one servant. For a while, Fannie Bond employed two servants to relieve her of some of the more mundane household chores so that she had more time to devote to mission work. Her response to the constraints imposed by the home seems entirely reasonable; yet other missionary women (or perhaps their husbands) considered the expense of a second servant inappropriate. Bond eventually discontinued the experiment and returned to a single servant. Thanks to her husband's support, she still found time to work outside the home. In addition to organizing a maternal association that met on Wednesdays (as all missionary wives did), the activities she most preferred were visiting the sick and traveling to organize women's meetings for Bible study. Missionaries praised her work as a Bible woman (a woman, American or local, although usually local, who read and interpreted the scriptures to other women). In William Locke's view, "so far as a Bible worker is concerned Mrs. Bond has not only no superior but no equal in our Mission."[64] Writing of her experiences after seven years in the town of Stara Zagora, she radiated exhilaration and optimism. "I do love this work more and more," she confided to her colleague Margaret Haskell.[65]

Bond was welcome with her Bible in the homes of Stara Zagora because she had a vocation to nurse sick people and an ability to heal them. She took care of her neighbors during an outbreak of typhus in the town when none of their family and friends would venture near them. Her neighbors recovered and were grateful. News spread about her ability to nurse people back to health and the Bulgarians among whom she lived came to have what she described as "an exaggerated opinion of my skill." Bond believed that her actions offered a good opportunity "to sow the seed of God's word" and had broken down prejudices against the missionaries.[66] She was instrumental in neutralizing the hostility of a local Orthodox priest after restoring his sick daughter to health.[67] When the Bonds moved to Bitola, their house had a room with a separate entrance where sick people could come to consult with Fannie Bond.[68] According to one of her colleagues in Bitola, she was "remarkably successful in the treatment of the sick."[69]

Bond's home arrangement enabled her to leave home for several days and even weeks at a time because her husband stayed home with the children so that she "might be perfectly free to work among the women." Lewis Bond sometimes accompanied her to her destination and then returned home. He seemed to relish the opportunity, boasting that he took excellent care of the children while she was gone.[70] The records provide no information to suggest what precisely made this couple different. Clearly, Lewis Bond supported his wife. She herself was a fearless individual. She was not afraid of visiting and caring for people who suffered from contagious diseases when their own families would not care for them for fear of infection. She disregarded local conventions for women by walking around town alone even when her husband was out of town, causing not a little consternation among her neighbors. In this experience, Bond was modeling not so much the Christian mother at the center of the Christian home as the independent married woman on a mission of her own.

Like Bond, Zoe Noyes Locke had a fulfilling missionary career, despite some of her public declarations to the contrary. A Mount Holyoke graduate, Locke ran her own school in Key Port, New York, before she married.[71] In her public letters to her classmates in her early years as a missionary wife she expressed her considerable frustrations. She lamented that domestic duties had prevented her from engaging in more meaningful work. On the occasion of her twenty-fifth class reunion at Mount Holyoke in 1884, she shared her disappointment about her work with her classmates: "I cannot say that all my dreams about missionary life have been realized. I have not had so much direct work among the people as I expected, family cares have taken up so much of my time." Among her many duties was the education of her own children in the absence of English-language schools. "I wonder," she wrote to her classmates, "if American mothers realize what a blessing they have in being able to send their children to school every day."[72]

In one respect, women of the second generation were less burdened than the first generation of missionary wives in that they gave birth to approximately half the number of babies. Whereas in the first generation wives had five to eight children; in the second generation they had three to four, a reflection of the mid-nineteenth-century demographic transition and perhaps an indication that some missionary wives were gaining control over the reproductive process.[73] Locke had only two children, probably a reflection of her age when she married; yet she claimed her domestic duties hindered her,

Fannie and Lewis Bond, ca. 1870. Courtesy Hilandar Research Library, Ohio State University.

including regular housekeeping, family sewing, educating her children, receiving visitors, and entertaining guests. She lamented her inability to find a suitable young woman to help with housework. Defeated by the daily round, she consoled herself with the idea that she supported her husband's work, acknowledging that her chief task was "to keep others in good condition for work, especially my husband."[74]

Locke's letters suggest that she felt constrained both by the work of home and by the need to mention it. Yet a private diary that she began after her daughters returned to the United States for schooling tells a different story, offering a narrative of social and moral reform work in the community. The diary confirms the unending domestic routine of the missionary wife, but it also describes a host of additional activities that show her engaging outside the home with Bulgarian women and girls in the town of Samokov. In the 1870s she attended a weekly mother's meeting and prayer meetings, taught Bible classes and Sunday school, and became involved with the mission benevolent society and a girls' literary society at the mission boarding school for girls. She was a member of the Women's Christian Temperance Union and subscribed to its publication, the *Union Signal*. Among her personal papers is a large scrapbook with newspaper cuttings, chiefly from the *Union Signal*, of women active in the temperance movement worldwide. Not until after her children were grown was she able to devote her time more fully to this interest. She organized a local temperance society in Samokov in 1887 and founded a Bulgarian affiliate of the World Women's Christian Temperance Union in 1890, for which she translated temperance tracts and songs for the Bulgarian Protestant community.[75] In her later life, Locke was fully engaged beyond the home in the work of moral reform.

Fannie Bond and Zoe Locke were at one end of a spectrum that illuminates the ways in which missionary wives adjusted to conditions and arranged their circumstances to organize home life and mission outreach. At the other end were women like Mary Van Lennep and Isabella Clarke, both of whom adjusted but neither of whom was able—because of poor health and different personal expectations—to soften the impact of their environments. The circumstances and activities of missionary wives help situate them along a spectrum between these outliers. The records of their experiences in the Near East, as in other parts of the world, confirm that few wives were able to achieve the freedom of action of Fannie Bond. By the 1860s, missionaries began increasingly to call for the employment of single women missionaries to work as teachers and train Bible women. The Christian home remained the justification for women's work, but the focus of that work began to move outside the home and demanded a new generation of mission workers.

Shoring Up the Mission Home

In 1873, an article in the *Missionary Herald* insisted that the missionary wife was the sine qua non of the success of all missionary work in the Ottoman Empire. In a particularly forceful display of Orientalism, the unnamed author described what some missionaries perceived to be the depravity of Ottoman society. The writer deplored the "ignorance, superstition, and degradation" of people who lived outside the major port cities of the Ottoman Empire and claimed that the influence of American missionaries had elevated the social life of its inhabitants. While acknowledging the contributions to missionary work of ordained ministers and single women, the article extolled the virtues of the Christian home and praised the missionary wife and mother as the backbone of mission and the instigator of a "moral revolution" in Ottoman society:

> It is the silent and steady home-life of the missionary wife and mother, who is content to be the light and solace of her husband's home, the true and constant help-meet of her husband's mission-ary life, training and educating her children to follow in their father's footsteps, watching, meantime, for all suitable and womanly opportunities to aid and bless her native sisters. It is this wife and mother who wields the greatest influence, and is perhaps the unconscious center and source of those elevating social forces which we see working in a manner so salutary all through the East. . . . [W]ithout the wife and mother in the missionary's home, the work would not have gone forward.[76]

This paean to the missionary wife emphasized a woman's self-sacrificing contribution as solace and helpmeet. Wives were the bedrock of the missionary enterprise: missionaries could not do their work without a wife in the home. According to this writer, single women were not the answer to the pressing need for personnel. In fact, the article was a forceful defense of apparently compliant wives in the context of a new working environment in which single women were attempting to exert more freedom of action.

Single women represented a challenge to the status quo of the missionary enterprise, a challenge that the article in the *Missionary Herald* recognized and attempted to parry. The American Board had been slow to appoint single women. Only after the Civil War did women in the United States begin to organize denominational women's missionary boards to support the work of single missionary women. Single women were, for the most part, women with professional experience. In the Near East Mission, they were hired to teach, supervise boarding schools, and train Bible women. They were asked to do the work that many married women had wanted to do but been unable to do. The arrival of single women in Istanbul and the Ottoman Balkans brought new challenges to the cultural formation of the Christian home and new uses of domestic discourse to support and promote the work of single women.

Individuals who wield power have the ability to manipulate the cultural symbols of their society to their own ends. Symbols can mean what people make them mean. The cultural formation of the Christian home, with the educated Christian wife and mother at its center, was a major trope of antebellum New England society. Rufus Anderson, who garnered considerable power within the American Board over three decades of service as foreign secretary, exploited it to justify the presence of women in the missionary endeavor. If he circumscribed their activities in the domestic realm by appealing to the authority of the scriptures, he nonetheless emphasized the need for them to work as models and teachers outside the family sphere. He shaped a sufficiently ambiguous policy to allow women— and men—to interpret the scope of women's contributions more narrowly or more broadly.

All missionaries—women and men—had their own visions of home and their expectations of the domestic circle. The work of home grounded those visions. Some tasks, such as the religious and intellectual instruction of their own children, were a prominent part of their work, but the porosity of home borders detracted from that vision and allowed for new interpretations. Other assignments, such as the supervision of boarding schools, became an extension of the domestic sphere, defined by the changing requirements of mission strategies and the everyday realities that missionaries experienced in their environments in Istanbul and other Ottoman towns. Such new duties created responsibilities that some missionary wives did not recognize as theirs but were obliged to accept. The additional work that missionary wives chose to do was driven by their vision of home but influenced by their personal preferences.

Negotiating the ambiguous policy of the American Board, the real burden of household duties, and the rhetoric of domestic discourse, missionary wives worked not so much to model the Christian home as to transplant the antebellum American culture of female moral authority across the Ottoman world. They organized prayer groups and benevolent societies, maternal associations and temperance societies, wrote mother's manuals, and built Mount Holyoke daughter seminaries. They carried the institutions of American civil society with them into Ottoman society. The concept of the Christian home and the gendered hierarchy it imposed in mission society was challenged by some missionary couples. Fannie and Lewis Bond represented an exceptional couple who had a vision of a more egalitarian home and an equal partnership.

Missionary domesticity was not a monolithic idea. It contained its own internal contradictions, which missionaries exploited in different contexts. In the following chapters, I examine the intellectual thought stream that was the Christian home in several locations in the Near East. Its complexity will emerge more forcefully as we see how the messages of domesticity were exported and transmitted through the broader Ottoman society and how American missionaries and Ottoman subjects negotiated and rearticulated them.

CHAPTER 2

Education, Conversion, and Bulgarian Orthodox Nationalism

On a late September day in 1867, a crowd of Bulgarian Orthodox Christians attacked the mission house of Charles Morse, a missionary with the American Board of Commissioners for Foreign Missions in the town of Stara Zagora. Rumors had spread among the Bulgarian community that Morse was holding a young Bulgarian girl against her will and had coerced her to convert to Protestantism. Several of the town's leading citizens sent a deputation to Morse to ask him to surrender the girl, Maria Gencheva, to her mother. When Morse refused, Maria's mother began to throw stones at his windows and, in her despair, took an axe to his door. Some young boys who were hanging around the house also began to throw stones. The crowd grew and the conflict escalated. Insults were hurled, bricks flung, and blows exchanged. Morse was accused of assaulting Maria's mother.[1]

Angered by the attack on his home and the mission school, Morse pursued the Bulgarians in court. In a punctilious account of the incident, he reported that a crowd of forty to a hundred people harassed the occupants of the mission house for four and a half hours. He estimated that two hundred stones were thrown; sixty-four stones entered the house, breaking sixty panes of glass.[2] Morse refused to believe that the action against the mission was spontaneous. He argued that the attack was planned with the knowledge and approval of some of the members of the local Bulgarian *obshtina,* or community council. He wrote to U.S. minister resident E. Joy Morris in Istanbul and appealed for his intercession with the Ottoman authorities to protect the mission and prosecute the offenders. Morris turned to the British ambassador, Sir Henry Elliot.

The ensuing legal confrontation, in which the British consul, John Blunt, represented Morse in an Ottoman court, permanently soured relations between Americans and Bulgarians in Stara Zagora. In the broader environment, it became a catalyst for debates in the Bulgarian national press about the dangers of what Bulgarians came to call "the Protestant propaganda." The attack on the mission house highlights the challenges that American missionaries and their ideal of the Christian home posed to Bulgarian Orthodox communities at a time of rapid social change when most Bulgarians clung to their religion as a significant marker of identity.

Conversion can be a disconcerting event for the cohesion of a community because it threatens traditional institutions and ideologies.[3] Apart from the spiritual experiences that lead an individual to adopt a new faith, switching religious affiliation is not a simple matter. Conversion occurs within a context.[4] The factors involved in the decision to convert are multiple, both personal and political, and the consequences are potentially destabilizing.

In the Ottoman Empire, the choice to convert was an expression of individual initiative over civic identity and community cohesion. Maria Gencheva's decision to become a Protestant was a response to her interactions with missionaries and an embrace of the opportunities that her new faith could offer. Her determination to leave the Orthodox community opposed the traditional Ottoman Bulgarian institutions of family, church, and local authority, and questioned local gender norms. By exercising her free will, she contested the authority of her parents and removed herself from the civil power of the Orthodox Church and the Stara Zagora *obshtina.* Her conversion also challenged the customs of Bulgarian society and Ottoman law, calling into question her civil, political, and national status. At a time when Bulgarian Orthodox Christians increasingly equated religion and nation—when to be Bulgarian was to be Orthodox—Gencheva's choice undermined the efforts of some Bulgarians to shape a national unity grounded in Orthodoxy. Her action exposed the fragility of the Bulgarian national project.

Gencheva's conversion illuminates the broader transformations in Ottoman society that shaped American-Bulgarian encounters, allowed Ottoman subjects to imagine new identities, and heightened intercommunity tensions. Her story emerges from the intersection of several converging political, social, and cultural developments in mid-nineteenth-century Ottoman society that made change possible but also created social and political instability. Chief among these are Ottoman community reforms, an emergent Bulgarian movement for national reform, and a drive in some quarters toward armed rebellion. American missionaries moved fast to intervene in this rapidly changing environment. Their ability to support religious and educational reform enabled them to take advantage of the dearth of educational opportunities for girls to extend their proselytizing activities among Ottoman Christians. They established a girls' school modeled on Mount Holyoke Female Seminary, a New England institution whose radical evangelical roots created opportunities for women in education and mission. As they opened up new prospects for women, missionaries contributed to greater disruption in Ottoman political life and in Bulgarian Orthodox communities. The choices made by young women like Gencheva helped lay the foundations of the first Bulgarian Protestant community and contributed to the shifting mosaic of Ottoman Bulgarian society.

Religion, Community, and Ottoman Reforms

Religion and community distinctiveness were intertwined in Ottoman society until new ideas about social identity began to unravel them and Ottoman reformers determined to separate them in the mid-nineteenth century. Internal and external pressures on the Ottoman state combined to shape an expansive imperial reform policy that sought to diminish the influence of religion in political life. Instead, it led to increasing sectarian tensions, facilitated missionary activities, and even sanctioned the existence of an Ottoman Protestant community, which further complicated the religious composition of the empire.

Historically, the Ottoman government did not recognize ethnic or national groups; instead, it organized subjects according to religion and state service.[5] Islam was the state religion. Sumptuary laws and tax laws, among others, ensured that adherents of other religions experienced reminders of their second-class status every day. The empire was nonetheless tolerant of other religions. Each recognized religious community, or *millet*, was headed by its own religious leader, who exercised spiritual and temporal control and was responsible for the administration of the group according to community laws and customs. Religious communities were largely left to manage their own affairs, particularly in the sphere of religion, family, and education. In a region of several religions, languages, nationalities, and ethnicities, mixed neighborhoods existed in towns and villages, yet most people tended to live and work with their co-religionists.

Since 1393, when the Bulgarian patriarchate lost its status after the fall of the medieval kingdom of Bulgaria to the Ottomans, Bulgarian Orthodox Christians had been under the jurisdiction of the Greek patriarch of Constantinople.[6] By the mid-eighteenth century, the Greek patriarch had ensured Greek control over all Christian Orthodox churches in the Balkans, and Greek replaced Church Slavic as the language of Bulgarian Orthodox churches. As Greeks dominated in ecclesiastical, educational, and commercial institutions, some Bulgarians began to embrace Greek language and culture. Individuals identified themselves by social position (official, merchant, peasant), religion (Muslim, Christian, Jew), and geographic region, rather than by ethnicity. Beginning in the eighteenth century, however, new ideas emerging from expanding economic contacts outside the empire encouraged Ottoman subjects, both Christian and Muslim, to envision new social and political identities that transcended, yet incorporated, traditional ones. By 1848, leading Bulgarians in Istanbul had persuaded the Ottoman government to grant approval to build a Bulgarian church (St. Stephen's) and print a Bulgarian newspaper (*Tsarigradski vestnik*) in the capital.[7] Ottoman approval was tantamount to recognition of separate ethnicity.

In their efforts to obtain increased religious and national recognition, Bulgarians sought, and received, support from their co-religionists in Russia. Official Russian policy was to maintain the ecumenical authority of the Greek patriarchate, but the Russian government and Russian volunteer associations worked to gain reforms for Bulgarians while expanding their influence in Ottoman domains.[8] At the same time, as some Christians in the Balkans turned to armed rebellion to end Ottoman rule, the European powers began to support what they perceived to be Christian nationalist movements. Russia, France, and Britain used the pretext of defending the rights of Ottoman Christians, including Serbians, Greeks, and Bulgarians, as a reason to intervene in Ottoman affairs to demand reform.

In response to internal and external calls for change, Ottoman statesmen inaugurated reforms that, among other things, began to dismantle community forms of identity connected to religious affiliation. In the mid-nineteenth century, reformers sought to restructure Ottoman society, including the Orthodox Church, through an expansive imperial reform policy known as the Tanzimat, which extended from 1839 to 1876.[9] Their goals were to reestablish the central authority of the sultan, legitimize the Ottoman state, and introduce a program of modernization that reached into all aspects of Ottoman society. As part of the restructuring process, civil reform guaranteed equality under the law for all Ottoman subjects and legislated freedom of religion for Muslims as well as non-Muslims. Freedom of religion was first granted by imperial edict in 1839 and reaffirmed in 1856.[10] By attempting to remove religion as a significant marker of difference, Ottoman reformers sought to develop a concept of Ottomanness (Osmanlılık) that they hoped would promote a more secular sense of modern citizenship with a dual connection among Ottoman subjects to the state as well as to a community of birth. Instead, the result was a greater fracturing of the polity.

The concept of freedom of religion within the Ottoman context requires some explanation. Christians and Jews had always been free to become Muslims, and some did, but conversion had never been an option for Muslims. Few Muslims chose to convert to what they considered an inferior religious and social position with limited rights. More relevant, perhaps, until the mid-nineteenth century apostasy for a Muslim was punishable by death. This reality explains why American missionaries early on understood that they could not proselytize among Muslims. Instead they turned their attention to what they saw as the "dead formalism" of the Eastern Christians and predicted that, with a reinvigorated and revitalized form of religion, the Eastern churches would return to "the pure faith of the Son of God."[11] In a period of extensive change, in the void between state promulgation of freedoms and their acceptance by the diverse communities, freedom of religion still posed a problem. Conversion was a thorny issue in all religious communities within the empire.[12] Court cases to determine whether conversions were forced or voluntary occurred not infrequently. Converts to Protestantism were dealt with harshly within their communities of birth.[13] If they declared themselves outside their community, or were expelled from it, they had no civil standing within a *millet,* might well lose their job or trade, would be ostracized by the community, and could not be baptized, married, or buried.

A solution to conversion or dissent that placed an individual outside a *millet* came to be seen as the establishment of a separate *millet.* An Ottoman imperial decree established a Catholic *millet* in 1831.[14] In 1847, with the aid of British diplomats, American Board missionaries in Constantinople gained recognition from the Ottoman state for a Protestant *millet* for converts from the Armenian community. Protestants obtained a charter that established their right to exercise their faith without fear of reprisals, choose a community leader to represent them, organize their affairs, levy and collect taxes, provide information to the appropriate authorities for a separate register of births and deaths, and petition for passports and permits of marriage. The charter, which was confirmed by imperial decree in 1850, was a radical departure from Ottoman community organization.[15] The Protestant *millet* was the only religious community that recognized a separation of church and state. It was led by a secular representative of the community, not a member of the clergy. As Protestants became an officially recognized community, they challenged the existing Ottoman legal structure and added to the empire's religious diversity.

Ironically, as Ottoman reformers worked to remove religious distinctions and shape a uniform Ottoman identity, they succeeded in undermining their goal.[16] As an unintended consequence of their reform efforts, religion took on a central role in emerging nationalist movements. Religious fragmentation increased among Ottoman subjects at a time when new ideas about nationalities were filtering into the empire. Among Bulgarian Orthodox Christians, religion and language became the dual pillars of an emerging vision of nationhood that encouraged escalating Bulgarian discontent within the Greek Orthodox *millet.*

Bulgarians were among those non-Greek populations within the Ottoman Empire who initially benefited from Greek education, Greek reform projects, and even the panhellenistic policies of the Greek state, but they eventually opposed Greek efforts to assimilate them.[17] Relations between Greeks and Bulgarians began to sour in the mid-1840s, however, when Greek cultural expansion became incompatible with budding Bulgarian national aspirations. Through expanding educational and commercial contacts within the Ottoman Empire and across Europe and southern Russia, a wealthy urban Bulgarian commercial class evolved that could support Bulgarian-language schools and a Bulgarian print culture and establish the foundations of a Bulgarian middle class with an appreciation for the accoutrements of national culture.[18] This middle class contributed to the forging of a new imagined community whose demands for social change challenged Greek cultural hegemony and the Ottoman concept of *Osmanlılık*.[19] Their activities came early on to the attention of American missionaries in Izmir and Istanbul.

Bulgarian Orthodox Christians were on the American Board's radar as early as 1840. They impressed the missionaries with their interest in the recently published New Testament in the modern Bulgarian vernacular sponsored by the British and Foreign Bible Society.[20] The successful sales of Bulgarian New Testaments at regional trade fairs first confirmed the promise of opportunity among the Bulgarians for the missionaries. Elias Riggs, among others, called for greater resources to be made available to publish reading material for Bulgarians. Writing from Izmir, he insisted on "the vast importance of good books in the machinery of modern missions" and argued for the need to expand the mission.[21]

Because Protestants believed that true Christians must be conversant with scripture, they placed great emphasis on literacy and familiarity with the Bible. The sixteenth-century Reformation had paved the way for vernacular translations of the Bible, which had hitherto been available only in Latin and Greek, but in the mid-nineteenth century no vernacular translation in Bulgarian existed. By providing the Bible and other reading materials in modern Bulgarian, the missionaries validated Bulgarian as a literary language and encouraged the Bulgarians in their demands for religious and educational reform.[22] Wittingly or not, American missionaries undermined Ottoman reform efforts and contributed to the further rupturing of the larger Orthodox community. When missionaries Harrison Dwight and Cyrus Hamlin submitted glowing accounts of Bulgarians following their travels through the Balkans after the Crimean War (1853–1856), their colleagues in Istanbul resumed their requests to expand their mission into Ottoman domains in Europe, where the largest population of ethnic Bulgarians (estimated at four to six million) lived.[23] They believed that Bulgarians' demands for the New Testament and their insistence on religious and educational reform were indicative of their openness to Protestant teachings. Among their new mission stations, they established a base in the town of Stara Zagora, in what is now south-central Bulgaria.

Bulgarian Women's Education

When American missionaries began to move into the Ottoman Balkans after the Crimean War, elementary schools for boys, and even some secondary schools, existed in most towns, but schools for girls were rare. Theodore Byington and his wife, Margaret, saw an opportunity. Potential converts to Protestantism must be able to read the Bible, but most girls were illiterate. American Board missionaries turned to teaching girls to ensure basic literacy among the young women they expected to be at the center of future Bulgarian Protestant homes. As leading members of the Protestant *millet*, the missionaries were authorized by the Ottoman state to open a school wherever they resided. Byington approached the leader of the *obshtina*, Khadzhi Gospodin Slavov, with a proposal to open a school for girls. Slavov was unimpressed. In his view, Bulgarians had "no need of foreigners doing good deeds." He told Byington to "go and enlighten the savages of Africa and other places who had no concern for the instruction and education of their youth."[24] It is unclear how Slavov came to think that the people of Africa were "savages," or whether Bulgarians in general shared the missionaries' belief that non-Christians were "savages." But Slavov's remark indicates that he was aware of a societal hierarchy based on race and education and that Bulgarians were not "savages" on either count. At a time when the Ottoman state had embarked on a program of modernization and Bulgarians were seeking to shape a new identity for themselves within the empire, the remark suggests that Bulgarian pride had been injured by Byington's plans. Despite Slavov's statement that Bulgarians were responsible for female education, the *obshtina* made no immediate plans to educate the young girls of their town. The idea that girls should be educated was only beginning to percolate into Ottoman society, whether Muslim, Christian, or Jewish.[25]

Ottoman reformers gave little thought to female education beyond the elementary level until the late nineteenth century. Not until the Public Education Law of 1869 did reforms mandate elementary education for girls as well as boys.[26] Even then, it was several decades before practice caught up with the law. But despite the lack of public education for girls, some Ottoman women in different societal strata did receive an education.[27] In elite households, governors and governesses were hired to teach basic literacy and the ornamental arts of music and conversation as well as household tasks. By the 1860s this practice extended to the households of the merchant classes. For nonelite families, religious institutions, charities, or individual clerics might organize schools in some neighborhoods: Muslim girls could attend Qur'an schools where Islamic scholars taught recitation; Christian girls could gain basic literacy in Old Slavic in the homes of priests or in convents. Girls might also learn to read from older brothers. Nonelite girls gained a domestic education to prepare them for future household duties from their mothers or neighbors. In the mid-1860s the Ottoman reformer Midhat Pasha organized industrial schools for orphaned girls to teach them to sew clothes for the military, a skill that would make them employable in the workshops and textile factories, even if work in this industry was poorly paid.[28] The mission school offered all girls the opportunity for a modern education. Education provided an opportunity for social mobility. As men in the commercial and administrative worlds sought educated girls as wives and looked to daughters to help in their work, an education might offer improved marriage prospects.[29] Orphaned girls who would be obliged to work might have a brighter future.

Recognizing that women, as mothers, were responsible for preserving cultural traditions, religious knowledge, and native language, some leading Bulgarian elites, including priests, had begun to call for girls to receive some schooling.[30] They recommended instruction in reading and religious education as a way to increase understanding of religious practices, eradicate superstitious beliefs, and raise future generations who would be free of superstition. According to this view, the future mothers of a fledgling Bulgarian nation needed an education to fit them to teach Bulgarian literacy, faith, and customs, but an education that was less rigorous than that for boys. Convent cell schools provided the origins of formal education for Bulgarian girls. Instruction was elementary and of little practical value. Girls were taught to read from prayer books in Old Church Slavic, the ancient language of religious texts that was no longer in everyday use. Some girls, particularly the daughters of priests and male teachers, attended school alongside boys. Generally speaking, however, it was considered inappropriate for girls to attend a mixed school.

Four obstacles prevented the development of education for Bulgarian girls in the 1840s and 50s. First, despite new ideas about the value of education, the general perception among Bulgarians was that girls did not need to be educated. Second, as few girls were educated, there were even fewer female teachers. Third, schoolbooks, or indeed instructional material of any kind, did not exist in modern Bulgarian. Finally, communities lacked funding for salaries and buildings. Attempts to organize female education in Stara Zagora came from men who had traveled abroad for their own education and appealed to Imperial Russia, as the perceived protector of Eastern Orthodoxy, to provide funds for female education.[31]

Among the first Bulgarian girls to study abroad were Anastasiya Mikhova (later Tosheva) and Alexandra Mikhaylova, who were thirteen years old when they left Stara Zagora in 1850 to study at a boarding school for the daughters of the Russian lesser nobility in Odessa.[32] Shortly after the young women returned in August 1857, the *obshtina* appointed them as schoolteachers in two of their parish churches.[33] A newspaper article about the school emphasized the importance of education for girls for their future duties as mothers and informed its readers that the teachers in Stara Zagora were ready to teach young girls everything they needed to be "a good mother and a good housekeeper."[34] The curriculum options at the new Bulgarian schools were inexpensive. The basic option was no different from the very elementary learning that girls received in convent schools. It included sewing, catechism, Old and New Testament, Christian prayers, and sums. A more rigorous curriculum included these subjects plus church history, writing, grammar (Bulgarian, Slavic, Greek, and Russian), geography, history, natural history, home economics, animal husbandry, rhetoric, logic, poetry, and literature.

Whatever the merits of the new Bulgarian schools in Stara Zagora, the teaching careers of Mikhova and Mikhaylova were brief and their hope to educate young girls short lived. Among the reasons for the closure of their schools after the first year were lack of parental interest, skepticism about the validity of the ambitious curriculum, doubts about the ability of the teachers, poor salaries, and the ambivalence of many Bulgarians about financing female education.[35] The basic obstacles to expanding educational opportunities for Bulgarian girls still prevailed. Theodore and Margaret Byington resolved to take advantage of the situation, all the more so as Theodore planned to discontinue preaching because his services were poorly attended. They were able to exploit a niche in Ottoman society to open a girls' school not only as a way to gain access to Bulgarian families to promote Protestant teachings, but also as a concrete example of their efforts to support the Bulgarian movement for education. They were initially successful precisely because no other opportunities existed in Stara Zagora for parents who wanted a modern education for their daughters.

American Interventions

Early on, American Board missionaries agreed that female education should represent the focus of their mission among Bulgarian Orthodox Christians and proposed as much to the American Board.[36] The missionaries saw an opportunity to respond to a need for female teachers and influence Bulgarian homes through daughters. A committee of Istanbul-based missionaries charged with reviewing the proposal recommended that a girls' school be founded at Stara Zagora as the most appropriate way for missionaries to gain access to Bulgarians and meeting their needs. They would train "Christian instructresses for their common schools."[37] The committee recommended that the school adopt a program on the model of Mount Holyoke Female Seminary. The curriculum, adapted for local needs, included reading, writing, arithmetic, grammar, geography, vocal music, needlework, health education, and Bible study.

Girls' boarding schools were a prominent feature of American missions, but their purpose was not to provide teachers for local communities. The objective of educating young women was to provide literate wives for the local men who became Protestant and trained as pastors and teachers.

Mission-school graduates were supposed to serve as models of good Protestant wives and mothers. The American Board reaffirmed this objective in a pamphlet that highlighted the centrality of the Christian home to Protestant communities. Every native community should have "at least one household illustrative of the fruits of Christian culture" because "the basis of a true Christian civilization must be laid in the *homes* as well as in the *hearts* of the people."[38] Yet the missionaries in the Ottoman Balkans saw the value in training female teachers. By meeting local needs, they would curry favor with the local community. While young girls were students, they would introduce Protestant teachings into their homes. Once they graduated as teachers, they would bring Protestantism to schools. Only later would they marry. American Board policy yielded to needs on the ground.

The Byingtons adapted one floor of their house for the school, which they opened in January 1863. Theodore acted as school supervisor and taught Bible instruction; Margaret took on the responsibility of supervising the boarding department as an extension of her domestic duties. Although missionary reports do not record Margaret's teaching activities, one Bulgarian source identifies her as among the school's teachers.[39] The American Board appointed Mary Esther Reynolds, a single woman, as the mission school's first official American teacher. Although she was not a Mount Holyoke graduate, Reynolds spent time there during the summer of 1862 to prepare for her task.[40]

Despite Slavov's brusque response to Byington's initial proposal, Bulgarians initially welcomed the mission school.[41] The thirty students included local day girls, boarders from surrounding towns and villages, and daughters of poorer families, whose tuition the missionaries waived. Bulgarian families were impressed that girls from as far away as Svishtov and Rusé on the Danube attended the school at a time when illiteracy was the norm among women. Parents were happy that their daughters learned to read and write and studied grammar, geography, and mathematics; they were glad to see the girls learn to sing by reading music, and they particularly appreciated the training in housekeeping. But they were concerned that their daughters sang Protestant hymns and did not learn Orthodox teachings and church history.[42] A Bulgarian nun prevented some girls from attending the school after she discovered that they were learning not to make the sign of the cross.[43] According to Slavov, members of the *obshtina* were worried that Protestantism would "take root in young girls' hearts." The *obshtina* had only recently overcome considerable discord in the town over a proposal for local Orthodox churches to join the Uniate movement—that is, to merge with the Roman Catholic Church.[44] They were not about to allow the young women of Stara Zagora to introduce Protestantism in the families of the town.

In June 1863, the *obshtina* opened a girls' school as a direct response to the mission school. Reflecting in his memoirs on the mission school and subsequent progress in Bulgarian education for girls, Slavov recalled that the missionaries shamed local people into following their example.[45] Anastasiya Mikhova Tosheva confirmed that the *obshtina* opened their school in an attempt to preserve the community from the inroads that Protestantism was making among their daughters. In language that highlights the intensification of nationalist feelings among Bulgarians, Tosheva recalled in her memoirs that the leading men intended to "eradicate the evil threatening our nation." Those men had made no effort to ensure that Tosheva's school remained open in 1859. Only four years later, however, they faced a different situation. They encouraged Tosheva to resume teaching and "oppose the foes of our Orthodox faith and nationality" lest "the curse of God" and "the scorn of the nation" befall her.[46] It is unclear when Tosheva wrote her memoirs, which were published in 1911, and she may have been influenced by subsequent political developments to use such strong language. There is no doubt, however, that because their faith was a fundamental element of their identity, some Bulgarians believed that Protestantism represented a threat to their emerging sense of nationhood.

The mission school and the *obshtina* school nevertheless continued to coexist amicably for several years. The Byingtons retained two young women from their first graduating class—Maria Gencheva and Elena Khadzhi Ivanova—as assistant teachers in the school, and Tosheva's school hired three mission-school graduates.[47] Other graduates of the mission school returned to their hometowns and villages to open elementary schools. Several girls organized a summer school in the nearby town of Kazanluk, where the missionaries had established a substation and a bookstore. There the girls taught older women to read. Some girls helped their fathers keep business correspondence and accounts, offering a novel and useful way to contribute to the household economy. News of the school's reputation spread. By 1866, forty-five girls were attending, of whom eighteen boarded from surrounding towns and villages and more distant locations, such as Samokov to the west.[48]

Pleased with the students' academic progress, Theodore Byington also reported that Protestant teachings at the school had encouraged some students to reject Orthodox practices. The mission's strategy appeared to be working; mission school graduates had begun to form a vanguard of religious reform. Yet Byington was obliged to acknowledge a basic problem: mission school graduates were willing to reject some of the outward signs of Orthodox customs, such as making the sign of the cross and kissing icons, but they could not proselytize openly and were unlikely to take action that would result in the strong disapproval of their parents and community. The Byingtons believed that the right teacher could help them create a spiritual awakening that would produce the conversions they so wished to see. They wanted to create a "Bulgarian South Hadley," a reference to the town where Mount Holyoke Female Seminary was located, and asked the American Board to appoint a graduate of the seminary.[49] Their request was granted when Roseltha Norcross arrived in Stara Zagora in the summer of 1867, but by then Maria Gencheva had already converted under the careful nurture of Mary Reynolds.

Despite the favorable news of Gencheva's conversion, the failure of the missionaries to convert larger numbers of Bulgarians highlighted preexisting tensions within the mission. A growing rift appeared between missionaries who insisted on holding fast to the American Board policy of direct evangelizing and those who believed that education was an appropriate mission tool for social change. Among those who believed that teaching must remain directly subservient to preaching was Charles Morse, who distanced himself from his former support for the girls' school. In his view, the mission would have produced more converts if Byington had been preaching instead of teaching. Morse observed that the original rationale for the school, to prepare teachers for Bulgarian schools, was "fallacious and even injurious" because teachers in Bulgarian schools were expected to model Orthodox practices for their students, particularly when they accompanied them to church.[50] Morse argued that Bulgarian communities would make conformity to Orthodox practices an issue of employment: mission school graduates who chose not to make the sign of the cross or revere icons would not be employed as teachers in Bulgarian schools. To counter Morse's argument, Byington reported that one graduate had taken Protestant practices into a Bulgarian school where she taught. Commenting on this not insignificant achievement for the mission, he described a Bulgarian school "in which the sign of the cross has not been made, nor pictures [icons] worshipped, nor the Church catechism taught."[51] But it was precisely the increasing practice of Protestantism among the girls of Stara Zagora that fuelled tensions between the mission and the *obshtina*. When Margaret Byington's continued poor health forced the couple to return to the United States in 1867, and Charles Morse and his wife, Eliza (also a Mount Holyoke graduate), replaced them, those tensions erupted in open conflict.

Maria Gencheva at the Center of National Strife

The conflict between the *obshtina* and the mission came only two months after the Morses arrived in Stara Zagora. Morse's handling of the confrontation marked a critical turning point in relations between the missionaries and the Bulgarian community and provoked a wave of anti-Protestant sentiment. The mission strategy of targeting young girls was on trial as a legal conflict focused international attention on missionary activities and signaled the end of the mission school in Stara Zagora. For Morse, freedom of religion and his rights before the courts were at stake. For the Bulgarian community, their religion and traditions were under threat. Although Gencheva stood at the center of this incident, she is largely absent from mission reports and the discussions of the court case and its consequences.

Maria Gencheva left no record of how she came to attend the mission school, but a memoir from a contemporary, Petrana Chirpanlieva, sheds some light on the status of orphans and the recruitment strategy of the missionaries. As a sickly orphan (a child without a father) in a primarily agricultural society, Chirpanlieva had little chance of marriage, in part because she was unable to offer a pair of hardworking hands to contribute to her potential in-laws' household economy. She had no hope of a future life "in a family among working people"; instead, her place was "in the monastery." Her fortunes seemed to change when Theodore Byington arrived in the small town of Shipka in 1863, when she was ten years old. He offered her a free education and told her mother that the teaching profession would guarantee her a living. Chirpanlieva was happy at the prospect but spent only one month at the mission school. Her brothers persuaded their mother to remove her from the school because they did not want to see their sister become a Protestant.[52]

Unlike Chirpanlieva, Gencheva remained at the mission school. She was among the school's first graduating class in 1865 and stayed on as an assistant teacher. She subsequently became engaged to Andrey Tsanoff, a convert to Protestantism who had graduated from the mission school for boys in Plovdiv and was an assistant teacher there. Morse described her as "a young lady of uncommon ability and decision of character."[53] Because the home was the site where the Bulgarian Protestant identity was to take shape, the Morses had taken Gencheva into the mission school, where they also made their home. She was being educated in the ways of American domesticity and trained to become the wife of a future Protestant helper. The records do not confirm how long Maria lived in the mission home, but it is likely that she moved there when the Morses arrived, and she brought her dowry of household items with her, indicating her intention to remain there until marriage.

At some point in September 1867, Gencheva's mother asked her to return home, and she did so. Morse believed that she was forcibly abducted. He had expected such an event and had previously instructed Gencheva what to do in case of abduction.[54] His expectation suggests that Gencheva's mother had not agreed to her daughter's move to the Morse home. Morse appealed to the local Ottoman administrator to return Gencheva to the mission home and uphold freedom of religion. At a meeting called by an Ottoman official, Maria declared her willingness to live with her mother as long as she could continue to practice the Protestant faith; however, she was apparently prevented by relatives from attending Protestant services. For this reason she chose to return to the mission house. Her decision caused no little consternation in Stara Zagora. It resulted in the attack on the mission house by her mother and several other Bulgarians, which led Morse to appeal to the U.S. minister resident in Istanbul to intercede with the Ottoman authorities on his behalf.

The United States had no consular offices in Balkan towns. Consequently, minister resident E. Joy Morris wrote to British ambassador Sir Henry Elliot, requesting that British vice-consul John Blunt in Edirne intercede on behalf of the missionaries. As part of his initial inquiry, Blunt urged the Ottoman governor-general at Edirne to take "proper measures for the protection of converts to Protestantism against persecution."[55] The governor-general replied that he had already received instructions by telegram from Istanbul to proceed to bring the guilty parties to justice.[56] He blamed the leading men of the *obshtina* for allowing matters to get out of hand. In his view, an incident that could have been dealt with quietly within the Bulgarian community had escalated to the point that Ottoman officials were compelled to take action.

By appealing to American and British diplomats to intercede with Ottoman authorities, Morse effectively removed the matter from Bulgarian control. Ottoman officials conducted hearings in Stara Zagora. Blunt, who attended the proceedings, reported that several Bulgarians accused by Morse had been held briefly in custody and released on bail pending investigation. They were reimprisoned during the trial that took place in December 1867. Blunt reviewed testimony from the trial and concluded that the proceedings were fair and impartial. In his view, the sentences imposed were likely to ensure the security of the missionaries and allow them to continue their work. The court determined that the attack was not premeditated. Based on the evidence, it seemed that the incident mostly involved women and children, and thus that leniency was in order. Blunt appealed to the Ottoman authorities to release the prisoners to "mitigate the embittered feelings of the Bulgarians."[57] Morse concurred.

Morse felt that he had made his point about freedom of religion and suggested that the Stara Zagorans still imprisoned at Christmas be released. The court granted the Bulgarian prisoners a pardon, and Morse believed that his plea for leniency was well received. But many Stara Zagorans remained resentful. Morse's intransigent approach toward the people among whom he worked sealed their determination to thwart the mission school. Morse scored a legal success but a moral failure.

Khadzhi Gospodin Slavov offered a Bulgarian perspective on the Gencheva affair.[58] His account did not dispute the basic details of the attack on the mission house provided in mission accounts, but he offered a defense of

Gencheva's mother. In his view, the missionaries promised that they would give Gencheva a good education and a paid position as a teacher so that her mother could enjoy her old age in comfort. But the missionaries forced the young woman to reject her family and the faith of her ancestors. When Gencheva converted, her mother was alienated. Gencheva was a poor girl. As Slavov saw things, the comforts of the mission home had turned her away from her own hearth and home. It seems that Gencheva had become engaged to Andrey Tsanoff without her mother's consent. The mother was obliged to reconcile herself to the idea that her daughter intended to remain a Protestant.

Slavov criticized the missionaries for converting young girls to Protestantism. Their goal, he realized, was to convert the girls then wait for them to marry, become mothers, and bring their husbands and children to Protestantism. Conversion was a painful personal issue for parents, as children embraced their new identity and distanced themselves from family and former acquaintances. It was a disturbing national issue for the *obshtina*, which was not about to sit idly by as Americans tried to turn more young women into Protestants. The townspeople of Stara Zagora took their cause to the national press, intending to warn Bulgarians across Ottoman domains about the missionaries' designs. Even before the court case, Slavov prepared a statement for *Makedoniya*, the most widely read Bulgarian-language newspaper of the late 1860s. In it, the town elders reported that they had recognized the missionaries' "murderous objective" to undermine their religious faith through indoctrination of their daughters. Local residents removed their daughters from the mission school and advised parents in other towns to take their daughters back home until such time as the *obshtina* could make arrangements for boarders.[59] The *obshtina* offered to provide free tuition for all children as long as parents provided for clothes and board. Petrana Chirpanlieva from Shipka, whose mother had removed her from the mission school in 1863 upon the insistence of the girl's brothers, was among the first students to be supported by the Stara Zagora *obshtina* in its boarding school.[60]

The Gencheva affair had repercussions beyond Stara Zagora, as prominent Bulgarians began to speak out publicly against Protestant proselytizing. Reports about the incident stoked criticism in the Bulgarian national press against "the Protestant propaganda." Russian consuls also reported on missionary activities, appealing to the Russian imperial government to do more to support education for Bulgarian girls as a way to counter Protestant ideas and Anglo-American influence.[61] Although Russian women in major Russian urban centers organized benevolent associations to raise funds to support Bulgarian girls in Russian schools, only twenty-four Bulgarian women studied in Russia in the 1860s and 1870s.[62] Moreover, based on press reports of schools in Moscow, the courses of study there were inferior to those offered at the mission school and at Tosheva's school.[63]

In a rare acknowledgement of Bulgarian public reaction, Morse reported that Petko Slaveykov, editor of the newspaper *Makedoniya,* had strongly condemned Morse's course of action in demanding Ottoman protection.[64] Slaveykov, a member of the provincial council charged by the Ottoman state with reform of the Orthodox Church from 1858 to 1860, was well known in missionary circles. He worked alongside American missionaries Elias Riggs and Albert Long in Istanbul to translate the Bible into modern Bulgarian, and his salary was paid by the British and Foreign Bible Society.[65] He sent his sons to Robert College, the educational institution for boys in Istanbul cofounded by former American Board missionary Cyrus Hamlin, and subsequently sent his daughter Penka to the Constantinople Home school.

Slaveykov's radical views on church reform and his close association with American missionaries may have earned him the suspicion of some Bulgarian critics that he leaned toward Protestantism.[66] In his openness to discussion about religious issues, he provided space in *Makedoniya* for articles by missionaries and Bulgarian converts to Protestantism. He was interested in new ideas but strenuously denied accusations that he was a tool of the missionaries or that *Makedoniya* was a Protestant paper. He supported the work of what he called the "Anglo-American Bible Society" to translate and publish the Bible and complimented mission publications for making available useful reading materials at reasonable prices for schools and individuals. He raged against the intrigues of the Greek Orthodox Church but also criticized what he called "Roman Catholic or Papist propaganda" and "Anglo-American or Protestant propaganda."[67]

Slaveykov generally wrote positively about American missionaries until the Gencheva affair, among other events that year, forced his hand. His commentary about events in Stara Zagora castigated the missionaries in that town. In his view, their objective was not enlightenment. He remonstrated against the "hypocritical fanaticism" of those who proselytized for "the domination of the Reformation."[68] He subsequently provided a forum in *Makedoniya* for a public debate on freedom of religion in which Gencheva's fiancé, Andrey Tsanoff, participated. In a lead article titled "Let's Move Forward," which appeared after the court case in Stara Zagora was resolved, Tsanoff urged all Bulgarians to put aside their differences. It mattered little, he wrote, whether Bulgarians were Orthodox, Protestant, or Catholic as long as they all worked for the common good.[69] Although Slaveykov defended Tsanoff's right to express this sentiment, he most certainly did not agree with it, and, in the fast-changing political reality of the late 1860s, he resolved to clarify his position.

Slaveykov was a major activist at the radical end of the peaceful Bulgarian movement for educational and ecclesiastical reform within the Ottoman polity, but other Bulgarian actors outside the Ottoman Empire looked to the prospects of armed rebellion to end Ottoman rule and establish Bulgarian political independence. Among these, in 1866 Georgi Rakovski helped found the Bulgarian Secret Central Committee in Bucharest, which organized armed bands to cross the Danube and carry out military attacks in 1867 and 1868.[70] In 1867 the committee also submitted a petition to the Ottoman sultan suggesting a political arrangement for Bulgaria within the Ottoman Empire on the model of the dual monarchy of Hungary and Austria. The attacks presented no real threat, but a combination of military and political action alarmed Ottomans and many Bulgarians. From the Ottoman perspective, the loyalty of Bulgarian subjects was in question.[71]

Bulgarian reformers believed that military action, political changes, and religious fracturing had the potential to destabilize their national project and call into question their allegiance. In the summer and autumn of 1868, leading Bulgarians in communities across the Balkans signed petitions of allegiance to the Ottoman sultan.[72] As loyal Bulgarians, they distinguished themselves from the insurrectionists who crossed the Danube, describing them as robbers and prisoners. The petitions expressed gratitude to the Ottoman government for protecting them from insurgents. Many leading

Bulgarians apparently believed that such expressions would earn apprecia-
tion from the sultan, who might then be more likely to press with the Greek
Patriarch the issue of greater autonomy for ethnic Bulgarians within the
Greek Orthodox Church.

Slaveykov chose this moment to make a personal profession of his faith
and his political loyalty. In the pages of *Makedoniya* he declared himself
staunchly Orthodox: "As a Bulgarian and a son of our holy orthodox church,
as in the past, so in the future," he wrote, "we shall respect and hold sacred
the following principle: Holding fast to the faith of our fathers and preserving religious unity is the first, greatest, and most important need of our
nation."[73] Slaveykov decried apostasy, urging his readers to remain united
in their Orthodox faith because religious unity was the only tie that held
them together. In his view, their patriotic duty had three elements: the first
was to the Ottoman Empire, the second was to religious unity, and the third
was to national education.

While he worked with American missionaries to translate the Bible into
modern Bulgarian, and appreciated American models for church and school
reform, Slaveykov reasserted his position as a Bulgarian Orthodox nationalist and reaffirmed the concept that to be Bulgarian one had to be Orthodox.
As a result of his encounter with American missionaries in a context in which
a small number of Bulgarians were resorting to military conflict to achieve
their aims, Slaveykov increased his commitment to the concept of reform
within the Ottoman polity and to Orthodox Christianity as an ideological
pillar of Bulgarian nationalism. Despite his friendship with and work for
American Protestant missionaries, Slaveykov was forced by political events
and the response to Maria Gencheva's conversion to take a public stand
against the inroads of Protestantism among Bulgarians.

Continuing Tensions in the Mission

The town elders in Stara Zagora hoped that by bringing the Gencheva affair
to the attention of a broader Bulgarian public through Slaveykov's newspaper
they could damage the reputation of the mission school and make parents
think twice before sending their daughters there. They hoped that by

reinforcing their own school and providing facilities for boarders they might compel the missionaries to close their school. The Bulgarians succeeded in removing local students from the mission school, but it took internal conflicts within the mission to force its final closure.

Charles Morse was again at the center of tensions that arose from a debate about the type of education that the mission school should offer girls. After the court case, the school's only pupils were out-of-town boarders. Morse focused his efforts on increasing the number of converts in the school. He viewed students not as future teachers but as "converting instruments" who could return to their homes to work as Bible women.[74] Morse's new strategy fit his philosophical stance that the mission should focus on evangelizing rather than educating, but it was shaped by the reality that Bulgarian schools would no longer hire mission-school graduates.

In this new environment, a dispute about the curriculum compounded ongoing tensions and contributed to a decision to close the mission school. The dispute ballooned into a debate not only about appropriate subjects of study for young women, but also about the independence of action of single women missionaries and overall mission management. In the face of dwindling numbers at the school, Roseltha Norcross launched an initiative to attract more young women by offering to teach English to advanced students outside of regular school hours. Opposing the idea, Morse asked rhetorically what the English language could do to make pupils "good Christian mothers," and he cited William Goodell's response to that same question in 1856: "Nothing, absolutely nothing."[75] Morse was among those missionaries who supported an emphasis on elementary education in the local vernacular language. He argued that the teaching of English wasted time that should be devoted to other duties. He believed that students who learned English would rise above their station, spurn missionary work, and seek more lucrative opportunities. To support his view, he referred to an American Board's report in 1856 that emphasized instruction in the vernacular to prepare a native ministry.[76]

The dispute poisoned relations within the mission. When poor health forced Mary Reynolds to leave Stara Zagora and return to the United States, Norcross wrote to the American Board advising against sending out a replacement. While Norcross welcomed the companionship of another single female teacher, she asked for the appointment of Reynolds's successor to be postponed "because we are not at present so amicably situated but that we look to another readjustment in the Spring and at this time the interests of the school are quite at stake."[77] The matter of English classes soon became moot, however. Roseltha Norcross died in late 1870, just three and a half years after she arrived in Stara Zagora.[78] Morse resigned, making good on his offer to withdraw from the mission over conflicts in the girls' school. Lacking leadership, the school operated in a fashion that was, as a mission report indicated, "rather spasmodic and less than optimal."[79]

In 1871, the American Board temporarily closed its mission station in Stara Zagora. The antagonism of the Bulgarian community toward the mission as a result of the legal battle surrounding the conversion of Maria Gencheva, conflicts within the mission about the form of education for girls, and a seriously depleted mission staff following the death of Norcross and the resignation of Morse all contributed to the decision. The experiences of the missionaries in Stara Zagora did not cause them to doubt the validity of their plan or their concept for change, however. The year they closed the school in Stara Zagora, they established a center of operations in Samokov, in the western reaches of the Ottoman empire. Maria Gencheva and her husband joined the new mission, where they worked as teachers in the mission schools.

The choice of Samokov for the new mission station was also dictated partly by changes in the local political situation and partly by a turnaround in mission fortunes. In 1870, Bulgarians finally succeeded in gaining from the Ottoman government agreement to recognize an independent Bulgarian Orthodox Church headed by an exarch. The decree established separate Bulgarian and Greek dioceses, and it stipulated that a diocese could join the Bulgarian exarchate if two-thirds of its inhabitants so voted. This stipulation guaranteed a continuation of intercommunity religious conflicts that missionaries hoped to exploit in mixed Greek and Bulgarian communities in the southwest Ottoman Balkans. The following year, a group of Bulgarians in the town of Bansko, also on the western edge of Ottoman domains not far from Samokov, established the first Bulgarian Protestant church, and from there the missionaries planned to extend their mission.

Gencheva and the Origins of Bulgarian Protestant Communities

When Rufus Anderson's successor as American Board foreign secretary, N. G. Clark, visited Stara Zagora with his wife, Elizabeth, in 1871, Maria Gencheva discussed her life and work with them. Elizabeth Clark reported in *Life and Light for Heathen Women* that Gencheva was grateful for Mary Reynolds's exertions on her behalf. "Only the judgment day can reveal what Miss Reynolds has done for me," she reportedly said. "When I think of what I was and what I am, I can never do enough to show my gratitude."[80] This account of a personal transformation engineered by a woman missionary confirmed the turning point of conversion that brought spiritual and intellectual change. It was certainly refracted through a missionary lens and intended to show the missionary endeavor in a positive light. It was undoubtedly a self-serving attempt by the missionaries to impress their supporters at home. Yet Gencheva's education at the mission school was a life-changing opportunity at a time of great social change in Ottoman Bulgarian society. She was able to avert the likely consequences of her orphan status to find personal and professional opportunities that would have been closed to her without her education at the mission school.

Long before the girls' mission school in Stara Zagora closed its doors, Maria Gencheva had become what Khadzhi Gospodin Slavov called in his memoirs "a great rarity."[81] She was a literate woman and a member of the first generation of Bulgarian women to exercise the professions of teacher and translator. Male missionaries had had little success among Orthodox Bulgarian Christians with their preaching and produced few graduates from their boys' school in Plovdiv. Gencheva was an important intermediary between the missionaries and the Bulgarians they hoped to reach.

The one detailed report of Gencheva's work is reflected through the prism of missionary translation. It nonetheless expresses her pride in her ability to discuss the Bible with other women who were as yet unable to read, and it shows that she helped establish the early Bulgarian Protestant communities through her work as an educator and Bible woman.[82] After graduation from the mission school, she divided her time between teaching and evangelizing in Stara Zagora. During the summers, she worked as a Bible woman in communities where American missionaries had established substations near the town. She spent the summer of 1870 in Bansko, five days' travel from Stara Zagora. Every morning Gencheva taught older women to read; in the afternoons she went visiting in the town to read the Bible and share her religious teachings with local women. It was the very next year that the inhabitants of the town founded the first Bulgarian Protestant Church.

The emphasis that Protestant communities placed on reading the Bible meant that women had to be literate, and Gencheva contributed to improving literacy among Bulgarian women. After she moved with her husband to Samokov, she began to translate evangelical and temperance tracts; she was one of only a handful of female translators in Ottoman Bulgarian society.[83] While Protestant communities made up only a very small percentage of the Bulgarian population, Protestant women were twice as likely to be literate as women in other religious groups.[84] Gencheva and young women like her were responsible for that statistic.

Maria Gencheva died in 1874. In an introduction to a tract that she translated, Andrey Tsanoff wrote that her only goal in life was to serve God and work for the good of her people. With her death, her mother had lost "a dear and worthy daughter," her husband had lost "a worthy friend, helper, comforter, and advisor," and her fatherland had lost "a true child."[85] From the perspective of the fledgling Bulgarian Protestant community, Tsanoff was at pains to emphasize that to be Protestant did not mean that one was not Bulgarian. Maria, as a Protestant, was also a "true child" of the nation, a true Bulgarian. Tsanoff disputed the claims of Orthodox nationalists that to be Bulgarian one had to be Orthodox.

As one of the first Bulgarian women to convert to Protestantism, Gencheva became a model for mission-school graduates and other converts. Although she experienced a temporary distancing from her mother, they were apparently reunited before her death. She found a new community with the Protestant mission center at Samokov, where she worked with her husband, and she remained there for the rest of her life. But she was not alienated from the Bulgarian community. Nor, ultimately, did Bulgarians reject Protestants from their midst. Bulgarian society was strong enough to counter Protestant proselytizing and flexible enough to accept individual Protestants among them. In 1879 Andrey Tsanoff became a representative to the first Bulgarian national assembly after Bulgarian independence from Ottoman rule the previous year. Unlike independent Greece, independent Bulgaria did not eject missionaries from their new state.

In an era of rapid social change, American missionaries were quick to exploit the uncertainties resulting from the dismantling of older forms of identity in Ottoman Bulgarian society. Their teachings offered an incomparable opportunity for young women whose futures, as orphans, looked bleak. But their attempt to transform a society at the very heart of its culture—in the home—provoked a backlash of mounting opposition from Orthodox Christians who were determined to defend their families, community, and religious practices. Conversion in the mission school succeeded in setting the Bulgarian Orthodox community against the missionaries and fomenting a defense of Bulgarian Orthodoxy that rejected the idea of religious freedom, further cementing the concept of a national Bulgarian religious affiliation.

Maria Gencheva's conversion highlights the complexities of the American-Bulgarian encounter. By converting to Protestantism, Gencheva made a spiritual, spatial, and legal move that marked her shifting religious and community identity. She worshipped at Protestant services instead of Orthodox services and taught at a Protestant school. She physically removed herself from her mother's home to the Morses' home. She transferred from the jurisdiction of the Ottoman Orthodox community to the Ottoman Protestant community. Her response to the social changes around her resulted in a change in personal identity that crossed religious, social, geographic, legal, and political boundaries. For the people of Stara Zagora, these changes represented a threat that transcended the purely personal. Conversion threatened the Bulgarian home, where Bulgarian culture was nurtured, and it threatened the growing sense of Bulgarian nationhood.

For women like Gencheva, conversion to a Protestant form of Christianity was inextricably linked to a redefinition of the domestic sphere and the community. Mount Holyoke Female Seminary was a powerful model for a school for Bulgarian Orthodox girls inasmuch as it emphasized home, religion, and a high level of education. Bulgarians who worked to promote female education agreed with the missionaries about the prominence of these three elements. In their view, however, the Christian home should be Orthodox, not Protestant. As missionaries sought to win the hearts and minds of the young women of Stara Zagora, the mission school became a site of confrontation. The Bulgarian Orthodox community mounted considerable resistance to the missionaries' efforts to transform their society and were successful in contributing to the closure of the mission school in their town. By bringing the activities of missionaries to the Bulgarian national press at a time when armed rebellion also threatened the status quo, the Stara Zagorans also contributed to provoking men like Petko Slaveykov to clarify their political position, not only vis-à-vis Protestant missionaries but also vis-à-vis an emerging revolutionary movement that saw military action as a solution to Bulgarian independence.

Home and school were the sites of missionary intervention, the locations of Orthodox nationalist resistance to that intervention, and the places where Bulgarian Protestantism was planted. Conversion to Protestantism and resistance to Protestantism were associated with new opportunities for young women as mothers and teachers. The mission school acted as a catalyst to restimulate efforts in Stara Zagora to improve female education. It was successful in educating several women in the first generation of female Bulgarian teachers. Mission school graduates worked alongside graduates from the *obshtina* school across the Ottoman Balkans, providing some of the earliest Bulgarian community schools with trained elementary school instructors. Young unmarried women had the mobility denied missionary wives to go out among the local population to preach and teach. Finally, the mission school trained the first generation of Bulgarian Bible women. Ultimately young women like Maria Gencheva established the bedrock of a nascent Bulgarian Protestant community. In the twenty-first century, as Bulgarian Protestants emerge from half a century of eclipse under Communist rule, they find the Bible women who were graduates of the Stara Zagora mission school at the origins of their communities.[86]

Whatever the spiritual motivation for Gencheva's conversion, she was aware of the social implications of her decision in a rapidly changing world that offered new prospects. Under Ottoman law Gencheva was technically an orphan. She lived with her mother but her father was absent, perhaps dead. An orphaned status promised a bleak future because a widowed mother was likely unable to provide a substantial dowry for her daughter or procure a good match for a future marriage. The convent was the only alternative to marriage until lay teaching became a professional option in the mid 1860s. The promise of education and employment was highly unusual at a time when the very idea of openings for paid employment for women outside of seasonal manual labor and cottage industries was new. By taking advantage of her mission school education and marrying a Bulgarian who had converted to Protestantism, Gencheva embraced an opportunity for herself that other Bulgarian women could emulate. As one of the first generation of trained Bulgarian women teachers, she promoted female literacy, contributed to the development of education in Bulgaria, and encouraged women to take an active role in learning about religion. She was a player in the nascent Bulgarian national home envisioned by Bulgarian nationalists and in the global Protestant community envisioned by American missionaries.

CHAPTER 3

The Mission Press and Bulgarian Domestic Reform

I n his annual report for 1869, missionary Albert Long commented on a
new development in Bulgarian society: Bulgarian Orthodox women had
begun to campaign publicly for improved access to education for their daughters. Across the Ottoman Balkans, they organized associations to raise funds
for schools and teachers' salaries. They read Martha Jane Riggs's *Letters to
Mothers,* and they subscribed to the mission magazine *Zornitsa* (*Day Star*),
which Long published. Their activities confirmed for Long that the efforts of
the missionaries in Istanbul to reach Bulgarian Orthodox women through
their publications had been successful. Missionaries now had an appreciative audience for their message. Long reported that Bulgarian women were
enthusiastic about the cause of education, and he expected to reap the benefits of their interest.[1] He believed that Bulgarian women would be attracted
to Protestantism as they became acquainted through the press with evangelical American ideas about home and society.

Long was correct that Bulgarian women were influenced by the ideas they
encountered in mission publications, but he was disappointed in his expectation that they would turn to Protestantism in large numbers. At a time of
increasing Bulgarian nationalism, when few Bulgarian women were literate
and most girls did not go to school, Bulgarian women saw in the Protestant

78

message an opportunity to demand respect for themselves and greater educational opportunities for their daughters so that they could contribute to the
progress of an emergent Bulgarian nation. In the process, they constructed a
hybrid message using a language that combined strains of American domesticity, Ottoman reform, and Bulgarian nationalism.

Mission publications were popular at a time when reading materials for
women in modern vernacular Bulgarian were sparse. An analysis of the place
of *Zornitsa* within the Ottoman Bulgarian press and the content of Riggs's
Letters to Mothers, which were first serialized in Bulgarian in *Zornitsa*, reveals
how missionaries promoted American cultural ideals to a broad audience
across the Ottoman Balkans. An exploration of their reception among Bulgarian Orthodox Christians highlights the purposes American ideals served and
why missionaries misjudged the outcome of their efforts to influence Orthodox Christian home life.

The American Mission Press and Ottoman–Bulgarian Print Culture

The earliest mission influence in Bulgarian print culture dates to the 1840s,
when Elias Riggs worked alongside Konstantin Fotinov in Izmir to translate
the Old Testament from modern Greek into Bulgarian. At the same time,
Riggs arranged for several mission tracts to be translated and printed in
Bulgarian, and Fotinov began to publish a Bulgarian version of the Greek-
language mission magazine.[2] According to Riggs, the Bulgarian magazine
was a direct result of mission work among the Greeks; it was sustained without mission expense and offered "one instance illustrative of the indirect
influence of missionary exertions in these parts."[3] Encouraged by Bulgarians'
earlier interest in the translated scriptures, he wrote to the American Board of
Commissioners for Foreign Missions urging an expansion of their mission
to include Bulgarians, reminding his colleagues in Boston that "reading
Christians will ever be the soundest Christians."[4]

Like Riggs, Long believed that the most promising avenue for American
missionaries would be to influence Bulgarian efforts to promote literacy.
Young Bulgarians were becoming "a reading generation," he noted, and
they needed good reading materials.[5] Long entertained literary ambitions
and believed he could bring Bulgarians to Protestantism through the printed

word; for "when these children grow up with our books in their hands," he wrote, "then will come the great harvest."[6] Like Theodore Byington, Long was disappointed by the poor results of his preaching. Interested in the study of language and literature, he saw an opportunity to fulfill his personal ambitions while attending to mission goals and meeting Bulgarian needs.

But Long needed a printing press, and here he encountered his first difficulty. Aware of the potentially subversive quality of the published word, the Ottoman government refused to authorize printing presses in its European domains. Even the first official Ottoman press in the Balkans was established only in 1865. Long first tried to work with Bulgarians to gain Ottoman authorization for a printing press in Turnovo, where he was stationed from 1859 to 1863. He and Pandeli Kissimov, the son of a prominent merchant in the town, made renewed applications to Ottoman authorities for permission to establish printing operations together. The Ottoman officials refused permission, granted it, subsequently revoked it, and finally left the matter in abeyance until Long and Kissimov gave up hope.[7] Long, who was originally commissioned by the Missionary Society of the Methodist Episcopal Church, saw an opportunity to achieve his ambitions by working with the American Board operations in Istanbul. In 1863, he joined Riggs and two Bulgarians, Petko Slaveykov and Khristodul Kostovich Sichan-Nikolov, to make up the translation team for the Bulgarian Bible, *Zornitsa, Letters to Mothers,* and other mission publications.

When he began his publishing activities in 1864, Albert Long became a player in the international effort to gain influence among Bulgarian Orthodox Christians. By the 1860s Istanbul had become a major center of publishing for all the religious and ethnic groups within the Ottoman Empire.[8] American missionaries, Ottoman officials, foreign diplomats, and Bulgarian nationalists all recognized and used the power of the press to introduce new ideas and shape public opinion and civic identity.[9] Using innovative print technology and distribution methods from the United States, missionaries expected to transform Ottoman society through the medium of the press.[10] Given that translating the Bible would be a very long task, they had published translations of shorter tracts, didactic materials, and magazines first. By the time they expanded their mission to the Bulgarians, they had printed millions of pages in several languages used in the Ottoman

Team of translators for the Bulgarian translation of the Bible sponsored by the British and Foreign Bible Society and printed in 1871. From left to right: Khristodul Kostovich Sichan-Nikolov, American Board missionary Elias Riggs, Methodist Episcopal Church missionary Albert Long, Petko Rachov Slaveykov, ca. 1860s. Courtesy Hilandar Research Library, Ohio State University.

empire through a publishing house owned by an Armenian Protestant family, the Minasians.[11]

The Bulgarian-language press also began to expand in the 1860s within a revitalized Bulgarian urban culture that evolved from commercial and proto-industrial development across Ottoman Europe.[12] Merchants, artisans, and the first generation of secular teachers had already opened schools for boys and organized reading rooms (*chitalishta*) for men, following a Greek model. These reading rooms subscribed to newspapers and periodicals and offered instruction in reading for adults who had not had the opportunity to attend school. They provided a new focal point outside the church, the marketplace, and the café, where men could meet, discuss the day's events, and read newspapers or listen to someone reading from them. No such public space existed where women could learn to read.

The overlapping interests of Americans and Bulgarians converged in *Zornitsa,* the monthly eight-page illustrated mission magazine that Long founded and edited from 1864 to 1871. *Zornitsa* was the longest-running Bulgarian periodical in magazine format until Bulgarians won independence from Ottoman rule in 1878. The magazine thrived in a precarious business environment at a time when the press was a novelty for most people in Ottoman domains. Several Bulgarian periodicals launched in the 1860s folded within twelve months, and newspapermen were frequently in debt and disillusioned about their prospects.[13] *Zornitsa* was a popular, long-running, well-circulated magazine because Long was able to avoid the obstacles that plagued other editors. The innovative content and format of *Zornitsa* contributed to its high circulation numbers, which also relied on low price and unique distribution channels.

Zornitsa was popular for a number of reasons. It was the only illustrated Bulgarian-language periodical in the 1860s. Designed as a family magazine, it included in almost every issue articles for and about women, which were rare in the few Bulgarian periodicals. The first women's journal in Ottoman Turkish, *Terakkı-ı Muhadderat,* did not appear until 1869.[14] The short-lived Bulgarian-language *Ruzhitsa* for women and *Pchelitsa* for children appeared only in 1871. In format and content, therefore, *Zornitsa* was unique.

The magazine was also popular because it offered a compendium of easy-to-read articles on religion and general educational topics and introduced Bulgarians to American life. In keeping with evangelical magazines published in the United States, *Zornitsa* carried stories from the Bible and articles about manners, moral virtues, and Christian duties. Natural history, science, and geography were also the subjects of many of the general articles. American social institutions—schools, the press, asylums, prisons, the American Bible Society—were showcased as successful symbols of a modern, prosperous nation. The lives of such major American political figures as George Washington and Benjamin Franklin appeared frequently and were held up as models to be emulated.

Circulation figures, which were considerably higher than most newspapers and periodicals in the 1860s, also point to the popularity of *Zornitsa*. Bulgarian publications rarely exceeded a circulation of several hundred. Only six months after he began publishing, Long claimed that all manner of Bulgarians were reading *Zornitsa* and that there was hardly a town where his "little sheet" was not carried.[15] On average, two thousand copies were printed each month, and the number of regular subscribers rose from a low of 700 in 1867 to a high of 1,480 in 1869.[16] By 1870, Long estimated that his reading and listening audience had reached three thousand.[17] In contrast, the Bulgarian conservative weekly *Suvetnik* (1863–65) had 1,000 subscribers in 1863, and the pro-government *Turtsiya* (1864–1873) began publication with 400 subscribers.[18] The official bilingual Ottoman gazette *Tuna/Dunav* (1865–1877) had 1,500 subscribers.[19] Only Petko Slaveykov's radical reform paper, *Makedoniya* (1866–1872), was more widely distributed (according to the localities where subscribers resided) and, with 3,600 subscribers, enjoyed a larger circulation than *Zornitsa*.[20] The radical revolutionary publications printed outside the Ottoman Empire circulated clandestinely and reached small numbers of Bulgarians.

Part of the success of *Zornitsa* can be attributed to its low cost and effective distribution channels. Compared with Bulgarian publications, *Zornitsa* was cheap, consistent with the broader mission pricing strategy. Providing inexpensive Bibles, books, tracts, and periodicals was the goal of the American Bible Society, the American Tract Society, the British and Foreign Bible Society, and British and American missionaries worldwide.[21] *Zornitsa* sold for five grosh (piasters) in Istanbul and twelve grosh elsewhere.[22] These prices considerably undercut other Bulgarian newspapers and periodicals published in Istanbul in the 1860s, which sold for between forty and eighty grosh.[23] The higher prices were frequently too much for the market to bear; both Petko Slaveykov (*Makedoniya*) and Ivan Naydenov (*Pravo*) complained about the failure of subscribers to pay their subscriptions.[24] In Shumen, where Methodist missionary Walter Prettyman settled in the 1860s and Bulgarian Iliya Bluskov was subscription agent for the daily *Pravo* and the monthly *Zornitsa*, the former had fifty subscribers, the latter two hundred.[25] People who might not be able to afford a daily newspaper could perhaps stretch to a monthly magazine.

Zornitsa was also widely distributed, despite the difficulties inherent in a region without a regular postal service. Here the mission press enjoyed a particular advantage: colporteurs (backpacking salesmen) of the British and Foreign Bible Society and the American Bible Society delivered *Zornitsa* to all towns where American missionaries had stations, substations, or bookstores, and to towns and villages that they traveled through en route. The colporteurs also sold the mission magazine to individuals and book handlers at inns and trade fairs throughout Bulgarian-speaking regions of the Ottoman Empire. As with all publications, readers could order by subscription and wait for family members or neighbors who lived part-time in Istanbul to deliver the magazine when they returned home. Wealthy urban and expatriate Bulgarians donated subscriptions to many Bulgarian villages.[26] Slaveykov sent copies of *Zornitsa* via travelers to his wife, Irina, in Tryavna, a small mountain town. He remarked that no reading materials were as widely distributed and sold as those of the missions and Bible societies.[27]

The same strong distribution channels ensured that *Letters to Mothers* would be widely read, and, like *Zornitsa,* the book was priced cheaply. The ways in which Bulgarian women and journalists took up the language of domesticity in the early 1870s confirm the existence of a broadly scattered audience. *Letters* was first serialized in *Zornitsa* between 1864 and 1869. As a result of the popularity of the articles, three separate Bulgarian-language editions were subsequently published, although evidence for the sales figures for each edition is harder to come by.[28] Most of the book titles published in the Bulgarian language in the 1860s and 1870s were textbooks, many of them primers, which were also eagerly purchased.[29] Given the dearth of general reading materials other than textbooks, a good price, and an expanding reading public, *Letters* would likely have sold well among a small but significant and appreciative audience. One Bulgarian educator, Atanas Iliev, noted in his memoirs that Riggs's *Letters* was the first book on child pedagogy that he read before leaving Stara Zagora for Prague to study pedagogy in 1869.[30]

Echoes of Domestic Discourse before 1864

Letters to Mothers resembled in content, format, and style the advice books in Martha Riggs's own library, which included works by popular antebellum writers, educators, and reformers, such as *The Child's Book on the Soul* and *The Mother's Primer, to Teach Her Child Its Letters and How to Read*, both by Thomas Gallaudet, *The Mother at Home*, by John Abbott, and Lydia Sigourney's *Letters to Mothers*, from which Riggs drew heavily for her own book.[31] Although *Zornitsa* provided the first Bulgarian-language outlet for Riggs's writings, the key themes in her writings had been circulating in mission publications since the 1830s and also found their way into Bulgarian newspapers and journals. Elias Riggs arranged for Gallaudet's works to be translated into Greek in Izmir in the 1830s and into Bulgarian in Odessa in 1840.[32]

Also in Izmir, Riggs arranged to publish the original Greek edition of his wife's book in 1842 and the second in 1844.[33] The first edition, published in a print run of five hundred copies, sold out rapidly.[34] The second edition bore the approval of the Society of the Friends of Education in Athens, among whose founders were John Kokkonis, who had studied with missionaries in Izmir, and Georgios Gennadios, father of the founder of the Gennadius Library in Athens.[35] This group promoted public education for girls in Greece and opened the first school for girls with subsidized fees and free tuition for poor families. The ideal of the mother-as-teacher appealed to these innovative Greek educators.

New ideas filtered into Bulgarian society chiefly through Greek publications. By the mid-nineteenth century Protestant tracts that promoted the ideal of the mother-as-teacher also appeared in translations from Russian and Serbian. They were translated by a very small number of urban Bulgarian women who had begun to emerge in public spaces as writers. In Belgrade in 1853, Stanka Nikolitsa published a translation into Bulgarian from Serbian of an original English text whose title she rendered in Bulgarian as *Famous Women*. The text used examples of prominent women from the past, chiefly from England, to argue that it was time for Bulgarian women to obtain an education and command more respect. *Famous Women* began with the notion that the status of women in any society was an index of social progress. As women made up half the human race, the argument went, they were consequently the cause of half or more of its prosperity if they were wise and good, and of its misfortunes if they were not.[36] Unlike Riggs's mothers, however, the majority of the women cited in *Famous Women* were praised as wives and daughters. In a postscript to her translation, Nikolitsa appealed to women to challenge the contemporary social order in the cause of women's education.

Shortly after she returned from Odessa to Stara Zagora in 1858, Aleksandra Mikhaylova translated a short tract, presumably from the Russian, titled "A Mother Who Gives a Useful Lesson to Her Daughter," which was published in the only Bulgarian-language newspaper in Istanbul at the time, *Tsarigradski vestnik* (1848–1862).[37] The text had clear American Protestant origins, fit squarely with Riggs's philosophy on the maternal teacher, and was an example of the kind of childrearing techniques Riggs promoted. It is a moral tale of a tussle of wills between a mother and her daughter, Mariyka, who must complete her sewing tasks before she can play, and it emphasizes the selflessness of "English-American lady teachers" as a model to follow. At a time when articles in *Tsarigradski vestnik* emphasized the responsibility of fathers, not mothers, to instruct and educate their children, Mikhaylova's article, with her byline in print, was a new development in ideas about education and the prominence of women in society.

Also in 1858, Bulgarian readers became acquainted with Harriet Beecher Stowe's *Uncle Tom's Cabin,* the first American novel to appear in Bulgarian translation. Dimitur Mutev, the editor of the journal *Bulgarski knizhitsi* (1858–1862), or perhaps his sister Elena, translated the work, most likely from Russian; it was initially published serially in that journal and then immediately thereafter in book form.[38] Stowe's novel introduced Bulgarian readers to strong images of protective mothers as guardian angels protecting the home, images they would recognize from their own culture.[39] In women like Rachel Halliday, they met a mother who was the epitome of maternal influence and Christian nurture in a Christian home, an example of a mother whose love and instruction could earn eternal salvation for her children.[40]

Not all writings in Bulgarian about women agreed with these sentiments, and not all writings about women came through mission sources, but these translations by Nikolitsa, Mikhaylova, and Mutev were early attempts to introduce the concept of maternal influence.[41] They may have allowed the ideas in *Zornitsa* to gain traction in the 1860s. With the Bulgarian translation team established in Istanbul, *Letters* took on new life among Bulgarian readers.

American Domestic Ideals in Letters for Mothers *and* Zornitsa

Patterned after popular advice manuals for girls and women in the antebellum United States, Riggs's *Letters to Mothers* provided a direct link between New England evangelical culture and Orthodox Christian culture in the mid-nineteenth century. The Riggses were mediators in introducing Orthodox Christians, Greek and Bulgarian, inside the Ottoman Empire and in the diaspora, to popular American writers, educators, and reformers. With her writing Riggs contributed successfully to the missionary enterprise and operated as a member of a transnational literacy network, yet retained her core identity as a maternal domestic teacher.[42]

Riggs's *Letters* emphasized the missionary credo that Christian home life was foundational to the development of Christianity and civilization. Three major themes from New England publications were interwoven into the advice contained in her twenty-four letters: the mother as nurturer and teacher, the status of women in Christian societies, and the association of educated womanhood with national progress.[43] With these themes, Riggs offered Bulgarian women a conceptual framework through which they could examine their status in Ottoman Bulgarian society and construct a new position of maternal power grounded in their everyday experiences. Riggs's focus was on women's duties, not their rights. The ongoing struggle for women's rights in the United States and Europe had no place in her world. What was innovative in her seemingly traditional message was the emphasis on child-rearing as a national task, the superiority of Christian women, and the contributions of women's domestic work to national prosperity.

Riggs's advice included an emphasis on the mother as nurturer and teacher: nurturing the soul, caring for the body, cultivating the mind, and shaping character. Hers was a holistic approach that encompassed the spiritual, physical, intellectual, and social development of the child. Within her overall theme of maternal influence, she constantly reiterated certain key phrases, including maternal love (*maychina lyubov*), maternal care (*maychina grizha*), and maternal duty (*maychina dluzhnost*).

Riggs assured her readers that only Christian mothers who were enlightened in both religious and secular matters could raise healthy children, gain eternal salvation for them, and nurture intelligent, useful and upright members of society. For missionary wives like Riggs, working to ensure the salvation of their children was their primary duty in life.[44] She promoted the idea of the lifelong process of nurturing, arguing that children would grow up as Christians and live their lives as useful citizens if their mothers provided a sound Christian environment and solid Christian teachings even into young adulthood. If she fulfilled her duty in all respects she could leave the consequences to Divine Providence. This advice was very much in tune with the ideas of the maternal associations of New England that received its clearest expression in Horace Bushnell's influential *Views of Christian Nurture* (1847).[45]

Riggs reassured Bulgarian women that they could acquire the necessary qualifications for their task. She advised her readers to organize meetings in which they could discuss childrearing issues and work for their own education. Anyone engaged in the instruction of others, she wrote, must follow the advice to "know thyself" and be responsible for oneself. She advised women to organize a "parents' association."[46] Given the significance of maternal associations to missionary wives, and the focus on mothers in *Letters to Mothers*, the suggestion of a parents' association, rather than a mothers' association, may seem strange; but the words "maternal" and "parental" were frequently used interchangeably in articles in *The Mother's Magazine* that missionary wives received.[47] Although Riggs's message was grounded in antebellum New England culture, she occasionally took aim against elements of Bulgarian culture. In recommending biblical stories as a source of appropriate childhood reading material, she directly criticized Bulgarian folklore, with its many superstitions and tales of nymphs and fairies. In her view, such stories were frivolous, unedifying, un-Christian, and unlikely to prepare children for the decisions they would need to make in their world. At a time when oral folk culture was strong, and when learned Bulgarians, following the German Romantics, were collecting and recording folklore, criticism of tales about nymphs and fairies was a rare missionary attack on Bulgarian cultural practices and Bulgarian nation-building activities. Riggs may not have appreciated that Bulgarian folk tales were part of the Bulgarian cosmology and helped them make sense of the world in which they lived.

Bulgarian religious didactic writings, such as the *damaskini* (popular sermons), were in agreement with her, however. They had also criticized popular interest in fairy tales in an effort to persuade ordinary Bulgarians to learn more about their Christian religion.[48]

Riggs also provided a primer on infant care and child development, discussing infant physiology and psychology, the mind-body connection, and the need for order and regulation in patterns of feeding and sleeping.[49] This approach suggests that she regarded maternal instincts as necessary but not sufficient for the work of motherhood. In a series of letters, she gave detailed, almost scientific, instructions on cleanliness, clothing, diet, exercise, and sleeping, including an occasional Franklin aphorism such as "Early to bed, early to rise." Finally, she chastised women who allowed servants to bring up their children while they gave themselves over to the pleasures of society, including fashion, the theater, and alcohol. Wasting their days in frivolous pursuits, she argued, would undermine their moral authority. Riggs was in tune with contemporary critics of conspicuous consumption, including Bulgarian satirical works, such as Dobri Voynikov's *Krivorazbranata tsivilizatsiya* (1871), that lampooned women who followed the latest French fashions (*alafranga*) and wasted their days in idle pastimes.

Throughout the letters, Riggs emphasized the need for mothers to shape the intellects of their children. *Constant* and *consistent* were her watchwords.[50] A mother should teach her children their letters and numbers and develop in them an understanding of shapes and colors, all of which could be done in a way that was amusing as well as instructive. She should constantly ask the children questions to help them develop the habit of observation and learn to name objects. When children asked questions, mothers should take time to answer them. Here Riggs was following the instructional models offered by Thomas Gallaudet, and since Gallaudet himself was influenced by the pedagogical approaches of Johann Pestalozzi, Riggs was returning European ideas to Europe imbued with New England sentiments.

Advice on character molding also took up a good deal of space in *Letters*.[51] The first lesson a child should learn, from its earliest age, was the lesson of obedience and submission to the will of its parents, which would prepare it for a life of obedience to God. Mothers should be gentle but firm in punishment, the purpose being to convince a child of wrongdoing and leave it to understand its action in its own conscience. Riggs crafted a number of vignettes that explained how to teach good behavior. Industriousness, she noted, was the duty of every member of society and thus every member of the family. She advised mothers that children should always tidy up their own books and toys and be found tasks commensurate with their age so that they learned as early as possible the adage "a place for everything, and everything in its place" and the notion that "there is no greater economy than economy of time." Riggs insisted that children had to learn that duty went before pleasure by completing their tasks before they were allowed outside to play. Boys and girls alike needed to learn these lessons.[52]

Although some of the other articles in *Zornitsa* spoke to a wife's relationship with her husband, most supported Riggs's opinions about maternal duties. For example, some articles encouraged women to take part in the great endeavor of educating their people. noting that those who could read could teach this skill to their neighbors. The task of education would not hinder women in their domestic duties; on the contrary, education was an integral part of their domestic work.[53] If one were to ask what Bulgaria needed most, the author of one article mused, the answer would have to be "mothers, not just girls in their ornaments and finery, but mothers, sober-minded, God-fearing, educated mothers." Bulgaria needed mothers who could do more than feed and clothe the bodies of their children; it needed mothers who could mold their children's spiritual character and prepare them for their civic responsibilities. The article clearly stated that the future of the Bulgarian nation depended "more on the current generation of Bulgarian women, and not so much on the men."[54] It was a strong affirmation of the power of maternal influence in modern society.

Riggs also articulated the American evangelical view that Christianity was responsible for the respected position of women in Christian societies. She argued that women owed everything to their Christian religion and, consequently, to their education. In contrast, she referred to some six hundred million inhabitants of the world who had not yet accepted Christianity. They were "deluded in the darkness of idolatry" and did not regard any woman as "a partner of man, a happy wife, a respected mother."[55] Using standard missionary rhetoric that exemplified a form of evangelical Orientalism, Riggs described the humiliating and degrading position of women in non-Christian societies, where polygamy, infanticide, and the enslavement of daughters were common. She wrote that nations such as India and China, where women lacked enlightenment and knowledge of Christ, were doomed to a vicious circle of perpetual misery and degradation unless women accepted Christianity and recognized their maternal duty. She encouraged Bulgarian women to reflect on images of women in India and China and then ponder the treatment of women in their own society.

Supporting articles in *Zornitsa* expounded the evangelical view expressed in Riggs's letters that national progress was a function of the status of women in society. They also emphasized the converse: wherever women remained uneducated and were not respected, nations failed to progress and prosper. Missionary stereotypes from non-Christian societies found their way into *Zornitsa*. One article described the practice of foot-binding and the neglect of girls' education in China.[56] Its message was that ignorance and superstition were the causes of Chinese women's low status, which in turn was the reason for China's failure to prosper. One particularly graphic illustration came from India. A sketch depicted a sari-clad woman cradling a baby while standing on the bank of a river. Barely concealed in the water lurked a wide-jawed crocodile that would likely devour the child before it had time to drown. The text that accompanied the image described the woman as an "Indian mother" who planned to send her daughter to an early death to save her from a life of degradation in a society that devalued women.[57] Had the newborn child been a boy, the article said, the parents would have celebrated. Another article on the gendered division of labor in Native American villages included a comment on a frequent sight in Bulgarian villages: a man riding a horse followed by women and children on foot carrying tools. The article condemned Native American gender relations as inappropriate and injurious to women and suggested that Bulgarian gender relations were also harmful: Bulgarian men were lazy and disrespectful toward their women, who bore the greater burden of field work.[58] The implication in *Zornitsa* was clear: Bulgarian society failed to prosper because Bulgarian women were neither respected nor educated to their tasks as Christian women.

Finally, Riggs emphasized the association of educated Christian women with

national progress. In a passage so similar to the words of Lydia Sigourney's
Letters to Mothers that it must have been directly copied, Riggs insisted that
to "exercise the office of maternal teacher" was the most powerful expression of enlightened Christianity and patriotism. Following Sigourney, Riggs
argued that "woman is surely more deeply indebted to the government that
protects her than man, who bears within his own person the elements of
self-defense." Consequently, "secluded as she wisely is from any share in the
administration of government," woman could do nothing more useful to put
her patriotism into action than "to teach by precept and example that wisdom, integrity, and peace which are the glory of a nation."[59] Here Riggs reiterated the message that Christian women had a responsibility to the nation
of which they were citizens. She argued that women "shaped the character of
nations as well as individuals."[60]

Emphasizing the need for female leadership, Riggs insisted that Bulgarian women had a great opportunity to exercise their moral and intellectual
abilities as they raised their children to be "useful members of society" who
would eventually take on their own responsibilities in life and contribute
to the progress of their community and nation.[61] She impressed upon her
readers that they should value spiritual and intellectual development more
highly than material goods. Education rather than ornamentation was her
recommendation for the preparation of daughters for their future responsibilities as mothers. Offering examples from ancient history, Riggs argued
that Semiramide and Cleopatra had conquered kings and emperors with
their feminine charms and wiles; as historical agents, however, they were
not recognized as worthy mothers of famous men. They could not command
the forces that a well-educated daughter would command. Neither wealth
nor fashion nor female charms could compete with the spiritual and intellectual development that shapes future generations.

Riggs's mention of Cleopatra and Semiramide revealed the fascination
of antebellum American women with the ancient world. But Riggs saw them
as poor role models because they relied on beauty and guile. The Roman
matron Cornelia was a much better example of an ideal mother from ancient
times. In a story told and retold in antebellum periodicals, one day a group
of Roman women who were admiring their jewelry asked Cornelia to show

her jewels. Cornelia presented her children and insisted that they were her true jewels.[62] Here again, Riggs was in tune with Bulgarian religious and secular teachings in the mid-nineteenth century, when the church and the *obshtinas* (town councils) tried to ban external displays of luxury, including the wearing of necklaces made of gold coins.[63] Cornelia offered an example of feminine civic virtue by rejecting material objects in favor of spiritual and intellectual growth. Daughter of the prominent general Scipio Africanus and wife of the consul Sempronius, she educated her daughter, Sempronia, to be a true Roman mother and prepared her sons Tiberius and Gaius for service to the Roman Republic.

Cornelia was an example that Riggs could use to good effect. Even though she was not a Christian, Cornelia understood what it meant to be a good and worthy mother. She was a splendid example of a maternal teacher from the ancient world, a great mother of great sons. Among other "great mothers of great sons," Riggs included Elena, the mother of Constantine the Great, "a learned woman of incalculable influence."[64] No one would argue, Riggs wrote, that Elena did not mold the character of the first Christian emperor of the Roman Empire. As the feast day of Saints Constantine and Elena was a prominent one on the Orthodox calendar, and as the capital Constantine founded had been under Muslim control since 1453, the significance of this example was likely not lost on educated Bulgarian women. Riggs argued that boys in particular needed the moral guidance of their mothers, and she urged Bulgarian women to disregard the erroneous opinion that they could have no influence on their sons. In her view, a mother's direction was essential: all the famous men in the world were molded and directed in their early years by their mothers.

Letters and *Zornitsa* contributed to making the idea of female authority and female education more visible in Ottoman Bulgarian society in the 1860s. Riggs encouraged her readers to channel their domestic responsibilities into new avenues of public reform. She tapped into a vein of interest by offering a positive model of motherhood that Bulgarian women recognized and could reconfigure for their own purposes at a time when female education was beginning to be discussed and women were starting to emerge into the public sphere as teachers and writers. Riggs's *Letters* and other articles in *Zornitsa* were popular precisely because they offered women a modern form of social identity alongside a task that resonated with their traditional contributions to society.

Bulgarian Rearticulations of Domestic Discourse

Like people in all of the communities of the Ottoman Empire, Bulgarians negotiated the social changes that resulted from Ottoman reforms, the growth of trade relations with Europe, and the infiltration of new ideas in the mid-nineteenth century.[65] In small towns across the Balkans, where middle-class groups began to emerge, women were able to take advantage of new ideas to restructure their female identity within a redefinition of Bulgarian domesticity. They began, as Albert Long reported, by organizing themselves in women's associations. In 1869 the first generation of literate Bulgarian women in an emerging urban middle class recognized in themselves the ideal of educated Christian motherhood. They saw a way to exercise their agency as mothers, work for change, and demand educational opportunities for their daughters. They embraced the concept of maternal moral authority celebrated in the language of domesticity and used it to organize women's associations as an entrance to the public sphere, where they could contribute to the emergent Bulgarian nation.

Traditional Bulgarian family structure recognized the authority of mothers, particularly mothers of sons, and their importance as conduits of culture. They gained respect as contributors to the household economy and were accustomed to running households at a time when husbands were frequently absent earning a living through seasonal migrant labor. Women in the countryside and small towns alike engaged in entrepreneurial activities—running inns, renting workshops, loaning money, and selling food to passing travelers. Women who were obliged to work outside the family economy hired themselves out for pay as servants, harvesters, and textile workers in fledgling proto-industrial workshops.[66] Only one or two generations removed from preindustrial society, most of the women who organized lived in small towns, where they became prominent members of this emerging middle class as the wives of artisans, merchants, and teachers. They attended church services with their families and visited local sites of pilgrimage. Outside of church services, however, women had no organizational structure beyond the home in which to operate until the idea of female education gained hold in the late 1860s. Building on traditions of charitable giving and new ideas about the value of education, Bulgarian women raised money for girls' schools, which then gave them a public space in which to gather and a new form of social identity.

Charitable donations fulfilled an important social function within Christianity and Islam. Few women had the wealth to exert much public influence, but by the mid-1860s some women began to support book publishing. Evidence from subscription lists suggests that a growing public of literate women helped support the publication of a wide range of reading materials.[67] Subscription lists guaranteed prepaid printing, and in return for subscribing an individual would receive one or more copies of the book. The lists provide a valuable perspective on the contribution of women to the provision of reading materials and the development of female education. Women's names began to appear in subscription lists in 1819 and increased in frequency over the next forty years. For the most part female subscribers were nuns who donated symbolic sums of money and widows who made more substantial donations. Wives and occasionally daughters were listed alongside husbands and fathers. By the late 1850s the names of teachers and even students appeared, and by the 1860s most lists included women subscribers.

Bulgarian women were eager to join and donate money to the women's associations that began to emerge across the Ottoman Balkans in 1869. From May to December that year, Bulgarian women founded fourteen associations based on the idea of maternal influence. Within three years the number had tripled.[68] They developed a public voice that evolved from their position as mothers. Among the names they chose most frequently for their associations were those reminiscent of the titles of Martha Riggs's *Letters:* Maternal Love (*Maychina lyubov*), Maternal Care (*Maychina grizha*), Maternal Duty (*Maychina dluzhnost*), Mother (*Mayka*), and Educated Mother (*Vuzpitana mayka*). They presented their objectives in printed pamphlets and circulars, promoted their activities in Bulgarian newspapers, subscribed to national newspapers and magazines, and opened women's treasuries to collect donations for female education. A typical goal was to open at least one girls' school in their town and provide the salary of a female teacher. If funds permitted, they opened girls' schools in surrounding villages as well. Some associations also aimed to raise money to send girls abroad for an education.[69]

Like subscription lists, the published lists of donations from the women's associations specifically for female education demonstrate the extent of women's engagement in the public sphere. Published in the press, the women's contributions made Bulgarian communities across the Balkans and in the Bulgarian diaspora aware of this new social movement and its impact. At the first meeting of the women's association in Kazanluk, forty-five women contributed. As one might expect, their status in the community determined the size of their contributions: old women and widows made small donations, teachers gave modest sums, wives of leading men gave large amounts, and the wealthiest women bequeathed property such as stores and workshops.[70] Anastasiya Tosheva commented that in Stara Zagora the townswomen tried to outdo each other in their eagerness to register and pay dues.[71]

Stara Zagora was the site of one of the earliest women's associations, *Maychina grizha,* which became a model for future associations. *Maychina grizha* provides a telling example because it illuminates the influence of missionary activities while at the same time revealing Bulgarian determination to resist Protestantism. Stara Zagora was the site of the mission school for girls founded by Margaret and Theodore Byington, which, in 1863, became a catalyst for renewed efforts among Bulgarian Orthodox Christians to develop education for girls in the town. Inspired by the language of domesticity, Anastasiya Tosheva was determined to counter the popularity of the mission school and Protestant teachings.[72] At the same time, Tosheva recognized the power of the Protestant message of maternal authority. She and Tonka Boycheva, a graduate of the Stara Zagora mission school, were among the founders of *Maychina grizha,* as was the wife of Khadzhi Gospodin Slavov, the leading member of the *obshtina* who sparred with Theodore Byington in their discussions about female education in the town.[73]

The name and founding date of the Stara Zagora association are disputed in the historical record, largely because the memoirs of the protagonists disagree: *Maychina grizha* (Maternal Care) and *Maychina lyubov* (Maternal Love) are both mentioned as names; 1865 and 1866 are both possible founding dates. By 1869, however, reports of the association's activities began to appear in the Bulgarian press. According to the newspaper *Makedoniya*, the women of Stara Zagora had recognized "their own want of learning" and decided to support six poor girls for four years in the recently opened Bulgarian girls' school in their town.[74] Since their purpose was to train the girls as teachers for outlying villages, the girls would be required to return to their hometowns and villages as teachers at the end of their education. By 1869 *Maychina grizha* supported the boarding school that the Stara Zagora *obshtina* opened that year in the wake of the Maria Gencheva affair. Newspaper reports of the Stara Zagora association served as an impetus for women in nearby towns, who rapidly formed maternal associations, not so much to resist Protestant inroads (although Protestant teachings were spreading as mission-school graduates began to work as teachers and Bible women in key towns) as to emulate the women who had already organized. The widespread geographic distribution of associations in towns across the Balkans by 1870—from Tulcea in the northeast to Veles in the southwest—suggests that word about maternal organizing spread fast.

In their speeches at gatherings, Bulgarian women took up all three themes emphasized by Martha Riggs: women were important first teachers of their children; women's status correlated with national progress; and educated women could make important contributions to national development. Their speeches always culminated in a plea for Bulgarian communities to do more to educate their daughters because they would be the future mothers of the nation.[75]

In Kazanluk, one schoolteacher, Rakhil Dushanova, a leading member of the women's association in that town, urged women to follow the example of the women who had organized in Stara Zagora and Lom. She closely patterned her foundation-day speech on Riggs's writings. Dushanova told her audience that women had the greatest influence in society. "Whether a home is good or bad, a community successful or not, a people prosperous or not," she said, "we are the ones who make it so." Like Riggs, Dushanova looked for female models in the ancient past and suggested the medieval Bulgarian princess Theodora, but she recommended that the women of Kazanluk look for contemporary models among themselves. Each of them in isolation would achieve little, she noted, but gathered together they could be a force for change.[76]

In Turnovo, Evgeniya Kissimova and like-minded women in the town founded an association called Women's Council (*Zhenski suvet*). Kissimova was the sister of Albert Long's friend Pandeli Kissimov. Although the name of the Turnovo organization differed from most maternal associations, Kissimova's speeches are typical of the ways Bulgarian women channeled the ideas that they encountered in *Letters* into support of Bulgarian national goals. In a speech at their inaugural meeting on September 8, 1869, Kissimova explained to her audience that the women of Turnovo had gathered to work together for the education of women. Their first duty as mothers was to prepare their daughters to become "worthy mothers," because only worthy mothers could raise "useful sons." She commended her members for beginning their work and implored them to continue to raise funds to educate Bulgarian girls and women.[77]

What was striking about Kissimova's speech, however, was her use of an image that had appeared in *Zornitsa*. She urged the women at the gathering to ponder the picture of an Indian mother who was about to kill her baby daughter by throwing her into a river. Then she asked them to reflect on how that woman might have behaved had she been raised in a society where women were educated and respected. Kissimova's borrowing of this stock missionary image came just three months after the graphic illustration appeared in *Zornitsa* for the second time, in June 1869, where Kissimova, who was a subscriber, had doubtless seen it. Similar images appeared not uncommonly in other American evangelical publications, particularly tracts aimed at children.[78] One such image found its way into one of the earliest Bulgarian books on geography (1843), which Konstantin Fotinov translated from an American geography book published in Greek by the missionaries.[79] There it was accompanied by text describing India as a colony to which the British and Americans brought Christianity and various aspects of civilization. The image was likely an unfamiliar one to most Bulgarians, who were used to comparing themselves with their local neighbors—Greeks, Turks, and Serbs in particular—but not with people who lived at greater distances.[80] Kissimova's inclusion of the missionary trope indicates that she was aware of some sort of racial or ethnic hierarchy. In this first speech, she addressed her audience as "my dear women of the same stock (*mili moy ednorodki*), which suggests an understanding of a common descent among Bulgarians.

In the Balkans, which had been crisscrossed by many different tribes and ethnicities in the distant past, a shared common descent was unlikely (as it was, and is, in many other places). Still, along with language and religion, the idea of a "same stock" offered the possibility of identification through a shared racial history that distinguished them from their neighbors.

A discourse of difference was useful to Kissimova as she sought to differentiate Bulgarian women as Christians within the Ottoman Empire. Her message was unmistakable: Bulgarian women did not wish to count themselves among the uneducated and despised women of the world. In her speech at the third meeting of the Turnovo women's association, Kissimova lamented the fact that Bulgarian women went without instruction while their menfolk were being educated at home and in Europe (that is, outside the Ottoman Empire). According to Kissimova, "our poor sex" remained "mired in ignorance," and she deplored Bulgarian women's "shameful level of education" compared to that of European women.[81] Her use of Europe as a comparison was a clear indication that women were looking outside the Ottoman Empire for sources of inspiration. As Bulgarian women negotiated new social and national identities within the empire, at a crossroads between Europe and Asia, they aspired to be counted among Europeans, not Asians. Kissimova argued that women owed it to themselves and their daughters to work for change. If they failed to act, they would be held in disdain. Reiterating a message from *Letters* and *Zornitsa,* Kissimova reminded her audience that "our dear Bulgaria has no greater need than for worthy, educated mothers."[82] To this end, she urged the women of Turnovo to do more than provide a material inheritance for their daughters. They needed to provide "the spiritual riches of learning and enlightenment," and a "spiritual dowry" that would never be consumed.[83] The Roman matron Cornelia was an appropriate model for Bulgarian Orthodox women.

In their speeches and writings, two of these women in particular — Evgeniya Kissimova and Anastasiya Tosheva—show an awareness of the larger context in which they had begun to organize. Like Petko Slaveykov, they also demonstrate a dual allegiance to the Ottoman state and the Bulgarian nation that puts them outside the Bulgarian revolutionary movement and within the framework of reforming Bulgarian nationalists who envisaged change within the Ottoman polity. Despite earlier radical leanings that had led to his exile from Ottoman domains in 1862, Evgeniya's brother Pandeli subscribed to the idea of a dual Ottoman-Bulgarian monarchy on the lines of the Hungarian monarchy within the Austrian empire.[84]

Kissimova recognized that the movement for Bulgarian-language education emerged from Bulgarian resistance to Greek cultural hegemony and Ottoman reforms. She thanked the ruler of the Ottoman empire, Sultan Abdülaziz, for granting Bulgarians freedom to learn and pray to God in their mother tongue. She also insisted that only worthy mothers could raise worthy sons who would be useful to their fatherland and to their sultan.[85] This appeal to the name of the sultan may have been a necessary encomium in view of Ottoman censorship, but such appeals were also a recognition of the contribution of the household to the Ottoman state.[86] At the same time, Kissimova likely wanted to assure the authorities of her loyalty. She may also have responded positively to Ottoman reforms that aimed to engender in Ottoman subjects a dual loyalty to the state as fatherland and to their ethnic nation.[87] In this respect her use of the word "fatherland" is interesting. Pandeli Kissimov published a radical Bulgarian-language newspaper, *Otechestvo* (Fatherland), in Bucharest. For the Kissimov family, "fatherland" meant Bulgaria. Kissimova made the distinction between the fatherland (the Bulgarian nation) and the Ottoman empire (represented by the sultan) and suggested that Bulgarian mothers could raise their sons to be loyal to both.

Anastasiya Tosheva likewise trod a careful path of dual allegiance. One of her few published articles, "An Incentive for Bulgarian Women toward Progress," is notable for its self-criticism in a mode of writing reminiscent of European and American Orientalism. It also expressed loyalty to the sultan and awareness of the larger Ottoman reform context. According to Tosheva, Bulgarian women were "engulfed in a cloud of prejudices" and needed to "wipe off the mud of benightedness" so that they could rise from the "abyss of ignorance."[88] Like Kissimova, Tosheva perceived Bulgarian women as backward and underdeveloped. She appealed to them to work through their women's associations to build schools where children would acquire learning that would be "of greater use to them than the material riches their parents left to them" and where their daughters would become "mothers worthy of their name, who would raise sons and daughters ready to sacrifice everything for the good of the fatherland and their Sovereign." She urged women to "search for the path illuminated by the dawn of revival and cooled by the light breeze emanating from the throne of our merciful Sultans, and set off along it taking our dear children with us, walking boldly and undeterred until we reach national consciousness." Tosheva's metaphors for the Bulgarian national movement and the progress of imperial reform are astute. The mental picture she created of women walking with their children along a path toward national consciousness accompanied by the wind of reform offers an image of dual allegiance, and its significance surely would not have been lost on her small audience of literate women and men. Tosheva's careful wake-up call was an appeal to women to promote the idea of Bulgarian progress within the Ottoman reform movement.

The rapidity with which Bulgarian women organized in 1869 confirms the national dimensions of their movement. With their choice of Orthodox feast days as founding days, they easily reconfigured the ideal of educated Christian womanhood to serve educated Orthodox womanhood. Popular dates for the founding of maternal associations and girls' schools included the Feast of the Transfiguration (August 6, the Gabrovo association Maternal Care), the Feast of the Birth of the Virgin Mary (September 8, the Turnovo association Women's Council), and the Day of the Annunciation (March 25, the Turnovo girls' school). The women of Kazanluk organized on May 11, the celebration of Saints Cyril and Methodius, patron saints of Slavic literacy and education, which was first celebrated as a national holiday in 1851.[89] Bulgarians also practiced the invention of traditions as they continued their nation-building activities in the mid-nineteenth century. By selecting the "national" day of May 11, the women of Kazanluk confirmed that they would contribute to the emerging national movement to promote Bulgarian education and the Orthodox faith.

Domestic discourse struck a chord with the first generation of urban educated Bulgarian women. Priests had argued that Bulgarians needed to educate girls because women were the preservers of cultural and religious traditions. But Bulgarian women drew from the language of domesticity more than the need to preserve traditions. They saw the value of women's education to national prosperity: educated mothers could make a modern and productive contribution to national progress by organizing and sustaining schools for girls who, as future mothers and teachers, would contribute to the spiritual and intellectual development of the Bulgarian nation and to its prosperity.

Bulgarian women who aligned themselves at the forefront of a movement for women's education in 1869 had a significant influence on national discourse, bringing the issue of education for girls to the national press. Articles about education, enlightenment, and national progress had been a staple of the Bulgarian press in Istanbul from its inception in 1848. Bulgarian newspapers and periodicals had sometimes extended this argument to women's education, but only sporadically before 1869.[90] It was not until women started to organize that women's education began to be featured prominently in the Bulgarian press. Within a year of the founding of the first women's associations and the publication of their speeches, "educated motherhood" became the mantra of prominent Bulgarian newspapers in Istanbul.

Like single women missionaries, however, married Bulgarian women experienced the limits of their success. In Turnovo, Evgeniya Kissimova's activities publicly challenged the power of the Bulgarian *obshtina* responsible for the provision of education. After failing to subsume her work into the *obshtina,* the men of Turnovo organized a campaign designed to discredit Kissimova. Anonymous critics reproached her for her ineffective emulation of Protestant missionaries, and they issued a public reprimand, arguing that she had used "all the mannerisms of Protestant missionaries from beginning to end, but without their accuracy, intelligence, and dignity."[91] They also accused her of mismanaging the funds she collected—a charge she denied by publishing her accounts—and they ultimately forced her to resign from the presidency of the Turnovo Women's Council.

In Stara Zagora, Anastasiya Tosheva also experienced the limits of female power. A new school board relieved her of her duties in 1870. Tosheva had carved out a position of power as head teacher, published author, and cofounder of the local women's association. It may be that more conservative members of the Stara Zagora *obshtina* were threatened by her emerging power base. It may also be that they no longer saw a need for a woman of her stature once the mission school had ceased to attract local girls. As Stara Zagora lost her services, however, the town of Gabrovo gained them. Mission-school graduate Tonka Boycheva was already in Gabrovo, and the two women contributed to organizing the women's association Maternal

Care and worked to develop a curriculum that was to make the Gabrovo girls' school the second, after Stara Zagora, to graduate students from a five-year course of post-elementary study.

Bulgarian Journalists and Domestic Discourse

Bulgarian women forced a debate in the national press about the contributions of women to Bulgarian society. By 1870 it was the rare Bulgarian newspaper that did not publish articles to promote women's education. Some even attributed Riggs's *Letters to Mothers* as the source of their content.[92] Publications across the political spectrum joined the debate. The pro-government newspaper *Turtsiya* opened its pages to Albert Long. The conservative yet pro-reform *Pravo* published articles that espoused the evangelical Protestant view of female education. The radical reform paper *Makedoniya* and the revolutionary *Svoboda* both advocated female education. Bulgarian historiography hails the reformer Petko Slaveykov and the revolutionary Lyuben Karavelov as major advocates of female education in the decade before Bulgarian independence from Ottoman rule.[93] Rather than being in the vanguard, however, they joined a movement that was well under way among literate women in 1869. Male journalists employed a language of domesticity to support the idea of female education only after women's activism made the issue prominent.

Karavelov, the editor of *Svoboda* (1869–1873), published in Bucharest, praised Bulgarian women for beginning to organize and admired them for promoting female education, but cynically asserted that women's associations would achieve nothing precisely because women were uneducated. Unless men joined as members, the associations would be "like a body without a soul."[94] Inverting the language of domesticity, Karavelov argued that the lack of worthy sons in Bulgaria was indicative of the lack of worthy mothers. Only in 1875, after he had repudiated his revolutionary political stance to focus on promoting education, did he begin to write in a more positive vein about women's potential to shape the nation.[95]

Like Karavelov, Slaveykov, the editor of *Makedoniya*, also published articles that initially expressed dismissive views of women in general and Bulgarian women in particular.[96] In 1867 he wrote that Bulgarian women had no concept of nationhood and thus could not be "mothers of the nation."[97] Like Karavelov, he was surprised by the emergence of women's associations. His mild consternation that women could act independently prompted him to wonder how Bulgarian women had advanced so rapidly. In August 1869 he praised Bulgarian women for their civic initiatives and was even emboldened to set an agenda for their associations, but his agenda reflected the goals the associations themselves had submitted to him for publication earlier in the year.[98] Slaveykov came to promote female education only after he became aware of Bulgarian women's activism.

The year 1869 marked a change in the discussion of women's education in the Bulgarian press. That year, the Ottoman government published a set of educational reforms developed in large part in response to the success of American Protestant mission schools. Ottoman administrators perceived Protestant efforts to educate Christian minorities within the empire as an attempt to undermine state legitimacy. The Ottoman Public Education Law of 1869 called for a massive restructuring of education across the empire.[99] Evolving from educational experiments in the Ottoman Balkans in the mid-1860s, it established compulsory education at the elementary level for all children in the empire. At the elementary level, children were to be educated in the language of their community. Beyond that level, all children who attended school were to be educated in Ottoman Turkish, regardless of their faith and ethnicity. Ottoman officials also proposed to establish teacher-training schools for girls to provide women teachers for girls' schools.

The proposals for post-elementary education, which were part of an ongoing effort by reform-minded officials to create a modern homogeneous Ottoman citizenship, were particularly disconcerting to Bulgarian nationalists. If Bulgarian children did not learn their faith and language at school, where would they learn them? As late as 1867, Slaveykov argued that educating children in Bulgarian was the job of priests.[100] By 1869 he no longer recommended priests as teachers. Shortly before translations of the Ottoman national education law appeared in *Pravo,* he decided that women should undertake the national task of teaching children the faith and language of their fathers. To this end, he argued that Bulgarians should do twice as much for the education of their daughters as for their sons. If they educated women, Bulgarians would educate the nation and consolidate their faith because women, as mothers and teachers, would raise future generations of Orthodox Bulgarians. According to Slaveykov, educated women would also offer a clear demonstration of the progress of the Bulgarian nation.[101]

When the Ottoman government established a quasi-autonomous Bulgarian Church by imperial decree in February 1870, it provided Bulgarians with a national institution around which they could coalesce as a national group. Bulgarians like Slaveykov who had worked tirelessly for church reform and educational advancement looked to this new institution to lead the way in Bulgarian education. Slaveykov immediately approached church representatives to take up the task of female education. It was a task for the nation, he wrote.[102] He requested that church funds be set aside to provide for schools of higher education to train girls to be teachers who would prepare better mothers for future generations. Only when Bulgarian women were educated and earned the respect of their menfolk could Bulgarians count on progress and enjoy "the true civilization of the gospel."[103] Slaveykov appealed for Orthodox reform using the Protestant ideology that permeated the Bulgarian press from the pages of *Letters* and *Zornitsa*. By 1871 he had embraced domestic ideology. He tailored American domesticity to fit his program of Bulgarian national reform in response to Ottoman proposals for a total restructuring of education within the empire.

Pravo, a reform-minded conservative newspaper, also embraced the message of domestic reform, publishing a series of articles on the education of women and children in 1869 and 1870. The articles fully represented the evangelical Protestant view of female education. They praised the conscientious mother who cherished her duty to care for her children physically and provide their spiritual, moral, and intellectual education. They suggested that despite the efforts made by many Bulgarian communities to build schools and provide education, Bulgarians had not achieved the results they desired because they had neglected education for girls. These articles asked Bulgarians to reflect on the philosophy of the Christian religion that had raised women from their inferior position in society. Again, the message was that Bulgarians needed to educate their girls, the mothers of future generations; otherwise, they would be destroying their chief means of progress.[104]

Pravo provided additional evidence that the concept of maternal influence resonated with Bulgarians and that the ideology of domesticity appealed to a broad political spectrum of Bulgarians. In 1872 the newspaper published a brief biography of the mother of Atanas Mikhaylov Chalakov, who became Exarch Antim I, the first Bulgarian leader of the autonomous Bulgarian Church established by the Ottoman government. A biography of a woman was in itself unusual, but it promoted the idea that the Bulgarian nation had mothers who could raise great sons for national leadership. According to the *Pravo* biography, Providence had ordained that Antim's mother, Baba Gena, should become "the worthy mother of a worthy son."[105] Baba Gena much regretted her illiteracy, and she ensured that her children received the best education she could arrange for them. She was the model of a great Bulgarian mother who had raised her son to be a leader of the Bulgarian Church.

American missionaries successfully exploited a need in Bulgarian society for reading material for women and girls in the 1860s. With *Zornitsa* and *Letters,* they contributed to a nascent Bulgarian-language press and worked to improve literacy, particularly female literacy. In targeting women, they expected to create a female audience for Protestant views and then shape the thinking of their new audience by appealing to their maternal authority. They were successful in creating an audience. Bulgarian women—and men—appreciated the ideal of the educated Christian woman whose child-rearing task took on national significance. Yet as women and the home became central to the idea of an emergent nation, where the Bulgarian language and the Orthodox faith were nurtured, missionaries failed to bring Bulgarian women and their households to Protestantism.

Through the pages of *Zornitsa,* Martha Jane Riggs and Albert Long promoted an American language of domesticity that resonated with the first generation of literate Bulgarian Orthodox women, who adapted it to bolster Orthodox nationalism. Women like Evgeniya Kissimova and Anastasiya Tosheva were easily able to convert the Protestant ideals they encountered in mission publications to Orthodox ends. They became the leaders of the first women's movement in the Ottoman Balkans and stood at the leading edge of a precarious alliance that sought to bolster Bulgarian Orthodoxy against the inroads of American Protestantism and the homogenizing tendencies of Ottoman reform. Like women in other colonial encounters, they found in the dual discourses of domesticity and nationalism a new subject position as conservers of tradition and harbingers of progress.[106] Entering the public sphere on a platform of maternal influence, Bulgarian women understood that they could work to change society. They injected a gendered language of reform into Bulgarian nationalism that newspapermen were quick to adapt for their challenge to Ottoman educational reform. Women's associations across Ottoman Europe raised funds for elementary girls' schools in the 1870s. Many towns established grade schools for girls before Bulgarian independence in 1878. In that small window of time, Bulgarian women did much to improve female education.

Yet the religious reform that Long hoped for did not materialize. Bulgarian interest in mission publications reflected curiosity about new ideas, but did not translate into commitment to Protestantism. Language and Orthodoxy were the two pillars of Bulgarian nationalism, and Bulgarians used domestic ideology as a resource to serve the vision of a Bulgarian Orthodox nation. The idea of women at the center of homes that provided microcosms of the nation held broad appeal. Because it was a nationalist discourse, the concept of educated Christian womanhood was sufficiently malleable to support the ideal of educated Bulgarian Orthodox womanhood. American missionaries were able to harness the power of the press, and they were able to influence the language of Bulgarian domestic reform, but they were unable to counter the power of Orthodox Christianity as a guiding force of Bulgarian nationalism.

CHAPTER 4

Unconventional Couples—Gender, Race, and Power in Mission Politics

During the early summer of 1876, tensions that had been festering for four years at the Samokov station of the American Board of Commissioners for Foreign Missions erupted into a major conflict that pitted two single American women missionaries and an Anglo-Bulgarian couple against the rest of the mission. The Christian home was at the heart of the crisis. Esther Maltbie and Anna Mumford had established unconventional domestic arrangements by setting up house together instead of living with a missionary family. The missionary couples at the station disagreed with the women's decision but did not prevent them from going ahead with their plan. When Maltbie and Mumford invited Elizabeth and Ivan Tonjoroff to stay with them for a short vacation, however, the married missionaries protested. In their view, the single women should have sought permission to invite the Tonjoroffs onto mission property. Maltbie subsequently complained about the missionaries' behavior to the American Board's foreign secretary, N. G. Clark. Maltbie used the language of home to reinforce their female authority and claim the right to make their own decisions about their household: "In our domestic arrangements and our merely personal affairs," she wrote, "we have felt that we ought to have the freedom and privileges of any other missionary family."[1] By setting up house together and asserting their rights

108

as a family unit, however, the two women disrupted the cultural formation of the ideal Christian home and challenged the gendered power structure of the mission.

Ostensibly about the management of mission property, the dispute masked a deeper issue. By insisting that the two women request permission to invite guests into their living space, male missionaries sought to control the activities of the single women and decide who they might and might not associate with. The missionaries disapproved of the women's friendship with the Tonjoroffs, who compromised the racial power structure of the mission. Their disapproval, as Tonjoroff learned to his surprise and regret, was connected to his marriage: "When two years ago Lord gave me a wonderfull helpmate in my English wife," he wrote to N. G. Clark in 1877, "great displeasure was felt by them, for what good reason, I do not know."[2] The reason was that the Tonjoroffs had a mixed marriage: Elizabeth Tonjoroff (née Bevan) was English, Ivan Tonjoroff was Bulgarian.

As Ann Laura Stoler has argued, mixed marriages threatened the order of colonial societies because they questioned the assumptions on which social categories were assigned, complicated recognition of national identity, and exposed the fault lines separating the promise of inclusion from the practices of exclusion.[3] Although American missionaries in the Near East did not operate within a formal American or British colonial context, they were products of a society that celebrated individuals of Anglo-Saxon descent as morally, socially, and intellectually superior to all other human beings. This belief was bolstered in colonial encounters at home and abroad and reinforced by global connections with the British.[4] New England missionaries shared the views of Europeans in other colonial contexts who believed that white women who married men of color were socially or morally deficient.[5] It was unthinkable to them that an individual of Anglo-Saxon Protestant descent would marry a non–Anglo-Saxon, even if a Protestant.

At the same time, by 1877 the very idea of whiteness had become contentious in the United States. Delineations of difference had long been established on the basis of color. In the final quarter of the nineteenth century, the legislatures of most southern and western states passed laws to prohibit marriage between individuals of European descent and individuals of African, Asian, Mexican, or American Indian descent. They were persuaded by "scientific" concepts of racial purity to believe that they could preserve the superiority of "whiteness" by preventing interracial sex and marriage between people deemed white and people deemed nonwhite.[6] But skin color alone did not determine racial difference. The notion of "variegated whiteness" evolved in the 1840s after large-scale migrations of Irish Catholics.[7] They appeared white, yet their Celtic culture and Catholic religion marked them as different from "native-born" Protestants and contributed to the perception that not all Europeans were "white." Later immigrants to the United States from central, southern, and eastern Europe discovered that whiteness presumed a hierarchy of races and civilizations that incorporated ideas about skin color, nationality, culture, religion, and gender. At the top of the hierarchy was the white Anglo-Saxon Protestant male. As a Bulgarian-born Orthodox Christian convert to Protestantism, Ivan Tonjoroff learned when he married Elizabeth Bevan that he was European and yet "not white"; he was Protestant and yet "not quite."[8]

The cultural formation of the Christian home also precluded the idea of marriage between Bevan and Tonjoroff. Anglo-American women were supposed to model the Christian home for the people among whom they worked; they were not supposed to become part of local homes. Women who defied the norm challenged the gendered and racial structure of missionary society. In that structure, a white Protestant woman was inferior by nature of her gender to her white Protestant husband, to whom she must be subservient; but she was racially and culturally superior to the "natives" (as missionaries everywhere called them) among whom she worked. If she married a native, a person perceived to be her inferior, how could she be subservient to him, even though he was her husband? In the eyes of the missionaries, Elizabeth Bevan was suspect. By marrying Ivan Tonjoroff, she had opened the door to foreign influences, rendered possible the idea of equality between American missionaries and their converts, and could no longer claim the privileges of Anglo-American culture. Her example posed a threat to missionaries' pretensions of superiority and offered a poor example to other single women in the mission community.[9]

Bevan, Maltbie, and Mumford envisaged a more egalitarian society. Bevan originally traveled to the Balkans to work as a governess in Plovdiv, where she met Tonjoroff. Before her marriage, she was occasionally acknowledged in missionary reports for "valuable services rendered" to the mission.[10] She accepted what the missionaries could not—an equal union of an English woman and a Bulgarian convert. When Maltbie and Mumford hosted the Tonjoroffs in their home, they demonstrated acceptance of the couple. In doing so, however, they transgressed the social boundaries of their missionary circle. This incident was only the last in a series of what the missionaries perceived to be their transgressions, but it was the most serious. It earned them the hostility of the mission as a whole and precipitated a serious rift that led to the women's departure for the United States and the Tonjoroffs' separation from the mission.

My analysis of the ways in which ideas about gender and race shaped this particular missionary encounter relies on discourse but also interrogates the behaviors of the parties involved. An examination of the aspirations of a new generation of professional single women reveals the challenges that single women posed to the authority of male missionaries. The attitudes of male missionaries toward single women and converts expose the inequalities that operated in mission circles. This chapter lays bare the gendered and racial framework of missionary society that denied women and converts access to material resources and prevented them from gaining social and professional standing among the missionaries. The resulting conflicts of power within the mission challenged the status quo but failed to dislodge it.

The Challenge of Professional Single Women

The missionaries' lack of success among Bulgarian Orthodox Christian men in the 1860s, combined with their greater success among young women and the inability of married women to do extensive Bible work, led them to make increasingly frequent requests to Boston for more single women as mission workers. Rufus Anderson was not generally well-disposed to appointing single women, but his successor, N. G. Clark, recognized their potential for mission work. In 1871, as missionaries established the headquarters of their newly created European Turkey Mission (a separation from the Western Turkey Mission) in Samokov, the American Board began to appoint larger numbers of single professional women who brought a new dynamic to mission arrangements. Established missionary families recognized that the advent of

Anna Mumford, ca. 1872. Courtesy Hilandar Research Library, Ohio State University.

single women missionaries complicated personal and professional relationships, but they were unprepared for their demands for independent action. When Maltbie and Mumford arrived in Samokov in the early spring of 1871 and 1872, respectively, the stage was set for conflict.

The change in policy at the American Board coincided with several social factors that opened new opportunities for ambitious single women after the American Civil War.[11] First, women's experiences in military hospitals,

Esther Maltbie, ca. 1880. Courtesy Hilandar Research Library, Ohio State University.

relief work, and family businesses during the war honed their organizational and managerial skills and shaped new expectations of what women might achieve after the war. Second, in the aftermath of the slaughter that deprived hundreds of thousands of men of their lives, and young women of their husbands, many women in the postwar generation might expect not to marry even if they wanted to. These women looked for fulfillment in occupations outside the family. Third, expanded educational opportunities continued to promote antebellum ideals developed by Catharine Beecher and Mary Lyon, among others, that teaching was the most appropriate field of endeavor for women. Fourth, expanded professional opportunities for men led to fewer men seeking ordination as ministers and consequently a reduction in the number of candidates applying to mission boards. Finally, women actively began to organize and promote women's work in mission, establishing denominational mission boards to provide female leadership and raise funds to support the work of single women. The Boston-based Woman's Board of Missions of the Congregational Church and the Chicago-based Woman's Board of Missions of the Interior sustained the work of the American Board and directed the labors of women missionaries. The women's boards resolved to fund single women appointed by the American Board, adopt those already under appointment, and assume responsibility for the girls' schools founded by American Board missionaries around the world.

Maltbie and Mumford belonged to this new generation of women missionaries. They were appointed to manage the mission school for girls in Samokov; Maltbie had oversight of assistant teachers, and Mumford ran the boarding department and supervised Bulgarian Bible women. They were well qualified for this work by virtue of their education and previous professional experience.

Unlike many of the missionary wives who were educated at Mount Holyoke Female Seminary and its daughter colleges, Maltbie and Mumford graduated from Oberlin College, an institution with different traditions.[12] Steeped in the culture of antebellum abolitionism, Oberlin was coeducational and admitted students of color. The college did not erase all the gendered and racial constraints of American society, but it offered an environment where students could imagine a less hierarchical society.[13] In addition to their alma mater, the two women had in common their experience of arduous work in the difficult conditions of the Civil War and its immediate aftermath. Following her graduation in 1862, Maltbie taught freedmen and women in the American South for eight years, an experience that likely contributed to her liberal attitudes toward race.[14] Mumford, a Civil War widow, taught in Michigan and Pennsylvania before her marriage, worked as a nurse in a hospital in Alexandria, Virginia, after her husband was injured at the battle of Bull Run, studied at Oberlin after her husband's death, and graduated in 1871.[15]

It was precisely the women's previous professional experience and independence of action that led to frictions with the missionary families. The tensions that developed between the single women and the married couples can in part be explained by the different expectations of the two groups, particularly as to the necessary qualifications for mission work. Missionary families had no professional expectations of single women. James Clarke believed that all a single woman would need was "a strong faith in Jesus, a warm, earnest heart, and readiness to work as providence should point out the way."[16] Similarly, according to Margaret Haskell "consecration to Christ and a love for perishing souls" were the only prerequisites.[17] In Haskell's view, the work was difficult, the qualifications were such that any pious woman could meet them, and the missionaries were disinclined to be critical or demanding. The divergence in expectations between missionaries already on the ground and the single women on their way was bound to cause difficulties. Several missionary families had been at their posts in the Ottoman Empire since the mid-1850s, and thus had not experienced at first hand the changes taking place on the domestic front in the United States. They had an entrenched perspective of antebellum society in New England. Conflict was all but inevitable.

The organizational structure of the mission also guaranteed a lack of independence of action for the single women. Single women were supported financially by the Woman's Board, but they were appointed by the American Board to a particular mission and were required to report through the lines of responsibility established within the mission. Although single women could be appointed to run girls' schools, they reported to the male trustees of those schools, who were chosen by the men of the local mission station. The men believed that they had ultimate responsibility for arrangements regarding the schools and insisted on making all important decisions. They argued that a missionary family be associated with the school, living either on one floor of the school or in a separate adjacent house. Single women were expected to board with missionary families. These arrangements, which effectively undermined the authority of single women, did not suit Maltbie and Mumford.

In the spring of 1873, Maltbie and Mumford proposed a fundamental change in living arrangements that challenged the supremacy of the male missionaries and subverted the idea of what constituted a missionary family. They proposed to set up house together. The women were almost certainly aware of plans for the Constantinople Home, a new center of women's missionary work in Istanbul funded by the Woman's Board of Missions that would include living quarters for single women missionaries. Maltbie and Mumford intended to make the same arrangements in the new construction to be built for the female boarding school in Samokov.

The men of the Samokov station understood the women's proposal for what it was—a radical departure from the norm and an attempt to establish some level of independence—and they determined to put a stop to the women's innovative views on life and work. The first missionary to warn his colleagues in Boston against the perceived unorthodoxies was William Locke, the husband of Zoe Noyes Locke. As he explained to N. G. Clark, "Our sisters Mrs. Mumford and Miss Maltbie claim that as they intend to keep house they shall constitute the missionary family" connected with the new female boarding school. According to Locke, the two women did not want another missionary family on the three-quarter-acre lot that the missionaries purchased for the school. Arguing against the women's plan, Locke wrote that "it seemed best to us *men* to buy as much land as we did that we might have it all under control."[18]

Chafing under the tight supervision of the Samokov station, Maltbie and Mumford certainly sought to gain some autonomy in their living arrangements and their work. They wrote to inform N. G. Clark of their intention of "keeping house" and asked his advice as to how best to go about it as their salaries were "too small to buy even a kitchen stove." They subsequently wrote to request clarification of their relations with the men of the station.[19] The women took care to emphasize that they were not stepping outside their bounds; they merely wished to be left alone to do the work assigned to them. In the first place, the women sought managerial control of Bible women. Second, they sought to manage and extend their space: they occupied the school building, planned to enlarge their sphere of operations by insisting that their Bible work extended beyond the Samokov station, and claimed greater mobility as they contended that they could travel at will, without seeking permission from male missionaries. Finally, they wanted a separate budget so that they could maintain financial control over their own work. Their letter suggests that the men of the station had attempted to control every aspect of their work and that they sought to establish their independent authority.

N. G. Clark's response essentially supported the women's position.[20] He confirmed that the plans for the new school building incorporated dwelling space for them as well as classrooms. They had a separate budget for their work in the school, it was their responsibility to supervise Bible women, and they could make their own decisions about travel. In all this they were not required to seek permission from the male missionaries in Samokov, but they were obliged to inform them of their plans and consult with them on practical matters. Despite Clark's clarification, the men of the mission found it difficult to accept the changing conditions.

The men of the Samokov station could not argue against the women's job description confirmed by Boston. Instead, they set about demonstrating to N. G. Clark that, despite their good qualities, Maltbie and Mumford were unsuitable and incompetent. According to the male missionaries, the two women adhered to unorthodox theologies that did not sit well with the more traditional Congregationalists in the mission. Among the most pernicious, in their view, was that both women believed in Christian Perfection and Mumford supported women's rights. Thus, beyond their failure to abide by customary living arrangements, Mumford and Maltbie challenged the religious and social tenets of the mission.

Christian Perfection, or Entire Sanctification, was a doctrine that had its origins in Wesleyan Methodism and led to the development of the Holiness Movement in the United States. At Oberlin, president Asa Mahan and his successor, Charles Grandison Finney, subscribed to the idea of Christian Perfection, which went beyond a belief in salvation through faith alone to assurance of salvation and the notion that an individual should and could strive to live a holy life entirely free of sin.[21] According to Locke, Maltbie and Mumford were too keen to teach perfectionism to their pupils. Apparently the missionaries had no objection to the women holding the doctrine if it gave them comfort, but they objected to their teaching it in the school. Locke was also concerned that the doctrine held weight with some of the missionaries. According to him, Lewis Bond "had the folly to preach on the subject at the annual sermon," and Locke feared that Henry Haskell would make it "a specialty in his teachings."[22] The more traditional theologians in the mission were determined to counter the unorthodox views that were filtering in.

Mumford was also tarred with the brush of women's rights. James Clarke reported that Mumford had bemoaned the fact that the women exerted no influence because they did not vote. Clarke neatly sidestepped the missionaries' objections to the idea of women voting (women did not even attend mission meetings) by stating that the missionaries understood that "the rules of the Board forbid" extending the vote to women.[23] Ironically, as Clarke was writing to Boston in the spring of 1874 to deny Maltbie and Mumford greater participation in the management of the mission, Minnie Beach, who had worked briefly in Samokov before Mumford's arrival, wrote to N. G. Clark from Marietta, Ohio, to proclaim women's achievements there: "The Temperance cause and the Woman's movement is the all absorbing topic of interest in Ohio now. It is wonderful. There can be no doubt that it is the Lord's work."[24] James Clarke did not agree with her sentiments about the woman's movement. He was not about to expand the reaches of women's rights into the mission. Ohio was a long way from Samokov.

The men's solution to what they perceived to be the shortcomings of the single women was to insist on more orthodox living arrangements where the women could be subsumed into a missionary family and relieved of their responsibilities. According to Clarke, instead of erecting a "high fence" between themselves and the missionary families, the women needed to join "the cheerful atmosphere of a mission family" and let the men "take the business off the hands" of the women. The male missionaries intended to restore traditional domestic and religious orthodoxy at the annual general meeting of the European Turkey Mission in June 1874. Clarke expressed the hope that experienced missionaries from the headquarters of the Near East Mission would be in attendance to advise them about relations with the women. "I trust," he wrote in the same letter, "we shall have the best wisdom Constantinople can spare at our Annual Meeting."[25]

Equally aware of the likely results of the annual meeting, Mumford appealed to N. G. Clark: "We learn that at the next Annual Meeting," she wrote, "they intend to have their control over us ensured to them beyond all controversy." The two women had no expectations of prevailing against the power of the annual meeting, where only ordained ministers were entitled to vote on resolutions. According to Mumford, the Samokov missionaries mocked the women for their lack of political power, arguing that they had no effective control over their work because they could not vote. Dismayed to see their decisions contested, the missionaries in Samokov relished the political power of the vote. They used it to undermine the single women missionaries and deflect their attempts to direct their own work. Mumford suggested that the male missionaries enjoyed antagonizing the women: "They have at times asked us in a manner savoring of *taunt,* if we wouldn't *like to vote.* This hurts, for we are not of the class who wishes to vote or to do the work of men, we only wish to do our own work, as the ladies in other fields do theirs, no more, no less, and we have freely advised with the brethren about it but they fail to recognize anything except they vote upon it."[26]

The specter of women's rights hung over the European Turkey Mission. Mumford strenuously denied any suffragist leanings, but her actions belied her protestations. In Mumford's view, the real issue was the inability of the male missionaries to adjust to the changing conditions of missionary work. Her chief criticisms were that the men refused to release to the women the funds that had been appropriated by the Woman's Board for their work. James Clarke in particular had ignored N. G. Clark's instructions that clarified the school teachers' supervision of Bible women. Without consulting Maltbie or Mumford, he had hired a Bulgarian Bible woman and insisted that she report to him. Both Clarke and Mumford sought to emphasize their own positions of authority by insisting on their control of Bulgarian women. Clearly aggrieved by the actions of male missionaries, Mumford indignantly reported a telling comment from the men: "They say *we* are no more missionaries than their *wives* are."[27] Yet Mumford and Maltbie were supported by auxiliaries to the Woman's Board of Missions of the Interior—Mumford by the Oberlin missionary society and Maltbie by an Ohio church auxiliary. The Woman's Board called the women "our missionaries,"[28] but the men of the mission did not recognize this designation applied to women.

Mumford's expectations of the results of the annual general meeting proved correct. After eighteen months of wrangling in missives that crisscrossed the Atlantic, the men of the mission took direct action to subsume the women's work under the specific control of the Samokov station. They argued that N. G. Clark's confirmation of the women's responsibilities could not override the constitution of their mission. They asserted that missionaries who acted as trustees of educational institutions exercised general control of them: they approved the curriculum, set rules of discipline, controlled funding, and wrote annual reports. They resolved that the Samokov school "exists for the Mission, that its work is a part of the work of the Mission and its fruits belong to the Mission." They insisted that the teachers at the school were responsible through the mission to the American Board. In a statement that suggested that women were too frail and vulnerable to fulfill duties other than instruction and "the minute affairs of the household," the missionaries contended that the women's "health, comfort, usefulness require that the burden of secular care and all large expenditures of funds should rest with the Trustees."[29] The missionaries ensured that there would be no devolution of power in Samokov. Maltbie and Mumford were effectively silenced.

These single women might have had more success in pressing their case had they garnered the support of the missionary wives, but wives resolutely supported their husbands.[30] When Mumford invited Zoe Locke to teach two half-hour classes in music at the girls' school for one semester, Locke refused. A graduate of Mount Holyoke Female Seminary, Locke was well qualified. She had taught before marriage; she could sing and play the organ. She nonetheless cited her domestic obligations as an obstacle to her teaching for two half-hour sessions a week. Mumford reconciled herself to the fact that she would "not be able to expect any help from our married sisters."[31] In contrast, Locke agreed to help run the school when Isabella Clarke (James Clarke's wife) requested her assistance after Mumford and Maltbie returned to the United States.[32] When it suited her, Locke exploited the language of domesticity as a screen to cover the antagonism between the Samokov station wives and the single women during the long-running conflict over the management of the school.

Without supporters in the mission, Maltbie and Mumford chose to return to the United States at the end of the spring semester 1876. Although the reasons for their departure are not entirely clear, a report from Maltbie suggests that Mumford's poor health and the unsettled political situation contributed to their decision.[33] In the spring of 1876 armed Bulgarian bands crossed the

Danube to foment revolution against the Ottomans. Their attempt failed and the Ottomans dealt swiftly and harshly with them. N. G. Clark complained about the expense of the women's travel and was indignant that they set out on their journey without prior approval but ultimately agreed to "a season of rest and recreation" for them.[34]

Clark used the women's return to the United States to impose a cooling off period in the Samokov station. He warned the women against speaking in public and advised them specifically not to speak to "mixed assemblies." That way, he assured them, they would spare themselves and the cause of missions from reproach and from any damage that could be done by individuals seeking to "ally our Womans Board with the Radical Come-outerism etc."[35] Women in radical evangelical causes had spoken to mixed audiences in the United States since the 1830s, but Clark was concerned to protect the American Board from association with radical causes.

While Maltbie and Mumford were in the United States, N. G. Clark corresponded with them and the men of the mission to determine the causes of the conflict and attempt to clarify their working arrangements. He also polled the mission's men to ascertain what changes might be made in the mission and whether the two women should return to Samokov. Clark suspected that the men had interfered unnecessarily in the women's work. In attempting to clarify the original tensions about living arrangements, he confirmed that single women living in the school have the freedom to arrange their own affairs, including hosting guests. He also clearly stated that the men of the mission were responsible for setting the strategy for the school (semester dates, curriculum, exams, and rules of conduct); women should manage the school on a practical day-to-day level. He expressed the hope that there would in future be less friction, more freedom for the women, and at the same time proper supervision from the school's trustees. He declared, however, that ultimately the men were responsible for overseeing the women.[36]

In their responses to Clark, the missionaries insisted on maintaining the hierarchical structures already in place and made detailed accusations against Maltbie and Mumford. They offered James Clarke as a scapegoat. Insinuating that he was the key protagonist at the center of the antagonism toward the single women, the missionaries made one concession: to remove him from his trusteeship at the girls' school. Apart from that they made several recommendations to settle the policies on single women. First, missionary families should supervise schools. Single women might teach but they should not be given the responsibility of management or oversight. Second, before leaving the United States, teachers should be required to agree to two conditions: the trustees of the mission were the "ruling power," and a teacher should never make a change or organize an event without seeking prior approval of the trustees. Third, female teachers should not assume Bible work or the supervision of Bible women. These recommendations indicate that the missionaries would not recognize the professional status of the single women. The men were unprepared to adjust their practices or make concessions to the new dynamic of single women exercising positions of responsibility within the mission. As one of the missionaries, Edward Jenney, acknowledged, "the settlement of the relations of the unmarried ladies with the Mission is the most difficult of all problems before any mission."[37] The missionaries' only solution was to deny the women participation on equal terms.

As to whether Maltbie and Mumford should return, the missionaries decided that Maltbie might be allowed to remain in the mission if she agreed to work in harmony with the missionaries, but that Mumford should not return. William Locke made the most forceful statement of this decision: "*It is the unanimous opinion of the members of this station, male and female, that it is best that Mrs. Mumford be not in any way connected with this mission,*" he wrote to N. G. Clark.[38] The men of the mission suggested that the women were responsible for a lack of harmony, but the concept of working in harmony appears to mean that the women must agree to follow the directions of the men. According to Lewis Bond, Maltbie and Mumford did not appreciate interference from the men of the mission. Bond, who had supported his own wife's ambitions, was the sole supporter of the single women. In a perceptive insight, he explained that the women were caught in a bind: if a teacher had "the necessary push in her," he wrote to Boston, she was sure to "butt against the missionaries," and if she did not have the push she would "do no better than a native teacher would do under the direction of the missionaries."[39] Recognizing the crux of the problem, Bond argued that single women would continue to experience difficulties unless the missionaries made fundamental changes at Samokov. He understood that this was unlikely.

Accusations from the missionaries against the women included a list of complaints about their strong personalities. Even Esther Maltbie seemed to agree that Anna Mumford was difficult to work with.[40] Several new charges against the women included allegations that they arranged engagements between couples at the mission schools, influenced pupils at the schools to travel to the United States for further education, traveled throughout the mission field inappropriately, and failed to exercise adequate financial control.[41] Not all missionaries joined in the accusations, and some discounted them. As one of the principles underpinning girls' mission schools was to provide wives for future pastors and native helpers, it was difficult to argue against pupils becoming acquainted and engaged under the guidance of their teachers. In general, however, missionaries were opposed to their pupils leaving for America because the young people would be unable to take up missionary work in their own communities. The issue of local travel was particularly sensitive and explained in part the missionaries' resolve to prevent single women from doing Bible work. The missionaries argued that it was not safe for single women to travel alone and it was inappropriate for them to travel with local people, both of which the women had done.[42]

Maltbie and Mumford defended themselves vigorously against these accusations. Maltbie declared that she had no intention of working independently of the missionaries but expected to work with them "untrammeled by unnecessary supervision."[43] Mumford placed the blame for the lack of harmony squarely with the men at Samokov, arguing that they refused to recognize her status and rights: "When they can accord to me privileges equal to those which they rightfully claim for themselves," she wrote, "there will be no cause for friction or difficulty."[44] Despite her earlier protestations to the contrary, Mumford's claim for equality earns her feminist credentials.

The two women strenuously denied the charge that they influenced male pupils to travel to the United States. Mumford conceded that she had counseled two young women to go to the United States because they could obtain "a better education there than at the missionary school."[45] Ethnic Bulgarians who had come into contact with missionaries were among the earliest Orthodox Christians from the Ottoman Balkans to emigrate to the United

States. They began to leave in very small numbers in the late 1860s, well before extensive migration from southeastern Europe in the final decade of the nineteenth century. By 1881, forty Bulgarian students from the Samokov mission school had gone to Britain or the United States for further study.[46] They followed a well-established pattern to travel abroad for education. Wealthy merchants could afford the experience for their children, mostly sons.[47] The Russian government as well as philanthropic Russian organizations had sponsored education for Bulgarians in Imperial Russia. The Ottoman government had sponsored the education of young men in Paris. If missionaries could find American sponsors, then Bulgarians would go to the United States. Mumford and Maltbie had arranged for congregations in Ohio to support Bulgarian women who wished to further their education in the United States.[48]

Missionaries around the world shared a concern that their converts and best pupils would emigrate. Esther Maltbie argued that young Bulgarians would continue to go to the United States of their own accord despite the best efforts of the missionaries to prevent them. In a rare acknowledgment of the limits of the missionary enterprise and the potential of Bulgarian people, she declared that the time had come when "*educated* Bulgarians christian or unchristian are to do far more to mold the future of that nation than foreigners."[49] Maltbie recognized the serious political changes taking place in the Ottoman Empire. The armed Bulgarian rebellions that began in the 1860s continued in the 1870s. The Ottomans dealt harshly with them, and several Bulgarian leaders lost their lives. Writing several months after the failed Bulgarian uprising of April 1876 against Ottoman rule, she exposed the conceit of mission objectives to transform Bulgarian society and her confidence in the ability of Bulgarians to shape their history.

In response to criticisms about her travel, Anna Mumford illuminated some of the sexual tensions that single women introduced into missionary circles and suggested that single women were vulnerable without the support of the married women in the mission. She had toured widely, sometimes alone and sometimes with Bulgarians, including Ivan Tonjoroff, but she refused to travel with male missionaries because their wives were jealous. In Mumford's view, Roseltha Norcross had hastened her early death by riding a two-day journey in only one day to avoid the need for an overnight stay when traveling with William Locke. Norcross apparently feared not Locke's advances but the disapproval of Zoe Locke, who questioned the propriety of single women traveling with married male missionaries.

Mumford's correspondence also highlights the racial undertones of the dispute between the single women and missionary couples. When Mumford registered her dismay about the missionaries' response to her friendship with the Tonjoroffs, she was surprised at the vehemence of Zoe Locke's response. Locke contended that the women had no rights: as teachers who lived in the mission school, they were obliged to obtain the consent of the mission for their actions. Their invitation to a "*native* pastor" was not to be tolerated. The missionaries apparently believed that Elizabeth Bevan should also be punished for her transgression of the frontiers of domesticity. As reported by Mumford, Locke argued that "Miss Bevan had married a *native* and deserved to suffer for it."[50] As punishment, Bevan was no longer welcome in missionary circles. Locke's reported use of the word "native" in this context indicates that the word was not simply a neutral designation for the people among whom missionaries worked. Instead, it marked clear distinctions between missionaries and their converts and established boundaries that should not be crossed. By befriending the Tonjoroffs, Maltbie and Mumford ignored the exclusionary practices of the larger mission and had to be disciplined as well.

Mumford's spirited defense of her behavior was written several months after N. G. Clark wrote to her "with great pain" to inform her that she would not be returning to Samokov. Acknowledging her "dismemberment from the A.B.C.F.M.," she declared her intention to return as an "independent worker."[51] Mumford was determined not to bend to the American Board.

The experiences of Esther Maltbie and Anna Mumford highlight the battles that missionaries fought over gender ideology. With the notable exception of Lewis Bond, the two women had no supporters within the mission. Quite the reverse: most male missionaries held fast to a strong patriarchal culture that assured them control of all aspects of missionary work, including women's work. That patriarchal culture prevailed against the challenges of single women and native pastors.

The Problem of Native Pastors

The reaction of the missionary couples to the friendship of Mumford and Maltbie with the Tonjoroffs offers a starting point from which to explore the challenge of native pastors to the mission hierarchy and missionaries' perceptions of the people among whom they worked. As Christians and second-class subjects in the Ottoman Empire, Bulgarians understood only too well constructions of difference that excluded them from greater access to positions of power within the Ottoman polity. They easily detected the attempts of missionaries to construct difference that excluded converts from positions of power and privilege within the mission, but in their daily contests with the missionaries for resources and access to greater mission management, Bulgarians made little progress.

For American Board missionaries, abstract conceptions of race based on skin color mattered but carried less importance than distinctions among people based on their perceived level of civilization. A classical education and a fascination with the ancient worlds of Rome and Greece shaped the ways missionaries framed the historical significance of their venture and viewed the inhabitants of the lands formerly occupied by Rome and Greece.[52] The missionaries' perspectives on history, their conceptual mappings of moral and political geography, and their views about the ranking of peoples and civilizations help explain their attitudes toward Bulgarians.

The prevailing view among missionaries was that the inhabitants of the Ottoman Balkans scored low on the civilization scale. Traveling through the predominantly Greek areas of the region in the 1830s, missionaries Henry Dwight and William Schauffler waxed eloquent about the former glories of ancient Rome and described the areas they passed through as sites of an ancient civilization that had collapsed into ruins.[53] One missionary map from 1847 color-coded the area as "Mohammedan." A popular American geography book from 1850 described the area as part of the "half civilized" sections of the globe.[54] Consequently, missionaries tended to ignore the region's recent history and used place names that harked back to ancient history, such as Constantinople, Adrianople, and Philippopolis.

Reflecting New England perspectives on culture and religion, missionaries also took a dim view of the Eastern Orthodox churches. They believed that they had become degenerate in their proximity with Islam. They shared the teachings of a popular antebellum Sunday School manual that Roman Catholic and Greek churches "propagate only a corrupt system, founded on tradition and superstition, restricting the circulation of the Bible."[55] Carrying their antebellum evangelical prejudices with them, missionaries characterized Orthodoxy as even worse than Catholicism. When he arrived in the Balkans in 1857, Albert Long remarked that in their dealings with Orthodox Christians the missionaries would have to contend with "all the distinctive features of Romanism, but yet attended perhaps by a still greater ignorance and superstition."[56]

By the time Istanbul-based missionaries traveled into the Balkans in the late 1850s, however, the picture of ruin had changed to one of industry and opportunity. Cyrus Hamlin was the first missionary to describe areas where Bulgarians predominated for readers of the *Missionary Herald*. Noting the industriousness of the Bulgarian inhabitants, he remarked that they needed only a reinvigorated form of Christianity and the tools of New England ingenuity to restore the region to a new age of glory. Bulgarians might be poor, but they were hard-working; though humble, their homes were clean and tidy; though uneducated, they expressed a keen interest in the scriptures. The Bulgarians, it seemed, had all the virtues of New Englanders. Hamlin expected that "the Christian sympathies of the Anglo-Saxon race" would prevail in reshaping the people and the region.[57] The *Missionary Herald* wrote that Bulgarians were "the chosen instruments of Providence" for the introduction of Protestantism into the Ottoman Balkans.[58]

Thus the missionaries initially had high hopes that Bulgarians would be the people to restore Christianity and civilization to the Ottoman Balkans by adopting Protestantism. Their early conversations with prominent leaders of Bulgarian communities in Istanbul, Edirne, Plovdiv, Stara Zagora, Shumen, Turnovo, and Sofia led them to expect that educated urban Bulgarians would be drawn to Protestantism. When Bulgarians did not respond to the missionaries' expectations within a short time, they expressed their disappointment in vitriolic rants against Bulgarian perfidy. Methodist missionary Wesley Prettyman in Shumen inveighed against "the insincerity and hypocrisy of the Orientals"; Albert Long in Turnovo lamented that the interest of some Bulgarians in Protestantism was pragmatic and political rather than spiritual. In his view, Bulgarians would consider any form of transformation if it met their own ends. They would become "Catholics, Turks, even Protestants," he wrote, as long as they could promote their national agenda.[59]

When the missionaries recognized that their task would be more difficult than they initially expected, they decided to turn to education to pursue their objectives. Missionaries in Plovdiv opened a school to train young Bulgarian men as pastors. They agreed that there was "no place where young men are more likely to be converted as in a school."[60] Unlike the girls' school in Stara Zagora, however, the boys' school in Plovdiv was a serious disappointment: it produced only three converts in a decade, Ivan Tonjoroff, Andrey Tsanoff, and Nikola Boyadjieff.[61] These young men were also the sole graduates of the mission school for boys who remained to work with the missionaries. James Clarke believed that this poor result was a consequence of inferior intellect accompanied by lack of religious freedom. He wrote after a decade in Plovdiv that "the wealthy, ignorant leaders, followed by the more ignorant of the masses wish to stifle all free thought."[62] When their efforts to convert young men in the school proved unsuccessful, the missionaries blamed the Bulgarians. The negative perceptions that missionaries began to express about Bulgarians extended to their converts and helped shape their attitudes toward them.

In the early days of the mission, missionaries rarely made specific remarks about their Bulgarian coworkers. Their perceptions of them must be gleaned from their behavior toward them—the ways they named them, how they paid them, the extent to which they associated with them, and the manner in which they excluded them from mission management. These practices—nomenclature, salary structures, and patterns of mission management and reporting—all contributed to shaping the gendered, racial, and class hierarchies of mission in the 1870s.

Missionaries often rendered Bulgarian men and women quasi-invisible by not using their full names or not naming them at all. Instead, job titles established social and professional locations on the occupational hierarchy.[63] Salaries corresponded to that status. Women and Bulgarian men took no part in mission management and made no formal reports to the American Board. When Bulgarian Bible women provided reports, they did so at the

Ivan Tonjoroff, ca. 1888. Courtesy Hilandar Research Library, Ohio State University.

explicit invitation of women missionaries, through whom their reports were filtered before being passed on to the board. These practices enabled the missionaries to maintain social distance, assert control of missionary activities, and gain the credit for any successes in their work.

An eloquent absence of Bulgarian names can be found in the records of the first annual meeting of the European Turkey Mission, which began on June 30, 1871, in Stara Zagora, shortly before the mission moved to Samokov. N. G. Clark traveled from Boston for this auspicious occasion, and Elias Riggs came from Istanbul. During the meeting, Riggs presented the first copy of the first edition of the modern Bulgarian translation of the Bible.

He wrote a commemorative inscription on the flyleaf, which he signed and dated July 4, 1871. All Americans in attendance signed their names, including the women who were present—Elizabeth Clark, Margaret Haskell, Fannie Bond, and Esther Maltbie.[64] Reporting on the event, Lewis Bond listed the names of everyone in attendance; not one Bulgarian name was given.[65] Neither the Bulgarian translators of the Bible, nor Bulgarian converts who taught in the mission schools were recorded as present. No Bulgarians signed the Bible. By choosing to present the Bible on July 4, Riggs made the event a particularly American celebration, yet the Bulgarian Bible was a cooperative venture. It may have been supervised by American missionaries, but it was financed by the British and Foreign Bible Society, and the work of translation could not have been completed without its Bulgarian translators: Konstantin Fotinov (who originally translated the Old Testament from modern Greek and died before this gathering took place), Neofit Rilski (who originally translated the New Testament from Old Church Slavic) and Petko Slaveykov, Khristodul Kostovich Sichan-Nikolov, and Nikola Mikhaylovski, all of whom worked to revise the previous translations.

The practice of not naming the people among whom they worked began with the missionaries' earliest encounters as they journeyed from Istanbul inland. In his first annual report from Stara Zagora, Theodore Byington informed the board that he was helped to find a house to rent by "a prominent Bulgarian . . . and a Greek physician."[66] The ways in which missionaries named Bulgarian converts changed as the converts progressed in the mission hierarchy. As students, they were rarely named but referred to simply as "one of the pupils." As they became assistant teachers or Bible women, women were sometimes referred to as "one of the assistants in the girls' school," but they were occasionally identified by their first names, usually in the diminutive form. Maria Gencheva, when she was named, was always referred to simply as Marika. Bible women were rarely mentioned by name in the annual reports of the Woman's Board of Missions.[67] Bulgarian men who converted were also usually identified only by their first names; however, men who attained professional status within the mission were rewarded with recognition of their status and referred to more formally. As a teacher in the Samokov boy's school, Andrey Tsanoff, if he was identified at all, was referred to as Mr. Tsanoff. Ivan Tonjoroff was always referred to formally as

Pastor Tonjoroff. His English wife was never referred to by her married name; she remained Miss Bevan. The missionaries refused to recognize the possibility of her mixed marriage by choosing not to use her Bulgarian married name.

The pattern of not identifying Bulgarians fully in official correspondence could not have been an effort on behalf of the missionaries to protect their converts. Bulgarian Protestants were well known in their own communities. They made a public display of their profession of faith by attending Protestant services, and on occasion they were verbally and physically attacked for their faith by Orthodox Christians. Their lack of recognition in the American records serves not to protect them but to limit their presence. Fortunately for historians, some of the Bulgarian Protestant communities kept good records. At the end of the twentieth century, attempts to recover the history of Protestantism among the Bulgarians have uncovered some of those early records and given names to these laborers in the work of evangelism.[68]

Work designations within the mission established the first order of hierarchy according to gender, education, and race. Only ordained American ministers were accorded the title "missionary." American women, whether married or single, were assistant missionaries, as were unordained American men (printers and teachers, for example). American men who preached were called ministers; American women who preached among women were called Bible women. Bulgarian men who preached were called native preachers or, if they were ordained, native pastors. Bulgarian women who worked within the mission were called native Bible women and native teachers. These designations were reflected in salaries, which provide another example of the hierarchical structure of the mission. Interestingly, the annual tabular summaries of workers and salaries provide the one record where workers were occasionally listed with their full names.

In the Ottoman Empire, as elsewhere around the world, male missionaries commanded the highest salaries within the missionary enterprise. Single women and local people earned considerably less. In 1879, budget estimates for the European Turkey Mission listed annual salaries for male missionaries in Samokov at 20,000 piasters.[69] In Plovdiv, a major city where living expenses were higher, Lewis Bond received a salary of 22,800 piasters. In contrast, the unnamed Bulgarian pastor in Plovdiv received 9,600 piasters, or less than half the salary for an American missionary. Preachers in smaller towns received only 4,800 piasters. The disparity between Americans and Bulgarians was even greater for women than for men. As a single American woman and a teacher, Esther Maltbie received a salary of 8,000 piasters, while Bulgarian female teachers at mission schools received 2,500, and Bible women toiled for 1,200.

A comparison with Bulgarian salaries in the secular sector is instructive.[70] Mission salaries were at the high end for the professional classes. The pastor's salary of 9,600 piasters in Plovdiv, a major town, was slightly lower than a male grade-school teacher's salary in Gabrovo, a midsized town, which ranged from 10,000 to 11,400 piasters and was perhaps a midlevel income among professionals such as teachers. Esther Maltbie earned less than male Bulgarian teachers but considerably more than female teachers. Bulgarian women who taught in the mission school in Samokov for 2,500 piasters earned less than female Bulgarian schoolteachers in other towns of similar size. Although data are sparse and comparisons difficult, graduates of the Bulgarian girls' school in Stara Zagora received salaries ranging from 3,500 to 4,800 piasters in Vidin in the 1870s.[71] According to their contracts, they also received housing, firewood, and travel expenses. The salaries of Bulgarian Bible women were below the level of Bulgarian female schoolteachers. Like other native assistants around the world, they earned considerably less working with the missionaries than they could have earned elsewhere.[72] Remuneration levels seemed unrelated to the importance of their work given the missions' need to spread the Gospel in local languages.

The American Board also argued that native preachers should look to their congregations for greater support. At the outset of the missionary endeavor among the Bulgarians, however, congregations were very small and could hardly be expected to sustain a pastor and his family, which meant that they remained under the control of the mission and within mission pay scales. The question, then, is whether the Bulgarian mission workers could sustain themselves on their salaries. Pastor Tonjoroff provides an illuminating example. Despite board policy that married men with families needed larger salaries, the missionaries did not accord Tonjoroff a salary increase when he married.[73] In an egregious example of the divergence of policy and practice, the missionaries punished Tonjoroff for marrying Elizabeth Bevan by not increasing his salary.

Mission management provided another mechanism through which male missionaries maintained power. Rufus Anderson had always argued that missionaries should follow the example of the early apostles by building self-supporting churches and communities and leaving them to manage themselves.[74] But most missionaries accepted the idea of self-government later rather than sooner. Missionaries in the Near East were no different from British and American missionaries elsewhere. They were reluctant to yield power and make themselves obsolete. The World Missionary Conference in Edinburgh in 1910 provides a telling statistic: of 1,215 official delegates at the conference, only nineteen were neither American nor European.[75]

Only ordained American ministers managed mission affairs. They enjoyed full reporting authority to the American Board and demanded that all other workers submit reports through them. Missionaries therefore controlled the information that flowed from the mission to the board. Missionaries discussed business matters on a regular basis in their mission stations and on an annual basis at their annual general meeting. At the first meeting of the European Turkey Mission in 1871, missionaries in attendance adopted a resolution, proposed by Elias Riggs, that "all male missionaries present at any annual meeting shall be voting members of the meeting."[76] Neither women nor Bulgarian pastors exercised a vote in mission affairs.

Married women, single women, and Bulgarian mission workers did not attend the business sessions of annual meetings, although missionaries at these meetings sometimes voted to extend special invitations for particular sessions, usually prayer sessions. Even Bulgarian Protestant pastors did not attend unless a vote was cast to issue a special invitation to them. Occasionally, the missionaries issued invitations to all the English speakers associated with the mission. In effect, these invitations excluded native helpers who spoke only Bulgarian, including some assistant teachers and most Bible women. The concept of vernacular education ensured that local workers remained to work among their own communities, but it also guaranteed that they would be excluded from participation in mission affairs.

Seeking greater participation in policy making and representation, the three Bulgarian pastors—Ivan Tonjoroff, Andrey Tsanoff, and Nikola Boyadjieff—in 1875 established the Bulgarian Evangelical Association. Tsanoff, who from 1868 to 1871 studied in the United States, seems to have been the prime mover in organizing the association. Despite this action, the missionaries remained unwilling to share power. They resolved at an annual meeting in 1880 that "we should throw on our Bulgarian brethren responsibilities as rapidly as they can assume them, but we do not deem it best to give them any more responsibility until they show by the management of their own affairs that they can bear greater burdens." This condescending language is a revealing example of their perceptions of the inadequacies of the Bulgarians, whom they themselves had trained over a period of nearly twenty years. Apparently they did not believe that twenty years was a long enough period of colonial tutelage. At the same meeting they also debated whether they should appoint a Bulgarian trustee on an annual basis to each of the school boards. They resolved against such an appointment, agreeing that "any such step be deferred for the present as we are not all assured that it is best."[77] The wording of their resolution suggests that some missionaries welcomed and encouraged greater participation of Bulgarians in the management of the mission. As a group, however, they voted instead that Bulgarians be invited to discuss with them the work of the Bulgarian Evangelical Society and that a committee be appointed to confer with the Bulgarians on behalf of the mission if the Bulgarians wished them to consider any matters at their larger meetings. This measure removed the Bulgarians even further from the annual meeting by inserting an intermediary committee.

The missionaries' treatment of Elizabeth and Ivan Tonjoroff offers another example of their use of colonial discourse to dismiss the qualities of their associates and control access to their society. Before Tonjoroff married Elizabeth Bevan, the missionaries praised his work and conduct as pastor of the first Bulgarian Protestant Church in Bansko. "He can reach and touch their *hearts* as we never can," wrote Locke.[78] After their marriage, however, the missionaries openly expressed their disdain for Tonjoroff by calling his masculinity into question, a common strategy in colonial rhetoric that cast colonized men as incompetent and effeminate.[79] When N. G. Clark asked the Samokov missionaries whether they would consider rehiring Tonjoroff after he left the mission, Locke used the language of domesticity to decline the opportunity: "Were Pastor T. the head of his family—which he is not— why the case would be other than it is."[80] Locke took pains to suggest that Tonjoroff was not sufficiently masculine and not sufficiently competent. Locke pointedly argued that Tonjoroffs' household did not assure him of domestic respectability. His wife's influence, particularly in discussions over salary, apparently exceeded the norm of the domestic ideal. These types of comments appear periodically in the mission archive. Ellen Stone, who joined the mission after Anna Mumford's departure, commented in 1888 that Tonjoroff was not "head of his house," and she wondered why her male colleagues did not speak to him about his domestic situation.[81]

The American Board could ill afford to lose Tonjoroff. He converted to Protestantism when he was a student at the mission school, and in August 1871 he became the first ordained Protestant pastor of the first Bulgarian Protestant Church, in Bansko, of which he was a founding member.[82] He translated mission tracts and American textbooks into Bulgarian for school use. He was a substantial member of the Bulgarian Protestant community and made a significant contribution to the work of evangelism across the Ottoman Balkans. The missionaries had made an investment in him, and he had repaid their trust. Their behavior when he married Elizabeth Bevan grieved him and ultimately persuaded him to leave the mission's employ, at least temporarily.

The Samokov missionaries reported that the Tonjoroffs left because Tonjoroff could not live on his salary and the climate in Bansko did not agree with his wife.[83] Tonjoroff concurred with these reasons but explained that they were incomplete. Writing to N. G. Clark (a rare occurrence in itself), Tonjoroff insisted that it was the treatment he received from the Samokov missionaries that persuaded him to leave their employ. He noted that he had been associated with the American Board missionaries for fifteen years, during which time he had had many frank and intense discussions with them, but their response to his marriage had soured their relations. Tonjoroff assured Clark that no one could say that Elizabeth Bevan had not fulfilled his highest hopes, "both as a wife and as a missionary."[84] He was clearly disappointed by the treatment meted out to him by the missionaries after his marriage.

Untidy Ends

The reaction of the missionaries to Tonjoroffs' marriage and his friendship with Anna Mumford and Esther Maltbie threatened to deprive the mission of the services of all four and ensured that tensions among them would continue. As it turned out, only Maltbie enjoyed a long career in the European Turkey mission. She returned after the Russo-Turkish War of 1877–1878 and became the principal of the American Board's female boarding school in Samokov after Bulgaria won its independence from the Ottoman Empire. She remained in Bulgaria for forty years. In 1911 a fundraising brochure of the Woman's Board of Missions of the Interior hailed her as "the Mary Lyon of Bulgaria."[85]

If the missionaries in Samokov thought that N. G. Clark's decision to remove Mumford from the European Turkey Mission would resolve their problems, they were wrong. She rejected Clark's offer of a position as assistant missionary in Micronesia, and returned to the Balkans in the summer of 1877, in the middle of the Russo-Turkish war. She journeyed to Samokov to retrieve her belongings and went on to Plovdiv to establish an independent faith mission. Faith missions lacked large bureaucratic support, but Mumford believed that she had been called by God to continue her work. In a stunning demonstration of her faith, will, and commitment, she wrote that she had continued her work through "faith and prayer, asking aid from no one but from God."[86]

Mumford's return exposed the American Board's sense of territoriality and revealed a serious lack of harmony among the missionaries. As the war played out, the missionaries left their posts and fled to the safety of Istanbul. Mumford stayed put, working in a hospital for the wounded and a sanctuary for refugees. After the war, she opened a girls' school. The missionaries believed that she was trespassing on their turf. They doubted her ability to succeed without the assistance of a man and predicted the early demise of her work. From 1877 to 1882 their correspondence is full of petty squabbles, unfounded rumors, and vicious insinuations about Mumford and some missionaries who chose to befriend her. A split occurred between the more authoritarian missionaries who sought to uphold the strict structure of the mission and those who were sufficiently free-thinking to welcome Mumford as a colleague in God's work. Brotherly love was nowhere to be found, however. Quite the reverse: the missionaries' reports reveal just what a petulant group of individuals they were and highlight the emptiness of their assertions that Maltbie and Mumford were the principle cause of earlier disharmony in the mission.

Writing from Istanbul, Theodore Byington and Elias Riggs commented despondently that matters had escalated out of all proportion to their significance. Mission work was suffering. Byington, who had been in the United States when the friction between the missionaries and the single women first emerged, believed that Mumford was "a good Christian, who honestly believes that her Master has a work for her to do among the Bulgarians." Writing to N. G. Clark to complain that the Bulgarians took a dim view of the confrontations in the mission, he noted, "Our Christian principles and our Christian spirit are now being put to a severe test before the people."[87] Christian spirit was once again in short supply. The behavior of the missionaries toward Mumford discredited them in the eyes of the small Bulgarian Protestant community, who remembered that she stood by them in times of real crisis during the recent war. The Tonjoroffs agreed with Byington that Mumford was doing God's work. They joined her in Plovdiv.

Mumford received considerable support for her faith mission from donors in the United States and Great Britain, raised funds to build a girls' school, and remained the school's principal for twenty-eight years.[88] In her early fundraising efforts she was aided by none other than Mrs. Asa Mahan, wife of the first president of Oberlin College, although some mission sources indicate that the Mahan-Mumford relationship may have been strained in later years.[89] Several women worked with Mumford for a number of years at different times to provide an elementary education and train teachers and Bible women. Among the teachers were Eunice Knapp and C. K. Doolittle, both Oberlin graduates, and Todka Stoikova, a graduate of the American College for Girls in Constantinople (the former Constantinople Home).[90]

When the Tonjoroffs first left the American Board they journeyed to England, but things did not work out as they had hoped. It seems that Elizabeth Bevan's marriage to Ivan Tonjoroff was not well viewed by her family either.[91] The couple returned to Plovdiv and began to work with Mumford. Subsequently, the local Protestant community invited Tonjoroff to be their pastor. He accepted their invitation and became an important member of the Bulgarian Protestant community in Plovdiv. He restored contact with the missionaries, but their relations remained cool. Elizabeth Tonjoroff went on to become a prominent philanthropist in the town, where she ran a small hospital and a dispensary. She became a Quaker and was supported at least in part by the Society of Friends in England.[92]

The Tonjoroffs' story does not have a happy ending. Zoe Locke's diary for August 25, 1890, reports, "The ugly secret out about the pastor," and on the following day Tonjoroff resigned.[93] He had been having an affair with a married woman in his congregation, and this was one unconventional arrangement that neither the missionaries nor Elizabeth Tonjoroff could tolerate. The missionaries called a special council at which Tonjoroff was dismissed from the ministry. Elizabeth Tonjoroff returned to England alone.

Missionaries in the Near East ordered themselves within a hierarchy that reveals the tensions between the inclusionary promise of the Protestant message of salvation and a brotherhood and sisterhood in Christ and the exclusionary conventions of Anglo-American society. They institutionalized a set of practices that were reminiscent of colonial society in that they marked the people with whom and among whom they worked as different, subordinate, in need of supervision, and excluded from full participation in the missionary enterprise. Differences had to be maintained. Male missionaries held fast to distinctions of gender, race, and class that placed educated males of Anglo-Saxon descent at the top of a social hierarchy. Women could labor alongside their husbands in mission, but they and their work went largely unrecognized by the American Board. These married women belonged to the mission but were excluded from its history. Single women, although their work was recognized in official histories, were subject to male authority. As women, they remained outside the power structure.

After the American Civil War, when they were no longer so willing to defer to male authority, single women disputed the power asymmetries operating in mission circles. The forcefulness of the response of male missionaries to their attempt to regulate their living arrangements and supervise their work confirmed that Maltbie and Mumford were missionaries, and yet "not quite." Converts, for their part, became "native helpers" and are barely visible in mission records; they were Protestant and yet "not quite." Ivan Tonjoroff converted to Protestantism; he became a pastor and joined the global evangelical endeavor—but he was a "native" pastor. Living in the heart of the Ottoman Empire, on the fringes of Europe, in what the missionaries called European Turkey, where they demarcated the European from the Asiatic, Bulgarians were European and yet "not white." As white Anglo-Saxons, women were inside the racial structure. Bulgarians remained outsiders.

Confronting the normative concept of the Christian home and the racial distinctions of Anglo-American society, Maltbie, Mumford, and the Tonjoroffs contested the ideological foundations of the mission. They offered a vision of alternative relationships that introduced the promise of a more inclusive missionary endeavor. The gendered and racial constraints of missionary society nonetheless repelled their attempts to breach the barricades erected against them. Missionaries brought Protestantism and American cultural norms to the Ottoman Empire and sought to transform Orthodox Christians in their own image, but they did not recognize them as equals. If they had, they would have lost their claim to superiority and recognition for the work that had been achieved. The promise of universal Christianity still lay in the future.

CHAPTER 5
The Constantinople Home

W hen the officers of the Woman's Board of Missions designed the
Constantinople Home in the early 1870s, they planned an ambitious institution for the center of women's missionary operations in Istanbul.
Envisaging a school for girls as the focal point of the building, they also
included plans for a dispensary and a city mission where American women
would work to improve the health and home life of Ottoman women. Equally
important, the officers saw the building as a place where single women could
experience domestic life and organize their professional affairs without interference from the men of the Western Turkey Mission. Brandishing the language of domesticity to justify this female space, the officers of the Woman's
Board stipulated that the women in the Home constituted "a family" and
appointed the principal of the Home school as its "recognized Head."[1] No
longer obliged to board with missionary couples, the single women who lived
in the Constantinople Home created an alternative space of belonging where
they developed a community of family, friends, and colleagues. Within this
space, which predated by a decade the settlement house communities founded
by single women in the United States, they sought to establish the authority
to manage themselves.[2]

The language of domesticity shaped the early development of the Constan-

tinople Home, which soon became a centerpiece of American education in
the Near East. In 1890 the school was renamed to reflect its earned reputation. That year, upon petition from the Woman's Board, the State of Massachusetts chartered the Home school as the American College for Girls in
Constantinople and awarded it the right to confer the degree of Bachelor
of Arts. The American College for Girls became the first institution to offer
a tertiary-level education in English for Armenian, Bulgarian, Greek, and
Turkish women, among others. Yet despite its success, in 1908 the officers
of the Woman's Board forfeited control of the institution they founded to
an independent board of trustees in New York City.

Why, at the height of its power, did the Woman's Board relinquish its
center of operations in Istanbul and transfer the property to a group of individuals who remained independent of the mission board? The answer to this
question lies in several interconnected factors that thrust the college on a
path of development that the Woman's Board was unable to support. The
Constantinople Home was, as its name suggests, embedded in a foreign context. It operated against a shifting global backdrop and was terminally troubled by conflicts about women's work that reverberated in Istanbul and Boston to the detriment of the Woman's Board.

Beginning as a modest mission school, the Home school evolved into a
prominent institution of higher education that celebrated its identity as an
American liberal arts college rather than its Protestant evangelical origins.[3]
Conflicts between Boston and Istanbul contributed to the shift, as leading
faculty members of the college, determined to respond to the needs of the
Ottoman capital, moved away from denominationalism to shape an emerging sense of feminist Christian internationalism at their institution. The faculty was supported financially by a new group of trustees who had close connections to American political and commercial interests. Unable to compete
with the fundraising potential of this group of wealthy East Coast philanthropists, the Woman's Board surrendered their institution to them.

The loss of the college was a contributing factor in the demise of the Woman's Board after World War I. The causes for the folding of women's separate missionary societies into the male societies in the 1920s and 1930s have
been largely attributed to domestic issues within the United States.[4] Increased
professionalization within American women's boards caused the officers to lose

touch with rank-and-file members, leading to a loss of financial contributions. At the same time, women's boards lost the battle in their power strug-
gles with male boards over the nature and autonomy of women's work. Yet
local environments were critical to shaping the development of missionary
institutions abroad.[5] I suggest that the demise of the Woman's Board began
in the nineteenth century when women missionaries developed ambitions
of their own, responded to the needs of local environments, and challenged
not only the institutional power of male missionaries but also the moral authority of their female officers. The experiences of women at the peripheries of
the American missionary endeavor challenged the denominational and hierarchical structures of the enterprise and contributed to undermining the
power of the Congregational Woman's Board.[6] At the same time, American
cultural expansion in the Near East, which for almost a century had been
largely the purview of American Protestant missionaries, entered a new phase
with its new backers as the United States began to exert its might on the
world stage in the decade before World War I.

Ambiguous Origins in Changing Times

The idea of building a girls' school as the focus of the Constantinople Home
took shape against a backdrop of continued Ottoman social reform, cultural
transformations, economic decline, a political shift toward more authoritarian imperial rule under Sultan Abdülhamid II, who ascended the throne in
1876, and devastating territorial losses for the empire in the Balkans as a
result of the Russo-Ottoman War of 1877–78 that, among other things,
resulted in Bulgarian independence. Most prominent for the missionaries
were Ottoman proposals to reform education and changing patterns of consumption among the new urban middle classes, Christian and Muslim, which
were also reflected spatially.[7] The Ottoman elite began to move from the
ancient center of Istanbul into the European quarters of Galata and Pera,
where modern residential areas were being developed, creating a distinction
between traditionalists and modernists and attempting to shape a "cosmopolitan identity."[8] Changing tastes among the elite reflected a growing interest in western goods and services. Schools were modern institutions that
opened up a new form of social space for young women. As women became

more visible in urban centers, the Ottoman middle classes were increasingly drawn toward the idea of a modern education for their daughters.

Proposals for Ottoman reform of education were debated openly in the 1860s. The Ottoman Public Education Law of 1869 included for the first time compulsory elementary education for girls throughout the empire and provision for a school in Istanbul to train female teachers.[9] Under this law, children would be educated in their native languages at the elementary-school level but in Ottoman Turkish at higher levels. At the same time, Ottoman statesmen crafted a new law that shaped a new concept of Ottoman citizenship, regardless of faith and ethnicity. The Ottoman educational law was promulgated in large part as a response to the successes of American education among Christian populations. The network of American mission schools was the largest foreign-school system in the empire. Yet the law also challenged American missionaries whose earlier progressive reputation for providing female education had to some extent been lost to Christian communities. Rufus Anderson, foreign secretary of the American Board of Commissioners for Foreign Missions, had moved the one mission school in Istanbul into an interior town in 1856 and insisted on training mission workers in the vernacular. Since that time the missionaries had not had a girls' school in the capital.[10]

Even though education for girls continued to remain poorly organized throughout the empire for the next two decades, Ottoman reforms and changing social and cultural circumstances were a major catalyst in the decision to build a new girls' school. Events in Boston made it possible. When Anderson retired in 1866, his replacement, N. G. Clark, supported the decision, but the American Board could not spare the funds. Recognizing an opportune moment, Clark turned to the newly established Woman's Board of Missions, on which, ironically, Anderson's wife, Eliza, served as vice president, to raise the required resources.

Founded in Boston in 1868, the Woman's Board of Missions appealed to evangelical Christian women to fulfill their "solemn duty of caring for their sex abroad" and support the cause of missions. It was no secret, they wrote, "that the degradation and wretchedness of women, in heathen and Moham-medan countries, is one of the greatest obstacles to the success of the missionary enterprise."[11] At their first annual general meeting, early in 1869, N. G. Clark and former American missionary George Washburn encouraged the women in attendance to take on the task of starting a girls' school in Istanbul. In pleading the case, Washburn in particular misled the women about conditions in the Ottoman Empire. Using the same exaggerated language of Protestant superiority that had a long tradition in evangelical circles, he appealed to the supposed superiority of Protestant American women who benefited from the advantages of Christian society that eluded heathens. He painted "a very dark and gloomy picture of the condition of women throughout Turkey," where, in his view, "every influence of religion and society tends to sink them below the level of the beasts." According to Washburn, the Turks did not believe it was possible for women to be educated. In contrast, the missionaries had learned through experience that Turkish women were "capable of elevation and education" if only they had "the influence of the gospel."[12]

Washburn's comments were misleading in two ways. First, as a missionary in Istanbul, Washburn was well aware of the complexity of Ottoman society and knew about the reforms that would expand educational opportunities for women. Second, he used the word "Turks," suggesting that Muslim girls would be a target of missionary activities. Ottoman Turks were unlikely to be among the women seeking education from missionary institutions, however. Washburn raised the specter of Islam purely for fundraising purposes. Missionaries had made few inroads into Islam and were unlikely to do so with the new girls' school in Istanbul. Their chief clients remained Orthodox Christian converts to Protestantism.

Raising the funds for the Constantinople Home became a priority for the Woman's Board. Led by board president Sarah Lamson Bowker (a former student of Mary Lyon), each officer pledged five hundred dollars as a gesture of confidence in their ability to raise the $58,000 deemed necessary for the project.[13] They envisaged a school at the center of the project, but planned to embrace a broader field of mission for American women. They hired Oberlin graduate Julia Rappleye as school principle and Mount Holyoke graduates Dr. Mary Wadsworth and Cora Welch to manage the dispensary and city mission, respectively. The school opened in temporary quarters in October 1871. According to N. G. Clark's wife, Elizabeth, who had toured the Ottoman empire with her husband in 1871, the school would to be "a seminary of high order, open to pupils of all nationalities," where "Christian culture" would be the first and highest object."[14]

At a time when the Woman's Board's annual budget was only $31,000, the sum required for the Home had to be raised independently of regular funds. It was this idea of a special fund for the Home that persuaded some of the original founders that the Home should be directed by the Woman's Board and remain financially independent of the Western Turkey Mission, a proposal that male missionaries in Istanbul subsequently challenged. Despite his initial support, N. G. Clark immediately began to signal his hesitation, declaring that "the whole thing" was "an experiment."[15] This tentative beginning left the enterprise open to indecision and ensured that the various parties to the discussion would champion different views of the project.

Mission correspondence during those early years illustrates the uncertainty surrounding the school's purpose and management. Former American Board missionary Cyrus Hamlin argued that the Home should have no connection to the mission but should aspire to be a college with an independent governing body, as was Robert College, which he had cofounded. Hamlin's progressive views on female education did not extend to female management, however. He wrote that he would "weep in secret places" if women had positions on the governing body of the women's school.[16] Clark, who believed the institution should be closely connected to the mission, vacillated between describing it as a high school and a mission training school for local helpers.

Interestingly, Clark's audience seemed to determine his point of view. Writing to Julia Rappleye and Mary Wadsworth in 1872, he favored the high school. Recognizing what he termed "the general progress in education in the empire," he was pleased to hear that the school would meet the high demands of the residents of Istanbul and expressed the hope that it would stay ahead of local progress by continuing to raise its standards.[17] Writing that same year to the men of the Western Turkey Mission, however, Clark supported the training school option.[18] By 1874, he was of the opinion that teachers at the school were moving away from "proper missionary work" toward "mere secular education."[19] Nor was Clark alone in his uncertainty. Division of opinion in Boston and Istanbul continued on almost every topic that related to the Constantinople Home. According to

Clark, the ambiguity was "embarrassing, paralyzing, and must cost a good deal of time and strength."[20] Clark, of course, had contributed to the lack of clarity. As late as 1880, he continued to have misgivings about the direction and level of education at the school.[21]

The threads of Clark's prolonged unease were sewn into the plan for the Home school. The plan expressed the tensions within the mission as it attempted to reconcile the differences between missionaries who wished to educate girls in the vernacular to become wives of pastors and teachers and those who argued that the missionaries should provide the highest level of education available in English to meet the needs of the Ottoman capital. These objectives were not mutually exclusive; they had been reconciled by Mary Lyon at Mount Holyoke Female Seminary. Lyon encouraged her students to become the wives of missionaries, but she also offered the highest education available to young women in Massachusetts, and she promoted the idea that her teachers and students should develop their own ambitions. In Istanbul, missionary George Wood insisted that the Home school "must be a missionary school in the broad view afforded by Mt. Holyoke Seminary."[22] The officers of the Woman's Board concurred.

When the Woman's Board presented their plan, they called for a building to accommodate one hundred fee-paying students, fifty boarders and fifty day students. The plan confirmed that the Home school should be all things to all people. The missionaries in Istanbul wanted "a school in Constantinople for Constantinople" that would demonstrate to Ottoman subjects the best type of education for girls. The Home school was to be "a model school" to attract families in the city who might otherwise send their daughters to local Armenian, Bulgarian, or Greek schools. The level of education it provided should enable its students to teach in schools in Istanbul and other cities across the empire. Graduates would be "well-qualified teachers of native female seminaries and higher schools." They should "command the respect and confidence" of the city's residents.

Missionaries believed that the school itself would command respect because students would be fee-paying. Charitable assistance with expectations of missionary work in return for education, which was the norm in mission training schools in the provinces, was not to be an option in the capital. A fee-paying institution offered three benefits: it would gain esteem for the missionaries, it would tend to influence the spread of other self-supporting schools throughout the empire, and it would not be a drain on mission finances. Missionaries knew that the imposition of fees would not present an obstacle, as more and more families in the Ottoman capital wanted their daughters to be educated and were prepared to pay for it.

At the same time, the plan stipulated that the school was subservient to mission needs. It was "directly auxiliary" to the mission station and the work of proselytizing. It was to be a "centre of Christian work," the purpose of which was "to train Christian workers." Students would be groomed for positions as wives of pastors and as Bible women. As a consequence they would learn to run "well-ordered Christian homes." Instruction would be provided in the vernacular, but English would be taught. In other words, the school was to be guided by missionary principles to provide basic training for mission helpers, but missionaries knew that such a school would not meet the needs of the Ottoman capital. From the outset, therefore, the school had a dual objective that in principle could be achieved but in practice created tensions within the mission between parties who favored one of the objectives over the other.

The final point in the plan established the chain of responsibility for the school. The institution was set "under the care of trustees, consisting of the Constantinople station." In other words, the Home school, a project founded and funded by the Woman's Board, would be controlled by male missionaries of the Western Turkey Mission in Istanbul, who were responsible only to the policy makers of the American Board. This point initially went unchallenged by the Woman's Board because its officers believed that local support and advice from experienced missionaries was appropriate. Reporting procedures soon became a contentious issue, however, as discussions ensued about who had ultimate authority to make decisions regarding the Home and its finances.

Public announcements in *Life and Light* made no mention of tensions. Articles included only positive reports of progress at the Home. After only two years in temporary quarters in the old part of the city, Julia Rappleye was forced by popular demand to rent a larger building because the original house could accommodate only twenty-five students. The school's first pupils were the daughters of Armenian converts, but soon Greeks and Turks also sought admission for their daughters, a very promising development. Rappleye reported that "patronage will come to us even before we are ready for it; she hoped soon to see "the tottering and speedy downfall of the might power of Islamism.[23] In Boston, the Woman's Board had raised $30,000 by 1874. They published a sketch of a three-floor building and invited their auxiliaries to adopt a room, name it, and donate the funds to build it. The naming opportunities yielded results. Among the donors were members of Union Church in Boston who provided funds for the physician's room, dispensary, and patients' room, and students and graduates of Mount Holyoke Female Seminary who donated funds for a teacher's room, which they named "the Mary Lyon Room."[24]

Unlike the public announcements, unpublished correspondence details strong undercurrents of anger at the Woman's Board about the men's actions in Istanbul. As women missionaries worked to develop the plan for the Home, they collided early on with the institutional power of male missionaries who recognized neither the authority of the officers of the Woman's Board nor the female-headed household in the Constantinople Home. The records of the early years of the school are full of recriminations, accusations, and counteraccusations from men and women missionaries about the work of women, the purpose of the school, what the women perceived to be intrusions of the men in their daily work, and what the men saw as the women's lack of deference. Negotiating these gendered conflicts would occupy the Women's Board for several years to come.

The first major tussle came when Woman's Board officers discovered, after the fact, that the male missionaries in Istanbul had not followed the construction plans for the Home but had eliminated the dispensary and the city mission. According to the men, it was not a good idea to invite sick people into a building where pupils were studying. In reality, the women's broader goal was at odds with male missionary expectations that focused on the school as a direct auxiliary to their work of evangelizing. They saw no purpose in looking after the physical and material needs of the city's women. In a letter of complaint to the Prudential Committee (the American Board's policy-making group), the women expressed their particular displeasure at the removal from the building plans of rooms for a female physician and a dispensary. They felt that the revised building plans represented "a viola-tion of good faith" for the women who had supported their original plans and donated funds specifically for those rooms.[25] Their protests were in vain, however; the men in Istanbul had already begun construction of the Home without space for the dispensary and the city mission.

The male missionaries also failed to report the progress of the building and declined to submit accounts for expenditures. They even vested owner-ship of the real estate of the Home in the American Board instead of the Woman's Board. The women's displeasure was palpable. In the same let-ter to the Prudential Committee, they insisted that American women had raised the funds for the building, planned the work, and would be respon-sible for sustaining it. In an assertion of their perceived equal status, the offi-cers insisted that they were not "simply collectors" for the American Board but were "an incorporated society working in unison." They demanded that accounts be sent to their treasury and argued vociferously that missionaries in Istanbul take steps to vest ownership of the Home in the Woman's Board. They also reiterated their understanding of the Home's family arrange-ments and the headship of its principal. They insisted that Julia Rappleye was accountable for the Home and invoked her spiritual authority: "Under her alone under God devolved the responsibility of success or failure," they wrote.[26] In the women's view, the tensions between the men and women mis-sionaries existed because the men did not recognize Rappleye's status.

The men of the American Board had not adjusted to the changes precipi-tated by the existence of the Woman's Board and the increasing numbers of single women missionaries with minds of their own. Although male mission-aries appreciated the women's fundraising abilities and were happy to share the costs of the missionary enterprise, they expressed no willingness to share power. They believed that single women missionaries were subordinate to male authority. Although the officers of the Woman's Board expressed their displeasure and requested a change in behavior from the trustees in Istan-bul, the men were slow to change their ways. As late as 1882, the Istanbul trustees continued to correspond with the American Board, not the Woman's Board, about issues at the Home. The men in Istanbul were not in a hurry to resolve the tensions.

In a bid to regain control of their institution, the Woman's Board

The Constantinople Home, 1876. Courtesy Mount Holyoke College Archives and Special Collections.

appointed a new team of teachers ready for the move into their new building early in 1876. Rappleye moved to Brusa to develop a new school there under the sponsorship of the Woman's Board of Missions of the Pacific. Clara (Kate) Pond Williams took Rappleye's place. A widow with two small children, Williams was a graduate of Mount Holyoke Female Seminary and had taught at Mount Holyoke and at the American Board mission school at Harpoot in eastern Anatolia. She was joined by three other teachers, Ellen Parsons (a Mount Holyoke graduate), Mary Mills Patrick, a teacher from the mission school at Erzurum also in eastern Anatolia, and Annie Bliss. They were subsequently joined by Clara Hamlin, daughter of Robert College founder Cyrus Hamlin. Patrick later recalled that they were "a group of unusual women."[27]

Shaping an International Institution

With the opening of the new three-story building in Üsküdar, on the eastern side of the Bosporus, Williams instituted significant changes at the Home. Chief among them was that English became the language of instruction, which allowed the faculty to achieve three critical goals to meet Ottoman needs rather than mission needs.[28] First, Williams indicated that the school would be open to the diverse ethnic and national groups in the empire. Bulgarian girls began to arrive after the Russo-Ottoman War of 1877–78. Second, teachers could use English-language textbooks, raising the level of education offered and making it possible for them to arrive from the United States and begin teaching immediately without the need to learning a foreign language before getting to work. Finally, and not inconsequentially in an era of European imperial rivalries in the Ottoman empire, she met the needs of parents who wanted their daughters to learn a European language, offering competition to the schools operated by Catholic nuns who taught in French. During Williams's tenure, the Constantinople Home began to evolve into an international educational institution that truly met the needs of the Ottoman capital and its hinterland. In conformance with Ottoman law, Ottoman Turkish was taught in all three years of instruction; Armenian, Bulgarian, and Greek students learned their own language, and all students could also study French.

By 1889, as a result of numerous changes at the school, Mary Mills Patrick became principal. The Woman's Board, encouraged by Kate Williams, who had been in the United States since 1883, planned a change in the status of their institution from school to college. The officers decided to "drop the misnomer of The Home," and, after discussing several options, selected the name American College for Girls.[29] Patrick agreed that it was a "dignified name" that expressed "the nationality of the founders and supporters of the college." She favored promoting the American identity of the college rather than its domestic philosophy or missionary connections. She also hoped that the connection between the college and the Woman's Board would be "more definite" and the reporting lines for the new college established "on a much more satisfactory basis" than the Home school.[30] She was to be disappointed.

Some of the male missionaries in Istanbul believed that the women had misjudged the moment for expansion of female education. While the Woman's Board in Boston proceeded to draft a constitution for the college, Albert Long and Henry Dwight in Istanbul insisted that the time had not yet come to offer an advanced level of education for women in the Ottoman Empire. In their view, raising the standard of education to that offered by a "Smith or Wellesley" would "tend to limit rather than to extend the usefulness of the institution." They argued that the lack of good preparatory schools in Constantinople meant that girls did not have the basic learning to study at college level, completely ignoring the fact that the Home school had always had a preparatory school. The girls themselves married young, they noted, which meant that they were unlikely to stay in school. The college would therefore have difficulty retaining young women "of mental powers sufficiently mature" to complete the course of study.[31] The Woman's Board paid no heed to the opinions of Long and Dwight, nor were the men's views borne out.

Not long after the Massachusetts Legislature passed the act incorporating the American College for Girls, the first meeting of the corporation (governing board) of the college took place, on March 6, 1890. The bylaws stipulated that only members of the board of directors of the Woman's Board could be elected trustees of the corporation. Augusta Smith was elected president, Abbie Child vice president, Caroline Borden secretary, and Ellen Carruth treasurer. Ten additional officers, all women, were elected to the corporation, including Mary Mills Patrick, who was appointed president of the college. To mark the occasion, and to close a chapter in the institution's trajectory, Caroline Borden published a brief history of the Constantinople Home.[32] She was to become a major player in the subsequent development of the college.

The Woman's Board was ahead of its time in placing overall management of the college in the hands of an all-woman corporation. Women were appointed to the governing board of Wellesley from its inception in 1875, and by 1884 women served on the board of Mount Holyoke Female Seminary, but neither institution had an all-female board. The record does not show whether Cyrus Hamlin "wept in secret places." The college's bylaws also retained the domestic language of the original working plan for the Home, stipulating that the college buildings were designed to be "the home of the Institution," where the faculty "constituted a family" and the president of the college was "the head of the family."[33]

Despite their radical move, however, the corporation saw fit to require the faculty of the college to administer the college jointly with a male advisory board in Istanbul and even to confer on the curriculum, thereby undermining the authority of the president and the faculty. The bylaws appeared to vest authority in the faculty and the Woman's Board, yet they ensured the

intervention of the male missionaries in Istanbul in the day-to-day operations of the college and also in control of its finances. A local advisory board
was necessary for matters that needed male representation, such as acting on
behalf of the college in matters relating to the Ottoman state, paying taxes,
managing the external relations of the college, and perhaps supervising the
property it occupied. Yet the responsibilities of the advisory board extended
into everyday administration and even curriculum design, matters that were
well within the purview of the president and faculty.

The language of domesticity that upheld female authority within the family of the college was an empty vessel. The Woman's Board still deferred to the
American Board, the female faculty of the college was required to defer to the
male missionaries in Istanbul, and the bylaws did nothing to reduce opportunities for continued conflict between the two groups. Renewed tensions rapidly arose regarding the purpose of the college, the status of the professors,
and finances. Downright hostility characterized the relations between the
faculty and the missionaries in Istanbul for the first decade of the life of the
new college.

In preparation for the first commencement ceremony of the American College for Girls, Mary Mills Patrick immediately moved to declare a shift in the
nature of the college. While the college remained steadfastly Protestant, and
Bible study continued throughout the four years of instruction, its first annual
calendar openly celebrated a move toward a nonsectarian, liberal arts institution that welcomed women of all faiths. The opening paragraph stated that
the college offered "to young women who desire to obtain a liberal education,
advantages and facilities of the highest grade." While foregrounding education, the calendar noted that the college aimed "to combine the highest
moral and Christian culture with the most complete mental discipline."[34] It
listed all the Home school graduates since 1875. Seventy-four young women
of nine nationalities and several different faiths had completed their education, including Jewish students and Christian Orthodox students who continued to attend their own churches. The calendar was a celebration of internationalism and freedom of religion.

The last graduating class of the Home included the institution's first
Muslim graduate, Gulistan Ismet Hanum. The graduation of a Muslim

The American College for Girls at Constantinople, 1890. From The American College for Girls, Calendar, 1889–1890 *(London: Sir Joseph Causton & Sons, 1890).*

student who remained Muslim speaks to Patrick's evolution from an evangelist to an educator who opened the institution's doors to young women of all faiths and permitted them to retain their religious practices. But the non-sectarian nature of the college caused discomfiture for the Ottoman state as well as the Istanbul missionaries. If the college was no longer a proselytizing arm of the mission, then it potentially held more appeal for Muslim students. In 1892 Sultan Abdülhamid issued an edict banning Muslims from attending mission schools.[35] Despite the edict, Halidé Edib attended the college as a day student in 1893–1894 until the sultan issued an edict pointedly prohibiting her from attending. Edib subsequently returned to the college, graduating with a B.A. in 1901.[36] She became a prominent alumna, public figure, and poster child for the college. Caroline Borden subsequently called her a "Princess of influence in both Diplomatic and Educational life in Constantinople."[37]

This international, nonevangelical shift at the college particularly antagonized Henry Dwight. He was provoked to ask pointedly whether the institution was an arm in the evangelical struggle for souls or an institution offering a liberal arts education for Ottoman women. In the increasingly difficult

Mary Mills Patrick, undated portrait. American College for Girls Records, Archival Collection, Rare Book and Manuscript Library, Columbia University in the City of New York. By permission of the Trustees of Robert College of Istanbul, New York.

work of evangelizing, Dwight regarded the American College for Girls as a potential recruiting environment for missionary work, and, as he saw it, the college needed to be squarely in the evangelizing corner and the faculty must operate within the confines of the Western Turkey Mission. He posed three questions: Had the missionary character of the college changed? Did members of the faculty remain assistant missionaries connected to the Western Turkey Mission? Should the Western Turkey Mission resolve questions affecting the annual support of faculty?[38]

At the American Board in Boston, the Prudential Committee responded affirmatively to all three of Dwight's questions. In their view, members of the college's faculty should return to the work of the mission. They were an integral part of the mission, supported by funds gathered for missionary work. The college must therefore "steadfastly and directly promote the aggressive missionary work amid which it stands."[39] In a statement not dissimilar to the one N. G. Clark made to Esther Maltbie in 1876, Clark's successor, Judson Smith, emphasized that faculty was responsible only to the trustees of the corporation and the Woman's Board, but their work was a part of the mission and they must report to the men of the mission in Istanbul. The female trustees endorsed his statement: the college remained a missionary institution, the faculty remained assistant missionaries of the American Board and members of the Western Turkey Mission, and, as such, should be treated in the same way as other assistant missionaries, particularly as regards salaries.[40] Thus the trustees confirmed the subservience of the faculty to the Western Turkey Mission—but the faculty refused to yield. In a letter to the college's trustees Patrick noted that the various nationalities in the Ottoman Empire were making progress in educational affairs. If the college did not maintain and improve its standing, it would be "left behind."[41]

Two issues confirmed that the faculty no longer considered themselves a proselytizing arm of the mission. In 1892 Lydia Giles, a Mount Holyoke graduate and a member of the faculty, announced her engagement to Stephen Panaretoff, a Bulgarian Orthodox Christian who was a faculty member at Robert College.[42] The couple planned an Orthodox wedding, followed by a Protestant ceremony at which Elias Riggs had apparently agreed to officiate. Riggs's willingness to marry the couple indicates that some members of the mission embraced a broader view of the Christian community. Comments from missionaries in several locations suggest, however, that they believed Giles must have been mentally unbalanced to even consider the idea of marriage to an Orthodox Christian. Dwight resigned his position on the college advisory board in protest. The marriage went ahead; the couple remained in Istanbul and subsequently traveled to the United States when Panaretoff was appointed Bulgarian ambassador to the United States in 1914.

The second issue was an attempt to smooth over the differences within the mission with a proposal from some of the men in Istanbul to remove the college from the work of proselytizing and the direct supervision of the Istanbul missionaries.[43] Patrick welcomed the proposal; however, the Prudential Committee rejected the conciliatory gesture, describing the proposal as "a virtual revolution, detaching the institution from the immediate sphere of approved missionary policy and administration."[44] With only three dissenting votes (one of which was Caroline Borden's), the corporation of the college concurred that it was unwise to make such changes because to do so would be a "violation of mission policy."[45] The officers of the Woman's Board continued to defend the patriarchal institutional traditions of mission policy. They had become precisely what the board's more radical founders had insisted they were not: merely a fundraising arm of the American Board.

Fissures now developed, not only between Patrick and her board but also within the board. Patrick was obliged to avow her loyalty to the Woman's Board and write to correct any impression that the faculty "wished to escape our obligations as missionaries of the Board."[46] She insisted that the faculty had never contemplated cutting their connection to the Woman's Board; they were merely concerned to secure funding for the college. For her part, Caroline Borden resigned her position as secretary to the corporation of the college. In her letter of resignation, she noted that she would not have agreed to serve as a member of the college' governing body if she had not "fully believed that the jurisdiction over the Institution and its Faculty was in the control of the Woman's Board of Missions."[47] Over the next few years, several individuals associated with the college made private and public efforts to assuage doubts at the Woman's Board about the Christian purpose of the college and Patrick's ability to purse it. According to one professor at the college, Patrick had succeeded in giving the students "a religious training which shall be positive and deep and strong" in a location where "broader religious tolerance is asked of us."[48]

Although the situation was much more complicated, Patrick and Borden laid the responsibility for the decision to place the college under the control of the Istanbul missionaries squarely at the door of Judson and Augusta Smith. In her memoirs, Patrick described their years in office as "the dark ages."[49] In Borden's view, by their action the college "lost its independence and was made subservient to the Missionary Boards."[50] As we've seen, Judson Smith was foreign secretary of the American Board, and his wife, Augusta, was president of the Woman's Board and the corporation of the American College for Girls. That these positions were held by a married couple assured the subjugation of the Woman's Board to the American Board. It could not be otherwise. The college never had been independent, although Borden believed that it was and argued that the Woman's Board should have supported the faculty position. Trapped within the hierarchical reporting structure of their organization, the officers of the Woman's Board voted against the faculty. Borden and Patrick were obliged to yield and bide their time, but they contrived to engineer their independence.

Paving the Way for Independence at a Global Ecumenical Moment

The rift between the women missionaries in Istanbul and their board officers in Boston could not be bridged. No longer willing to be deferential, faculty members began to question the moral authority of their female officers and planned to seek independence from the Woman's Board. Although they were members of the missionary enterprise, the faculty believed that the institution they had developed should not be subservient to the goals of the mission. As professional educators, they argued for the right to conduct their own affairs and promote nonsectarian education. In the ensuing struggle the lines were not drawn hard and fast; some members of the corporation and some male missionaries in Istanbul supported the faculty.

Three factors paved the way for independence. In 1895, the sultan granted the college an imperial *irade* that provided an Ottoman charter for the college, recognized the corporation's ownership of the college, and held the faculty strictly to educational work, in return for which the college obtained tax-exempt status, even from religious taxes.[51] The college was now recognized and licensed by the Ottoman government.

Although bureaucracy proceeded slowly in the Ottoman Empire, the timing of the charter requires some comment. The Ottoman Education Law of 1869 stipulated that foreign schools must obtain a license from the government to operate. This requirement had most often been observed in the breech. College records and Patrick's memoir suggest that the sultan finally agreed to grant the charter to deflect attention from massacres of Armenians by Ottoman irregulars that had begun in Anatolia in 1894 in response to

Armenian revolutionary activities and were reported in European and U.S. newspapers.[52] The sultan hoped that the granting of the license would be reported in U.S. newspapers and would soften the outrage among Americans over the massacres.

The college's faculty worked continually to improve standards and develop the college's curriculum, which was similar to that of women's colleges in the United States. General courses included English literature, mathematics, geography, zoology, botany, physiology and hygiene, chemistry, geology, physics, astronomy, history, psychology and ethics, and the history of art. French and music were optional. Armenian, Bulgarian, and Greek girls also pursued studies in their own language, although Ottoman Turkish was no longer offered. Faculty members also worked to upgrade their qualifications; Mary Mills Patrick herself earned a Ph.D. from the University of Berne in 1897.

A final factor was Patrick's successful fundraising tour in the United States in 1899–1900. It had become clear to all parties that the Woman's Board could no longer support the growing expenses of the college. Appropriations from the Woman's Board rarely exceeded $5,000 annually to cover salaries, scholarships, and incidental expenses. The college's only other source of income was small donations and fees for tuition and board. Faculty salaries remained the same in 1892 as they were in 1871. Only in 1901, thirty years after the Constantinople Home first opened its doors, did the faculty receive a substantial increase, from $440 to $572 annually.[53] Patrick and Borden determined to secure other sources of funding.

While previously the two women had sought separation from the Western Turkey Mission, the continuing deterioration of the college campus pressed Patrick to look for separation from the corporation and independence from the Woman's Board. Patrick began in 1896 by suggesting that the college publish a fundraising pamphlet to attract donations for building maintenance.[54] By early 1899 talk in Istanbul had turned to the idea of raising an endowment. Patrick attributed the idea to U.S. consul-general Charles Dickinson, who pledged $1,000 to begin the endowment. He planned to appeal to friends in New York State, but thought that his business acquaintances would be unfavorably impressed by the complicated management of the college.[55] Whatever the practical difficulties, in the absence of a clear commitment to change from the corporation, some of the men in Istanbul floated the idea of an independent endowment and contemplated the separation of the college from the Woman's Board. Patrick expressed the hope that the college would soon have its own funds and that the Woman's Board would not have to "carry the heavy expenses of this College for many years longer."[56]

Patrick spent the academic year 1899–1900 in the United States on a fundraising tour organized in part by Caroline Borden. On the way she attended, as a delegate of the college, the meeting of the International Council of Women in London, a clear indication of her internationalist credentials.[57] In New York, Borden introduced Patrick to individuals from the worlds of business and education who could provide the funds to support the college. In addition to meeting wealthy potential patrons on the East Coast, Patrick traveled across the United States from New York via Chicago to Iowa, lecturing on the topic "Higher Education for Women in the Orient." Around this time, articles also began to appear in the New England and New York press promoting the college.[58]

Patrick made several noteworthy public appearances during her American tour, including a presentation at the ecumenical missionary conference in New York, where the conflicts at the American College for Girls were reflected in tensions in the larger missionary movement about women's work and social and religious changes in the United States. These tensions were already apparent at the Centenary Mission Conference held in London in 1888, as delegates debated the goal of education in mission and the relationship of women missionaries and their work to men in missions. Retired American Board foreign secretary N. G. Clark sparred with his replacement, Judson Smith, who questioned whether the missionary education system in "Turkey" belonged in any mission field. Rev. J. N. Murdock of the American Baptist Missionary Union argued that women's work for women was irrelevant. In his view the great point to be maintained in missionary work was "the headship of man."[59] The conservative bent of the American Board and the majority of trustees of the college corporation was reflected in a speech given by vice president Abbie Child, who discussed education in very general evangelical terms and made no mention of the American College for Girls.

By 1900, however, at the Ecumenical Missionary Conference in New

York, many more women gave presentations that defended women's work. Among them, Patrick emphasized the international nature of the college. Its students came, she said, "from Athens on the west; from Russia, Roumania, and Bulgaria on the north; and from the east as far as the Tigris and Euphrates Rivers, and from Egypt, Syria, and the Greek Islands on the south."[60] Their achievements were not restricted to work in the mission; instead they aimed higher. According to Patrick, the women of the Near East were ready to engage in professional careers. Some aspired to be physicians and translators. Clearly Patrick's goals for the college had deviated completely from those missionaries who wanted the institution to be an auxiliary to the mission. This transition was accomplished through changes in the views of the female faculty, particularly Patrick herself, about the purpose of the school and the willingness to challenge male authority, and shifts in U.S. society and within the missionary movement that demonstrated a growing sense of Christian ecumenical internationalism. In everything, Patrick was solidly supported by Caroline Borden in Boston.

While in the United States, Patrick also aired her feminist credentials. On October 18, 1899, at Yale University, she marched as one of only four women in the procession of college presidents at the inauguration of Yale's new president. Her impression from that event occasioned a comment that there was "progress at Yale—when women have been rather at a discount in times past."[61] This remark identifies Patrick as a New Woman, one who was confident, assertive, and independent in pursuit of her goals. A well-educated single woman who valued independence, professional advancement, and fulfillment through a career rather than through marriage and self-sacrifice, during her tour Patrick crystallized her feminist, Christian internationalist views and promoted herself as a prominent American educator in the Near East.

The prospect of raising a large endowment once again forced the Woman's Board to broach the question of whether the college should be separated from the Western Turkey Mission. In the spring of 1901, Harriet Stanwood, secretary of the corporation in Boston, wrote to missionaries and other individuals associated with the work of mission in the Ottoman Empire to seek their opinion. Her query caused a flurry of letter-writing from across the empire. The opinions of the correspondents ranged from those in favor of separation because the college diverted the mission from its true objectives and was "not proper work" for the Woman's Board, to those who argued against a separation so that the college could "stand as the Queen in our educational system."[62] In the face of this divergence of opinion from male missionaries, the officers of the Woman's Board made no decisions. The status quo continued at the Woman's Board, but Patrick's fundraising tour set in motion a trend that could not be stopped.

Patrick's trip marked a move away from the Woman's Board toward a new group of patrons from among the wealthy philanthropists of the New York commercial classes. From 1890, when the college was incorporated, to 1899, when she began to raise an endowment, the gifts Patrick listed in her annual president's reports were typically small and represented donations from the base of the Woman's Board; for example, $5 from a Mrs. Louisa P. Turnbull in Philadelphia, $30 from the Ladies' Society in Binghamton, New York, and $50 from Mount Holyoke College. Modest sums were also raised by the alumnae association that Caroline Borden founded after the first commencement. Larger sums were sometimes given, but they were not actively courted on a regular basis. That changed in 1900, when Patrick's annual report established specific donor categories. For $500, a donor became a patron for life of the college; for $1,000, one would be recognized as a patron in perpetuity of the college. Among the new donors were such well-known figures as Mrs. Russell Sage and John D. Rockefeller. Wealthy individuals like Sage and Rockefeller gave thousands and, in some cases, tens of thousands of dollars to the college.[63]

A new power emerged from these new financial backers. Borden recalled in her notes for 1904 that they "made a rift in the portending darkness by organizing an Advisory Committee." This group, headed by Charles Cuthbert Hall, president of the interdenominational Union Theological Seminary in New York City, intended to make decisions about how donors' money was spent.[64] In the face of donations of hundreds of thousands of dollars to an endowment that remained outside the control of the American Board, the officers of the Woman's Board were forced into a position where they had to contemplate relinquishing the college.

When Augusta Smith died in 1906, Borden wrote in her notes, "Death of Mrs. Judson Smith—Freedom!" Borden believed that Augusta Smith was chiefly responsible for insisting on the deference of the faculty to the men of the local advisory board in Istanbul and viewed her as a major obstacle to the progress of the college. On her death, the Woman's Board removed the requirement that members of the corporation be members of the board of directors of the Woman's Board of Missions at the time of their election. According to Borden, the removal of this requirement was "the bomb that dismembered the woman's board." Such a macabre description was perhaps an expression of the anger and frustration Borden had felt as she toiled for so many years on behalf of the college against the more conservative elements of the Woman's Board and the American Board. She expected more support from the new financial backers.

The new board of trustees for the college, based in New York, comprised sixteen members, only four of whom were women, including Caroline Borden and Mary Mills Patrick. The two women seem to have exchanged missionary patriarchy for capitalist patriarchy. A new auxiliary association, charged with the responsibility to raise funds, was headed by Talcott Williams, stepson of former Home school principal Kate Pond Williams, and it included such prominent figures as U.S. Supreme Court Justice David Brewer (son of missionaries Amelia and Josiah Brewer), former U.S. diplomat Oscar S. Straus, Mrs. John Hay (widow of the former U.S. secretary of state), and the well-known feminist reformer Julia Ward Howe. These prominent individuals had the social position to raise funds from wealthy donors in the commercial and philanthropic worlds who had connections to national political power. In a new imperial age of expansive American military and political power in the wake of the Spanish-American War of 1898, these people were more able than mission boards to wield American influence and project American power abroad.

On the last day of 1908, the American College for Girls ceased to be an institution associated with the Woman's Board. On January 1, 1909, the Woman's Board officially transferred to them the property and buildings of the college in Istanbul.

Caroline Borden and Mary Mills Patrick built their power base in a separate female institution established on the foundations of American domesticity, but they could realize the full potential of that institution only by reaching out beyond it—and beyond the denominational mission that shaped it. In the process the concept of the Christian home at the center of the Constantinople Home yielded to an English-language liberal arts education in the American College for Girls. The notion of a woman as head of family in the Constantinople Home ran counter to the logic of American domesticity, in which women shape the character of home and nation but must be submissive to men who ruled families, missions, and states. The idea that single women would manage their own work in an educational institution was at odds with the intrinsic hierarchy of the American Board, where the Woman's Board of Missions served as an auxiliary to the American Board, women ranked as "assistant missionaries" to ordained male missionaries, and education was subservient to the work of evangelizing. The single women at the Home rejected the submissive role of the missionary wife. Living together in an institutional household where a woman, not a man, held authority, the women resembled Catholic nuns and struggled in the same way as nuns against the patriarchal hierarchy of their organization.[65] The deep personal and professional friendships they formed within the Home seemed to threaten the men of the mission.

Differences of opinion as to the development of the Home and the position of the American College for Girls within the missionary enterprise shaped the relationship of the faculty within the Western Turkey Mission and eventually brought an end to its relationship with the Woman's Board. Ultimately, the officers of the Woman's Board were obliged to recognize that they could not provide for the financial needs of the college. When Borden and Patrick sought other sponsors, they succeeded in working across gender and denominational lines to wrest the college away from the Woman's Board by appealing to a broad, interdenominational group of wealthy men and women who appreciated the significance of female education in order to promote American values through an American liberal arts college.

Borden and Patrick's goal went far beyond the project that the Woman's Board envisioned. Their success indicates that the demise of the Woman's Board was not so much a result of the board's loss of connection with rank-and-file churchwomen as an indication of the board's unwillingness or inability to support its missionaries at the periphery. Patrick and Borden responded to the needs of the Ottoman surroundings to provide the best education for women that American women could offer in an international environment. In

her memoirs, Patrick frequently commented that the young women of different nationalities got along just fine within the college, even if the nations to
which they belonged were at war. Her experiences in Istanbul led her to criti-
cize identities based on religion and extreme nationalism. In an interesting
insight to her views about international cooperation, she argued that Ottoman
reformer Midhat Pasha's short-lived Ottoman constitution of 1876 was "one of
the most profound plans for the advancement of internationalism ever designed." Patrick was not convinced that Midhat Pasha intended to "Otto-
manize" all the groups in the empire; she thought that the people in the Near
East could have evolved under the new constitution had they been "free from
national and religious jealousy."[66] These insights help explain her trajectory
from evangelist to professional educator and her commitment to work for
international understanding.

The year that the Woman's Board ceded its institution, 1908, also brought
the Young Turk Revolution. Patrick missed experiencing that political upheaval, as she was once again in the United States. In her memoirs, she connected the changes at the college with the political changes taking place in
the Ottoman Empire and elsewhere. In her view, changes in the college were
"symptoms of general transformations taking place in world affairs" that
were "especially marked in Turkey."[67] Patrick's view that the transfer of
authority at the college was part of a broader global movement gives added
meaning to her perception of her place and the place of the college in world
affairs. Only ten years later, in the aftermath of World War I, pamphlets
advertising the college promoted it as a "fortress of Americanism."[68] The college became a new instrument of American cultural expansion in a new age
of American global power. Female education was now too important to be
left to mission boards.

Conclusion

In an era of massive political disruption, Protestantism and Ottomanism alike extended to Bulgarian Orthodox Christians the option of a supranational identity that transcended traditional markers of distinctiveness. American missionaries worked to bring Bulgarians into a global community of Protestant Christians, but they succeeded in exacerbating the splintering of Ottoman society by adding to religious segmentation. Ottoman reformers tried to mold the sultan's subjects into Ottoman citizens, regardless of religion and ethnicity, but they succeeded in facilitating increasing expressions of nationalism among the expanding middle classes, which the missionaries then supported through their work of translation and education. The missionaries and the Ottomans failed in the face of an encroaching nationalism that exploited religion and language as long as they were useful to unify Bulgarians against Ottoman reforms. Bulgarian nationalists found that a gendered language of religious reform in the service of the home and nation served their purposes admirably to thwart both Protestant and Ottoman pressures. At the same time, women missionaries turned this domestic discourse into an instrument of Christian feminism to promote their own internationalist goals.

From 1831 to 1908, the shifting fissures in American and Ottoman society delineated the possibilities and limits of American cultural and religious expansion in the Ottoman Balkans and the Near East. In Istanbul and other towns, Protestant-Orthodox encounters reveal the connections among evangelical Protestant traditions, American imperial culture, Balkan nationalisms, Ottoman imperial reforms, and an emergent Christian feminist internationalism. They illuminate the ways in which American ideas about gender, religion, and race cross boundaries and are redeployed by new actors in diverse contexts. A transnational approach to the study of these events, which span a period of tremendous social change in the United States and the Ottoman Balkans, broadens the debate about the substance, extent, and impact of the American Protestant empire.

Gender, religion, and race were central to understandings of the American Christian home and nation in the United States in the nineteenth century. The educated Christian (Protestant) mother stood at the center of both, shaping the character of the family, guarding the borders of home and nation, contributing to national progress, and justifying continental expansion. In the preceding chapters I have traced the cultural formation of the Christian home to the Ottoman Balkans, where American Protestant missionaries employed a language of domesticity to shape their mission culture and to win Christian Orthodox women to Protestantism. As the encounters analyzed here indicate, the Christian home was a very flexible construct. It contained inherent contradictions that proved useful to a wide range of individuals, men as well as women, Orthodox as well as Protestant, Bulgarian as well as American. The language of domesticity was redeployed in contexts unimagined by those who originally articulated it, and its adaptability helps explain its durability.

The cultural formation of the Christian home remained a steadfast ideal of the missionary enterprise even as the flexibility of domestic discourse was negotiated and manipulated to shape a myriad of expressions and behaviors. When Elizabeth Dwight was concerned about the character of her children growing up in Istanbul in the 1830s, she shared her worries with readers in the United States. Emphasizing the loneliness and the difficulty of her task, she wrote that "a mother must be the model, and almost the only model of virtue and religion her children will have."[1] Martha Jane Riggs somewhat more optimistically shared her views about the connections of motherhood to religion and national progress when she urged her Bulgarian readers to prepare themselves for their responsibilities. They had the duty to shape "the character of nations as well as individuals," she wrote.[2] Nowhere were ideas about home, family, and nation more intensely experienced than by missionary wives as they sought to serve as examples to the women among whom they labored while nurturing their own children in their New England faith and culture.

Within the patriarchal order of missionary society, wives were expected to exert their moral authority, but they were also expected to be deferential to the male head of the household. Male and female missionaries alike extolled the virtues of American women as shapers of modern families and civilized nations, yet few men saw the contradiction in demanding that wives extend their domestic sphere to include supervision of a boarding school. Most men looked to their wives to support them in their own work. Men like Lewis Bond, who supported Fannie Bond's ambitions, were few and far between.

Social changes in the United States led to women looking for more fulfilling independent careers in mission. The women's movement of the mid-nineteenth century, women's experiences in the Civil War, and greater educational opportunities all created a context in which single women in particular expected to exert more authority. Women missionaries were not immune to these changes. Yet the language of domesticity and ideas that linked women, family, and national progress remained a robust discourse even as those ideas were challenged by single women. In an extension of the male headship model, single women missionaries were also expected to defer to male missionaries. When Esther Maltbie and Anna Mumford claimed "the privileges of any other missionary family" and officers of the Women's Board of Missions stipulated that the single women in the Constantinople Home would "constitute a family," they retained the language of domesticity even as they contested the gendered structures of mission society and set new goals for their educational institutions.[3] Family and home were constant, yet flexible, concepts in the clear face of change. Discursive strategies remained the same; practices varied and altered. But a community of single, educated, ambitious women was a particularly threatening idea to married male missionaries, who, as the chapters on Samokov and the Constantinople Home demonstrate, did their utmost to prevent the women's independence of action.

The tensions at the center of discussions about single women worked themselves out in ways that had long-lasting effects within the mission, in the lives of women missionaries, in the local environment, and back in Boston. Conflicts of power in Istanbul and other Ottoman cities and towns contributed to redefining understandings about gender among missionaries. Single women viewed themselves as professionals from the outset, and their officers invoked a higher spiritual authority to support their claims. "Under her alone under God devolved the responsibility of success or failure," wrote the original officers of the Woman's Board in support of Julia Rappleye, whose authority male missionaries in Istanbul refused to acknowledge.[4] Faced by male intransigence, single women increasingly challenged the structures of missionary society that claimed to offer spiritual equality but denied equal access to social status, decision making, and material resources.

Single women were unwilling to be deferential, but they found it difficult to break down the invisible yet resilient webs of patriarchal power that thwarted them in Istanbul and seemed to constrain their officers in Boston. The first group of officers of the Woman's Board, who operated in the 1870s and 1880s, were more progressive and demanding of recognition than the group that became trustees of the American College for Girls in the 1890s. The cultural formation of the Christian home constrained Augusta Smith at the Woman's Board in Boston, even as it liberated Mary Mills Patrick in a different environment in Istanbul.

The cultural encounters analyzed here also demonstrate that missionary institutions were embedded in local environments and missionaries responded to local conditions. American ideas were welcome in Istanbul and the Ottoman Balkans because changes in Ottoman society made possible the infiltration of new goods, services, and ideas, most of which were perceived as modern. Under internal and external pressures, Ottoman statesmen implemented far-reaching programs of reform that facilitated the extension of American ideas about women and society. The increasing intervention of European powers in the affairs of the Ottoman state and the strengthening of trade links with Europe created interest in things European among Ottoman subjects. As missionaries Elias Riggs, Albert Long, and Theodore Byington realized that Bulgarians were not interested in their preaching but wanted to own the Bible, read mission magazines, and send their daughters to mission schools, they reconsidered their strategy and tried to achieve their own goals by meeting Bulgarians' needs.

Missionaries persistently clung to the idea that, directly or indirectly, they would prepare new generations of leaders in the Near East by shaping the moral values of home life, their own and other people's. As Orthodox Christian girls were educated in Mount Holyoke clones, Protestant ideals seeped through schools into Bulgarian homes and through the pages of the missionary magazine *Zornitsa* into the Bulgarian press. They echoed in the communities where mission-school graduates taught and worked as Bible women, and through the maternal associations organized by Bulgarian women across the Ottoman Balkans from 1869 to 1876.

As the idea of the Christian home wended its way through Ottoman domains, however, it frequently took surprising turns that could be neither predicted nor controlled. Missionaries certainly did not encourage armed rebellion, but their work furthered the causes of Bulgarian Orthodox nationalism and undermined Ottoman reforms. Their publication of the Bible, *Zornitsa, Letters to Mothers,* tracts, and textbooks at a time when there were few works published in Bulgarian confirmed the usefulness of the Bulgarian language as a vehicle of national expression and endorsed the compelling prospect of a Bulgarian national identity separate from Greek and Ottoman. Their project to transform religion and society by attempting to improve the status of women threatened the patriarchal framework of Orthodox society (as it did missionary society), the cohesion of Orthodox communities, and, ultimately, the spiritual and temporal power structures of the Ottoman state.

Bulgarians redeployed American domesticity to recast the significance of gendered, racial, and religious markers of identity, which created profound changes in Ottoman society. In the hands of Bulgarians who sought evolutionary, rather than revolutionary, change in the Ottoman Balkans, American domesticity became an anticolonial tool that contributed to shaping Bulgarian nationalist aspirations. Urban educated Bulgarians grafted American domesticity onto their own conceptions of women's contributions to society. At a time when Bulgarians sought a way to achieve greater national recognition within the Ottoman polity, they promoted the view that well-educated

Christian women could raise children to become engaged citizens who would build a strong modern nation while retaining their allegiance to the Ottoman state.

For women in Ottoman domains, as in New England, the private space of the home, grounded in religious ideology, became the springboard for a public sphere of action. Women like Maria Gencheva, Anastasiya Tosheva, and Evgeniya Kissimova were cross-cultural thinkers who could shape a complex yet comfortable identity from the languages of American domesticity, Ottoman reform, and Bulgarian nationalism. Whether or not they chose to convert, they were able to construct a platform for their own personal and political ends. They stretched the contours of Ottoman Bulgarian society, challenged or supported the influences of Protestantism in their communities, contributed to different strands of Bulgarian nationalism or internationalism, and contemplated the possibility of multiple identities and allegiances. Through them, gender also became a central component of the nationalist narratives of Orthodox Bulgarians in the late 1860s. Women's education became a vehicle to train mothers and teachers who would shape homes and citizens to lead an emergent Bulgarian nation into a new historical moment. The promise of the Bulgarian women's movement was cut short by the Bulgarian uprising of 1876 that led to war between Russia and the Ottoman Empire the following year. Bulgaria gained independence as a consequence of this war, but it also led women to return to auxiliary associations that emphasized their nurturing role. In that brief window of time between 1869 and 1876, however, Bulgarian women demonstrated the power and flexibility of American domestic discourse.

Protestant missionaries acted as agents of American cultural and religious expansion and as one among many catalysts for change in Ottoman society. The influence of missionary institutions, particularly schools and the press, in contributing ideas about women and the home to new expressions of Orthodox nationalism that undermined Ottoman reform is a significant consequence of the American-Bulgarian encounter in the region. The positive reception of some aspects of Anglo-American Protestant culture among urban educated Orthodox Bulgarians across the Ottoman Balkans shows that cultures were not always destroyed in their encounters with the

Protestant missionary enterprise. American-Bulgarian interactions demonstrate the strength of local cultures when communities unified to confront the engine of Protestant reform.

Religion as faith, as a sign of difference, and as an expression of national belonging was an elemental component of the worldview of individuals caught up on all sides of missionary encounters. The spread of Protestantism in the Near East was therefore constrained by people's ideas about their personal, religious, and civic affiliations to community and state. It was also tested by American ideas about home life that shaped the colonial structure of missionary society and rejected converts as equals. The promises of a pan-Protestant universal Christian community that offered spiritual equality in the sight of God did not translate into social equalities in the here and now. Bulgarian Orthodox Christians understood the meaning of second-class citizenship in the Ottoman Empire, where Islam was the dominant religion. They were not attracted to another form of inferiority within a minority Protestant community. Few Bulgarians responded to the opportunity to convert in the 1860s and 1870s. Those who did convert found meaning in their new identities and created vibrant spiritual communities that still exist today, yet they found themselves at the margins of missionary society and struggled to be included in the larger Protestant community. Converts like Ivan Tonjoroff took the promise of a brotherhood and sisterhood in Christ to its logical conclusion, and their actions offer a glimpse into a more egalitarian Christian community. But neither Bulgarian converts nor those missionaries who shared more equitable views of society were able to breach the paternalistic and racial structures of missionary colonialism. Indeed, those who tried were ostracized. The forcefulness of the missionary response to the marriage of Elizabeth Bevan and Ivan Tonjoroff reveals the dominant Anglo-Saxon attitudes that prevailed in the late nineteenth century against a more tolerant perspective of the missionary enterprise; yet the divided views within the mission about the marriage of Lydia Giles and Stephen Panaretoff demonstrate the changing perspectives on race, gender, culture, and Christianity among some missionaries.

The Constantinople Home demonstrates most clearly the shifting interpretations of the Christian home within the missionary enterprise and the impact of the local environment on the missionaries and the board back in

Boston. American women refashioned the language of domesticity not merely to adapt to the local environment, nor even to change it, but to use it to build an American-Ottoman institution that served both American and Ottoman needs. On the fringes of power, single women missionaries were well placed to see the connections that would enable them to create opportunities for themselves. More than testing the patriarchal contours of missionary society, they contested its evangelical philosophy. The determination of the faculty at the American College for Girls to be professional educators first, Protestants second, and proselytizers not at all led to their loss of confidence in their officers in Boston and to a decision to split from the Woman's Board of Missions. That split caused a loss of prestige for the women in Boston and carved the beginnings of a path that contributed to the demise of the Woman's Board, which was eventually incorporated into the larger American Board of Commissioners for Foreign Missions. Looking back at the split from the comfort of her retirement, Mary Mills Patrick argued that it came because the women in Boston had "a narrower conception of the best way to cooperate in world improvement."[5] In 1908, Patrick was on the leading edge of a movement of Christian feminist internationalism, one that took on new relevance after World War I. She embraced internationalism well before the liberal wing of the missionary movement in the 1920s. Dissent at the periphery, rather than at the center, provoked change at home.

Mary Mills Patrick and Carolyn Borden achieved what male missionaries and Ottoman reformers could not: a cosmopolitan, multinational community of educated women that embraced religious liberty, decried sectarianism, and tolerated all faiths. Yet the American College for Girls in Istanbul remained a Christian institution, founded on domestic discourse, shaped by faith and feminism, and imbued with the perception of American Protestant superiority that was shaped by New England culture and celebrated by wealthy East Coast philanthropists. The trajectory of the college helps us to see the complexity of the missionary enterprise, the challenges it faced at home and abroad, and the cultures of American expansionism it transplanted in the Near East.

Notes

Introduction

1. "The Constantinople Home," *Life and Light for Woman* (from 1869 to 1873 titled *Life and Light for Heathen Women*), October 1876, 289–98.

2. "Extension of our Work," *Life and Light for Heathen Women*, September 1869, 94.

3. N. G. Clark, "The Gospel in the Ottoman Empire," in *Proceedings of the General Conference on Foreign Missions Held at the Conference Hall, in Mildmay Park, London, in October, 1878,* ed. The Secretaries to the Conference (London: John F. Shaw, 1879), 107–15, quotations on 111.

4. On the concept of American domesticity, see Kathryn Kish Sklar, *Catharine Beecher: A Study in American Domesticity* (1973; repr., New York: Norton, 1976). The language of Protestant superiority offers an American version of the European Orientalism first illuminated by Edward Said in *Orientalism* (New York: Pantheon, 1978). Although Said has been much criticized since the publication of his book for his ahistorical approach, his work remains useful as a study of how cultures perceive each other. On the entwined discourses, see Lisa Joy Pruitt, *A Looking-Glass for Ladies: American Protestant Women and the Orient in the Nineteenth Century* (Macon, Ga.: Mercer University Press, 2005).

5. The scholarship on nineteenth-century Ottoman reforms is voluminous. For a recent interpretation that includes a bibliography of earlier works see M. Şükrü Hanioğlu, *A Brief History of the Late Ottoman Empire* (Princeton: Princeton University Press, 2008).

6. Charles Jelavich and Barbara Jelavich, *The Establishment of the Balkan National States, 1804–1920* (Seattle: University of Washington Press, 1977), chaps. 2 and 3.

7. The scholarship on Bulgarian national movements is also voluminous. For syntheses, see Roumen Daskalov, *Kak se misli bulgarskoto Vuzrazhdane* (Sofia: Izdatelstvo Lik, 2002), in

English as *The Making of a Nation in the Balkans: Historiography of the Bulgarian Revival* (Budapest: Central European University Press, 2004); and Nikolay Genchev, *Bulgarskoto Vuzrazhdane*, 4th ed. (Sofia: Ivan Vazov, 1995).

8. William G. Schauffler, *Autobiography of William G. Schauffler, for Forty-Nine Years a Missionary in the Orient* (New York: Anson D. F. Randolph, 1887), 134.

9. Nathan J. Citino, "The Global Frontier: Comparative History and the Frontier-Borderlands Approach in American Foreign Relations," *Diplomatic History* 25, no. 4 (2001): 677–93.

10. For critical perspectives, see Paul W. Harris, "Cultural Imperialism and American Protestant Missionaries: Collaboration and Dependency in Mid-Nineteenth-Century China," *Pacific Historical Review* 60, no. 3 (1991): 309–38; and Arthur Schlesinger Jr., "The Missionary Enterprise and Theories of Imperialism," in *The Missionary Enterprise in China and America*, ed. John K. Fairbank (Cambridge: Harvard University Press, 1974), 336–73. For a scholarly debate that focuses on the Ottoman empire and its successor states, see Eleanor H. Tejirian and Reeva Spector Simon, eds., *Altruism and Imperialism: Western Cultural and Religious Missions in the Middle East* (New York: Middle East Institute, Columbia University, 2002).

11. See, for example, Ryan Dunch, "Beyond Cultural Imperialism: Cultural Theory, Christian Missions, and Global Modernity," *History and Theory* 41, no. 3 (2002): 301–25; Maina Chawla Singh, *Gender, Religion, and "Heathen Lands": American Missionary Women in South Asia (1860s–1940s)* (New York: Garland, 2000); and Peter Van der Veer, *Imperial Encounters: Religion and Modernity in India and Britain* (Princeton: Princeton University Press, 2001).

12. See, for example, Jane Hunter, *The Gospel of Gentility: America Women Missionaries in Turn-of-the-Century China* (New Haven: Yale University Press, 1984); and Ian Tyrrell, *Woman's World, Woman's Empire: The Woman's Christian Temperance Movement in International Perspective, 1880–1930* (Chapel Hill: University of North Carolina Press, 1991).

13. Ann Laura Stoler and Frederick Cooper, "Between Metropole and Colony: Rethinking a Research Agenda," in *Tensions of Empire: Colonial Cultures in a Bourgeois World*, ed. Cooper and Stoler (Berkeley: University of California Press, 1997), 1–56.

14. See, for example, Hyaeweol Choi, *Gender and Mission Encounters in Korea: New Women, Old Ways* (Berkeley: University of California Press, 2009); Noriko Kawamura Ishii, *American Women Missionaries at Kobe College, 1873–1909* (New York: Routledge, 2004); and the essays collected in Barbara Reeves-Ellington, Kathryn Kish Sklar, and Connie Shemo, eds., *Competing Kingdoms: Women, Mission, Nation, and the American Protestant Empire, 1812–1960* (Durham, N.C.: Duke University Press, 2010).

15. For an interesting analysis of what counts as archives for imperial history, see Antoinette Burton, *Dwelling in the Archive: Women Writing House, Home, and History in Late Colonial India* (New York: Oxford University Press, 2003).

16. Ussama Makdisi, *Artillery of Heaven: American Missionaries and the Failed Conversion of the Middle East* (Ithaca: Cornell University Press, 2008); Heather Sharkey, *American Evangelicals in Egypt: Missionary Encounters in an Age of Empire* (Princeton: Princeton University Press, 2008); Hans-Lukas Kieser, *Nearest East: American Millennialism and Mission to the Middle East* (Philadelphia: Temple University Press, 2010).

17. Nikolay Nachov, *Tsarigrad kato kulturen tsentur na bulgarite do 1877g* (Sofia: Pechatnitsa P. Glushkov, 1925); Toncho Zhechev, *Bulgarskiyat velikden, ili strastite bulgarski,* 6th ed. (Sofia: Prof. Marin Drinov, 1995).

18. For the theological perspectives that motivated the American Board, see David W. Kling, "The New Divinity and the Origins of the American Board of Commissioners for Foreign Missions," in *North American Foreign Missions, 1810–1914: Theology, Theory, and Policy,* ed. Wilbert R. Shenk (Grand Rapids, Mich.: William B. Eerdmans, 2004), 11–38. For an early history of the American Board, see Clifton Jackson Phillips, *Protestant America and the Pagan World: The First Half Century of the American Board of Commissioners of Foreign Missions, 1810–1860* (Cambridge: East Asian Research Center of Harvard University, 1969). For a comparison of resources spent on the missionary enterprise, see James A. Field Jr., "Near East Notes and Far East Queries," in *The Missionary Enterprise in China and America,* ed. John K. Fairbank (Cambridge: Harvard University Press, 1974), 23–55.

19. Rufus Anderson, *The Promised Advent of the Spirit for the World's Conversion* (Boston: Crocker & Brewster, 1841), 5. Anderson served as the American Board's foreign secretary from 1832 to 1866.

20. Dana Robert, *American Women in Mission: A Social History of Their Thought and Practice* (Macon, Ga.: Mercer University Press, 1997), and "The 'Christian Home' as a Cornerstone of Anglo-American Missionary Thought and Practice," in *Converting Colonialism: Visions and Realities in Mission History, 1706–1914,* ed. Dana Robert (Grand Rapids, Mich.: William B. Eerdmans, 2008), 134–65.

21. Sklar, *Catharine Beecher.*

22. Amy Kaplan, "Manifest Domesticity," *American Literature* 70, no. 3 (1998): 581–606.

23. Derek Chang, *Citizens of a Christian Nation: Evangelical Missions and the Problem of Race in the Nineteenth Century* (Philadelphia: University of Pennsylvania Press, 2010).

24. Women missionaries have not usually been included in histories of feminist internationalism. See, for example, Leila J. Rupp, *Worlds of Women: The Making of an International Women's Movement* (Princeton: Princeton University Press, 1997).

25. Matthew Frye Jacobson, *Whiteness of a Different Color: European Immigrants and the Alchemy of Race* (Cambridge: Harvard University Press, 1998).

26. Selim Deringil, *The Well-Protected Domains: Ideology and the Legitimation of Power in the Ottoman Empire, 1876–1909* (London: I. B. Tauris, 1998). For the implications of this perception in relation to Armenian Christians, see Jeremy Salt, *Imperialism, Evangelism, and the Ottoman Armenians, 1878–1896* (London: Frank Cass, 1993).

27. William Webster Hall Jr., *Puritans in the Balkans: The American Board Mission in Bulgaria, 1878–1918, a Study in Purpose and Procedure* (Sofia: Kultura Printing House, 1938); James F. Clarke, *The Pen and the Sword: Studies in Bulgarian History,* ed. Dennis Hupchick (Boulder, Colo.: East European Monographs, 1988); Ivan Ilchev, "Robert kolezh i formiraneto na bulgarska inteligentsiya, 1863–1878g," *Istoricheski pregled* 1, no. 1 (1981): 50–62.

28. Andrey Pantev, *Istoricheski pregled kum bulgaristika v Angliya i Sasht, 1856–1919* (Sofia: Nauka i izkustvo, 1986); Petko Petkov, "Amerikanski misioneri v bulgarskite zemi, XIX do nachaloto na XX v.," *Istoricheski pregled* 46, no. 5 (1990): 18–32.

29. Tatyana Nestorova, *American Missionaries among the Bulgarians (1858–1912)* (Boulder, Colo.: East European Monographs, 1987), 135.

30. For critiques of Bulgarian historiography, see Thomas A. Meininger, "A Troubled Transition: Bulgarian Historiography, 1989–1994," *Contemporary European History* 5, no. 1 (1996): 103–8; and Maria Todorova, "Historiography of the Countries of Eastern Europe: Bulgaria," *American Historical Review* 97, no. 4 (1992): 1105–17.

31. Boris Kozhukharov, *Purvata evangelska tsurkva v Bulgaria: Deynostta na amerikanskite misioneri* (Sofia: Nov chovek, 1998); Khristo Kulichev, *Vestiteli na istinata: Istoriya na evangelskite tsurkvi v Bulgaria* (Sofia: Bulgarsko bibleysko obshtestvo, 1994); Khristo Kulichev, *Zaslugite na protestantite za bulgarskiya narod* (Sofia: Universitetsko izdatelstvo "Sv. Kliment Okhridski," 2008). See also George Dimitrov's website *History of the Bulgarian Protestants (Evangelicals)* at http://reocities.com/Paris/Jardin/4656/ and his blog at http://muntzer2.blog.bg/.

32. For the usefulness of expanding the concept of conversion from a narrow spiritual perspective, see Dennis Washburn and A. Kevin Reinhart, eds., *Converting Cultures: Religion, Ideology and Transformations of Modernity* (Leiden: E. J. Brill, 2007).

1. Missionary Families and the Contested Concept of Home

1. Louisa Fisher Hawes, *Memoir of Mrs. Mary Van Lennep, Only Daughter of the Rev. Joel Hawes, D.D., and Wife of the Rev. Henry J. Van Lennep, Missionary in Turkey* (Hartford, Conn.: Belknap & Hamersley, 1848), 240–41.

2. Ibid., 263, 262.

3. Ibid., 261–62.

4. Dana Robert, "The 'Christian Home' as a Cornerstone of Anglo-American Missionary Thought and Practice," in *Converting Colonialism: Visions and Realities in Mission History, 1706–1914*, ed. Dana Robert (Grand Rapids, Mich.: William B. Eerdmans, 2008), 134–65. For a study that explores the ways in which the meanings of the mission home were affected by the local environment, particularly spatial and architectural dimensions, among American missionaries in Syria, see Christine Lindner, "The Flexibility of Home: Exploring the Spaces and Definitions of the Home and Family Employed by the ABCFM Missionaries in Ottoman Syria from 1823 to 1860," in *American Missionaries and the Middle East: Foundational Encounters*, ed. Mehmet Ali Doğan and Heather J. Sharkey (Salt Lake City: University of Utah Press, 2011), 33–62. For a study of the home that explores the ways in which British missionary families shaped and changed the British missionary enterprise, see Emily J. Manktelow, "Missionary Families and the Formation of the Missionary Enterprise: The London Missionary Society and the Family, 1795–1875" (Ph.D. diss., King's College, London, 2010).

5. Joseph A. Conforti, *Jonathan Edwards, Religious Tradition, and American Culture* (Chapel Hill: University of North Carolina Press, 1995), 64.

6. Mary Kupiec Cayton, "Canonizing Harriet Newell: Women, the Evangelical Press, and the Foreign Mission Movement in New England, 1800–1840," in *Competing Kingdoms: Women, Mission, Nation, and the American Protestant Empire, 1812–1960*, ed. Barbara Reeves-Ellington, Kathryn Kish Sklar, and Connie Shemo (Durham, N.C.: Duke University Press, 2010), 69–93.

7. Ruth H. Bloch, "American Feminine Ideals in Transition: The Rise of the Moral Mother, 1785–1815," *Feminist Studies* 4, no. 2 (1978): 101–26.

8. Ann Douglas, *Feminization of American Culture* (New York: Alfred A. Knopf, 1977); Barbara Welter, "The Feminization of American Religion: 1800–1860," in *Clio's Consciousness Raised: New Perspectives on the History of Women*, ed. Mary S. Hartman and Lois W. Banner (New York: Harper Torchbooks, 1974), 137–57.

9. Richard A. Meckel, "Educating a Ministry of Mothers: Evangelical Maternal Associations, 1815–1860," *Journal of the Early Republic* 2, no. 4 (1982): 402–3; Mary P. Ryan, *Cradle of the Middle Class: The Family in Oneida County, New York, 1790–1865* (Cambridge: Harvard University Press, 1981).

10. Anne L. Kuhn, *The Mother's Role in Childhood Education: New England Concepts, 1830–1860* (New Haven: Yale University Press, 1947), v.

11. Mary P. Ryan, *The Empire of the Mother: American Writing about Domesticity, 1830–1860* (New York: Haworth Press, 1982); the phrase "vast army of mothers" is from "Address to Mothers," *The Mother's Magazine*, April 1841, 1.

12. Kathryn Kish Sklar, *Catharine Beecher: A Study in American Domesticity* (1973; repr., New York: W. W. Norton, 1976), quotation on 159.

13. Amy Kaplan, "Manifest Domesticity," *American Literature* 70, no. 3 (1998): 581–606.

14. Lisa Joy Pruitt, *A Looking-Glass for Ladies: American Protestant Women and the Orient in the Nineteenth Century* (Macon, Ga.: Mercer University Press, 2005).

15. Amy Kaplan first made explicit the connection between the discourse of domesticity and manifest destiny; Edward Said first alerted scholars to European discourses of Orientalism; Lisa Joy Pruitt, among others, has explored the facets of American Orientalism within the missionary enterprise. See Kaplan, "Manifest Domesticity"; Pruitt, *A Looking-Glass;* Edward W. Said, *Orientalism* (New York: Pantheon, 1978).

16. On domestic discourse, moral reform, and early women's activism in New England, see, for example, Nancy F. Cott, *The Bonds of Womanhood: "Woman's Sphere" in New England, 1780–1835*, 2nd ed. (New Haven: Yale University Press, 1997); Nancy A. Hewitt, *Women's Activism and Social Change: Rochester, New York, 1822–1872* (Ithaca: Cornell University Press, 1984); Carolyn J. Lawes, *Women and Reform in a New England Community, 1815–1860* (Lexington: University Press of Kentucky, 2000).

17. Scholars differ in their assessments as to whether women embraced the domestic sphere and thereby shaped mission policy or whether they were obliged by circumstances to accept a more restrictive perspective of the empire of the mother. Dana Robert, *American Women in Mission: A Social History of Their Thought and Practice* (Macon: Ga.: Mercer University Press, 1997), chap. 2; Patricia Grimshaw, *Paths of Duty: American Missionary Wives in Nineteenth-Century Hawaii* (Honolulu: University of Hawaii Press, 1989); and Mary Zwiep, *Pilgrim Path: The First Company of Women Missionaries to Hawaii* (Madison: University of Wisconsin Press, 1991).

18. Rufus Anderson, "Introductory Essay on the Marriage of Missionaries," in *Memoir of Mrs. Mary Mercy Ellis*, ed. William Ellis (Boston: Crocker & Brewster, 1836), vii–xxii.

19. All quotations in this and the following three paragraphs are from Anderson, "Introductory Essay," viii–xii.

20. Grimshaw, *Paths of Duty*, 6; Niel Gunson, *Messengers of Grace: Evangelical Missionaries*

in the South Seas, 1797–1860 (Melbourne: Oxford University Press, 1978), 147–66. Emily Manktelow argues that the London Missionary Society had no objection to their male missionaries marrying local women as long as the women were converts. Their objection was to sex outside marriage and marriage to non-Protestant women. See Manktelow, "Missionary Families."

21. See, in particular, Pruitt, *A Looking-Glass;* and Robert, *American Women in Mission.*

22. Anderson recounted his travels in *Observations upon the Peloponnesus and Greek Islands, Made in 1829* (Boston: Crocker & Brewster, 1830), 187, 231–42, 249.

23. Anderson, "Introductory Essay," xii–xiv.

24. American Board, *Manual for Missionary Candidates* (Boston: Crocker and Brewster, 1837), 17–18.

25. The Vinton Books, Congregational Library, Congregational Christian Historical Society, Boston, available at www.congregationallibrary.org/resources/digital/vinton.

26. E. D. G. Prime, *Forty Years in the Turkish Empire; or, Memoirs of Rev. William Goodell, D.D., Late Missionary of the A.B.C.F.M. at Constantinople.* (New York: Robert Carter and Brothers, 1876), 189–90.

27. Harrison Gray Otis Dwight, *Memoir of Mrs. Elizabeth B. Dwight, including an Account of the Plague of 1837; with a Sketch of the Life of Mrs. Judith S. Grant* (New York: M. W. Dodd, 1840), 156–57.

28. Paul William Harris, *Nothing but Christ: Rufus Anderson and the Ideology of Protestant Foreign Missions* (New York: Oxford University Press, 1999).

29. Elias Riggs, "A Missionary for Fifty-Five Years," *Missionary Herald,* February 1888, 59–62.

30. Dwight, *Memoir of Mrs. Elizabeth B. Dwight,* 145, 148.

31. Hawes, *Memoir of Mrs. Mary Van Lennep,* 147, 183.

32. Margarette Woods Lawrence, *Light on the Dark River; or, Memorials of Mrs. Henrietta A. L. Hamlin, Missionary in Turkey* (Boston: Ticknor, Reed & Fields, 1854), 84.

33. "Letter from Mrs. Dwight to Mrs. H.," *The Mother's Magazine,* January 1836, 13–16, quotation on 14.

34. Grimshaw, *Paths of Duty;* Jane Hunter, *The Gospel of Gentility: American Women Missionaries in Turn-of-the-Century China* (New Haven: Yale University Press, 1984).

35. "Letter from Mrs. Dwight to Mrs. H.," 15.

36. "Letter of Mrs. Dwight," *The Mother's Magazine,* December 1836, 188–90, quotation on 189.

37. H. Read, "Appeal to Mothers on the Subject of Missions," *The Mother's Magazine,* December 1836, 177–80, quotations on 179.

38. Constitution of the "Maternal Association" of Utica, adopted June 30, 1824, New York State Library, Albany.

39. Horace Bushnell, *Views of Christian Nurture, and of Subjects Adjacent Thereto* (New York: Edwin Hunt, 1847).

40. "Letter from Mrs. Dwight to Mrs. H."

41. Martha E. Temple, "For the Mother's Magazine," *The Mother's Magazine,* July 1838, 181–84.

42. "Donations for the Wives of Missionaries," *The Mother's Magazine,* April 1839, 96.

43. The information about the translations comes from Riggs, "A Missionary for Fifty-Five

Years," 61. Riggs's book was published in English, but for convenience I use the title *Letters to Mothers* when referring to all editions.

44. Christine Lindner coined the term "mosaic families" to describe this phenomenon. See Lindner, "The Flexibility of Home," 34.

45. Extracts from American Board 26th annual report, *Missionary Herald*, January 1836, 1; extracts from Elias Riggs's journal, *Missionary Herald*, February 1836, 56–57; January 1837, 7; February 1837, 70.

46. Constantia Kiskira, " 'Evangelising' the Orient: New England Womanhood in the Ottoman Empire, 1830–1930," *Archivum Ottomanicum* 16 (1998): 279–94; Barbara Merguerian, "Mt. Holyoke Seminary in Bitlis: Providing an American Education for Armenian Women," *Armenian Review* 43 (1990): 31–65; Barbara Reeves-Ellington, "A Vision of Mount Holyoke in the Ottoman Balkans: American Cultural Transfer, Bulgarian Nation-Building and Women's Educational Reform, 1858–1870," *Gender & History* 16, no. 1 (2004): 146–71; Ellen Fleischmann, "Evangelization or Education: American Protestant Missionaries, the American Board, and the Girls and Women of Syria (1830–1920)," in *New Faith in Ancient Lands: Western Missions in the Middle East in the Nineteenth and Early Twentieth Centuries*, ed. Heleen Murre-van den Berg (Boston: Brill, 2006), 263–80.

47. This assumption of superiority led American women missionaries to take promising students into their homes in other locations in the Near and Middle East. It was also a prominent factor in removing Native American children from their parents to educate them in boarding schools. Nor was the assumption a particularly American conceit. German women missionaries in the Near East believed that they could improve family life by removing children into orphanages. See Lindner, "The Flexibility of Home"; Julia Hauser, "Waisen gewinnen: Mission zwischen Programmatik und Praxis in der Erziehungsanstalt der Kaiserswerther Diakonissen in Beirut seit 1860," *Werkstatt Geschichte* 57 (2011): 9–30; David Wallace Adams, *Education for Extinction: American Indians and the Boarding School Experience, 1875–1928* (Lawrence: University Press of Kansas, 1995); and Clyde Ellis, *To Change Them Forever: Indian Education at the Rainy Mountain Boarding School, 1893–1920* (Norman: University of Oklahoma Press, 1996).

48. Lawrence, *Light on the Dark River*, 166.

49. Annual report from Stara Zagora, 1870, ABC:16.9.4, item 24, Papers of the American Board of Commissioners for Foreign Missions, Houghton Library, Harvard University (hereafter cited as ABCFM).

50. Mary Gladding Benjamin, *The Missionary Sisters: A Memorial of Mrs. Seraphina Haynes Everett, and Mrs. Harriet Martha Hamlin, Late Missionaries of the American Board of Commissioners for Foreign Missions at Constantinople* (Boston: American Tract Society, 1860), 64.

51. George L. Marsh, "The Story of an Eventful Life," ABC Individual Biographies, box 40:17, ABCFM; Zoe Noyes Locke, extracts from letter of May 12, 1884, in *Sixth Class Letter of the Lulasti, Mt. Holyoke Seminary, South Hadley, Mass.: A Record from October, 1876, to June, 1885* (Boston: Beacon Press, 1885), 45. A copy of *Sixth Class Letter of the Lulasti* is held in the Locke Family Papers, Archives and Special Collections, Mount Holyoke College, South Hadley, Mass. (hereafter cited as MHC).

52. William F. Arms to Rufus Anderson, September 18, 1861, ABC:16.9.4, item 66, ABCFM.

53. Jasper Ball to Rufus Anderson, May 20, 1864, ABC:16.9.4, item 88, ABCFM.

54. Locke, extracts from letter of May 12, 1884, in *Sixth Class Letter of the Lulasti*, 45.

55. Rev. H. C. Haskell, "In Memoriam—Mrs. J. F. Clarke," *Missionary Herald*, May 1894, 194–95.

56. On Ottoman household economies, see Donald Quataert, "Ottoman Women, Households, and Textile Manufacturing, 1800–1914," in *Women in Middle Eastern History: Shifting Boundaries in Sex and Gender*, ed. Nikki R. Keddie and Beth Baron (New Haven: Yale University Press, 1991), 161–76.

57. On the college's founding and early history see Elizabeth Alden Green, *Mary Lyon and Mount Holyoke: Opening the Gates* (Hanover, N.H.: University Press of New England, 1979); Louise Porter, *Seminary Militant: An Account of the Missionary Movement at Mount Holyoke Seminary and College* (South Hadley, Mass.: Mount Holyoke College, 1937); and Kathryn Kish Sklar, "The Founding of Mount Holyoke College," in *Women of America: A History*, ed. Carol Ruth Berkin and Mary Beth Norton (Boston: Houghton Mifflin, 1979), 177–201.

58. Helen Lefkowitz Horowitz, *Alma Mater: Design and Experience in the Women's Colleges from Their Nineteenth-Century Beginnings to the 1930s* (New York: Alfred A. Knopf, 1984), 27.

59. Mary W. Chopin to the Prudential Committee, October 27, 1855, ABC:6.23, item 130; Charles F. Morse to the Prudential Committee of the ABCFM, October 12, 1855, ABC:6.23, item 117, ABCFM; Eliza D. Winter, Class letters for 1856, Alumnae files, MHC.

60. Rev. Norman Hallock to the Prudential Committee, August 3, 1858, ABC:6.20, item 440, ABCFM.

61. Letter from Moses Day, June 13, 1858, ABC:6.23, item 76, ABCFM.

62. Letters to the Prudential Committee from Rev. P. C. Headley, November 21, 1859, L. D. Seymour, M.D., November 18, 1859, and Anna Hovey, November 26, 1859, ABC:6.20, items 130, 131, 133, ABCFM.

63. Clara Pond Williams to her mother, June 26, 1867, Pond, Clara C. (Mrs. Williams, F. Williams) Class of 1857, Teacher 1857–64, Biographical Materials, 1 of 4, MHC.

64. Edwin Locke to N. G. Clark, April 8, 1876, ABC:16.9.6, item 138, ABCFM.

65. Extracts from Fannie Bond to Margaret Haskell, October 2, 1875, ABC Individual Biographies, box 9:12, Bond, ABCFM.

66. Ibid.

67. Annual Report from Stara Zagora, 1877, ABC:16.9.5, item 56, ABCFM.

68. "Bulgaria. Letter from Mrs. Bond, of Monastir," *Life and Light*, September 1884, 326–29.

69. Harriet Cole, Reports of the Girls' Boarding School, Monastir, 1885 and 1886, ABC: 16.9.7, items 141 and 142, ABCFM.

70. Lewis Bond to N. G. Clark, June 25, 1880, ABC:16.9.5, item 225, ABCFM.

71. "Keyport Young Ladies' Seminary, Keyport, N.J." (printed advertisement), Locke Family Papers, MHC.

72. Locke, extracts from letter of May 12, 1884, *Sixth Class Letter of the Lulasti*, 44–45.

73. For fertility data see J. David Hacker, "Rethinking the 'Early' Decline of Marital Fertility in the United States," *Demography* 40, no. 4 (2003): 605–20.

74. Locke, extracts from letter of May 12, 1884, *Sixth Class Letter of the Lulasti*, 45.

75. Diary of Zoe Noyes Locke, 1886–1924, and alumnae questionnaire, January 4, 1924, both in box 1, folder 1, and *Temperance Work in Bulgaria: Its Success* (Samokov: Evangelical School Press, 1909), box 2, folder 2, Locke Family Papers, MHC.

76. "Influence of American Missionaries on the Social Life of the East," *Missionary Herald*, June 1873, 187–90, quotation on 190.

2. Education, Conversion, and Bulgarian Orthodox Nationalism

1. The narrative can be pieced together from the reports of two key players, Charles Morse and Khadzhi Gospodin Slavov, a leading member of the *obshtina*, or Bulgarian community council.

2. Annual Report from Stara Zagora, 1868, ABC:16.9.4, item 22, Papers of the American Board of Commissioners for Foreign Missions, Houghton Library, Harvard University (hereafter cited as ABCFM).

3. Gauri Viswanathan, *Outside the Fold: Conversion, Modernity, and Belief* (Princeton: Princeton University Press, 1998).

4. In my interpretation, I have been influenced by Lewis R. Rambo, *Understanding Religious Conversion* (New Haven: Yale University Press, 1993).

5. Rifa'at Ali Abou-El Haj, *Formation of the Modern State: The Ottoman Empire, Sixteenth to Eighteenth Centuries* (Albany: State University of New York Press, 1991); Benjamin Braude and Bernard Lewis, eds., *Christians and Jews in the Ottoman Empire: The Functioning of a Plural Society* (New York: Holmes & Meier, 1982); Kemal Karpat, *An Inquiry into the Social Foundations of Nationalism in the Ottoman State: From Social Estates to Classes, from Millets to Nations* (Princeton: Center of International Studies, Princeton University, 1973).

6. For a basic history of Bulgaria in English, see Richard J. Crampton, *A Concise History of Bulgaria* (Cambridge: Cambridge University Press, 1997). For a general history of the Balkans, see Barbara Jelavich, *History of the Balkans: Eighteenth and Nineteenth Centuries*, vol. 1 (Cambridge: Cambridge University Press, 1983). For the late medieval Balkans, see John V. A. Fine Jr., *The Late Medieval Balkans: A Critical Survey from the Late Twelfth Century to the Ottoman Conquest* (Ann Arbor: University of Michigan Press, 1994).

7. Petur Nikov, *Vuzrazhdane na bulgarskiya narod: Tsurkovno-natsionalni borbi* (Sofia: Nauka i izkustvo, 1971), 96–97.

8. On Russian interventions, see Barbara Jelavich, *Russia's Balkan Entanglements, 1806–1914* (Cambridge: Cambridge University Press, 1991); and Thomas A. Meininger, *Ignatiev and the Establishment of the Bulgarian Exarchate, 1864–1872: A Study in Personal Diplomacy* (Madison: State Historical Society of Wisconsin, 1970).

9. A considerable literature exists on Ottoman reform. For a recent interpretation that includes a bibliography of earlier works, see M. Şükrü Hanioğlu, *A Brief History of the Late Ottoman Empire* (Princeton: Princeton University Press, 2008). For a study of Tanzimat reforms in the Ottoman Balkans, see Milen V. Petrov, "Tanzimat for the Countryside: Midhat Paşa and the Vilayet of Danube, 1864–1868" (Ph.D. diss., Princeton University,

2006). On reform of the Orthodox Church, see Jack Fairey, "The Great Game of Improvements: European Diplomacy and the Reform of the Orthodox Church" (Ph.D. diss., University of Toronto, 2004).

10. For English translations of the edicts of 1839 (*Hatt-ı Şerif Gülhane*) and 1856 (*Hatt-ı Hümâyun*, or *Islahat Fermanı*), see J. C. Hurewitz, *Diplomacy in the Near and Middle East: A Documentary Record, 1535–1914* (Princeton: D. Van Nostrand, 1956), 113–16, 149–53.

11. William Goodell, *The Old and the New; or, The Changes of Thirty Years in the East, with Some Allusions to Oriental Customs as Elucidating Scripture* (New York: M. W. Dodd, 1853), v–viii.

12. Selim Deringil, " 'There Is No Compulsion in Religion': On Conversion and Apostasy in the Late Ottoman Empire, 1839–1856," *Comparative Studies in Society and History* 42, no. 3 (2000): 547–75.

13. Charles A. Frazee, *Catholics and Sultans: The Church and the Ottoman Empire, 1453–1923* (Cambridge: Cambridge University Press, 1983); Ussama Makdisi, *Artillery of Heaven: American Missionaries and the Failed Conversion of the Middle East* (Ithaca: Cornell University Press, 2008).

14. Frazee, *Catholics and Sultans*, 259.

15. For English translations of Ottoman Protestant charters see Harrison Gray Otis Dwight, "Translation of the Firman of His Imperial Majesty Abd-El-Mejid, Granted in Favor of His Protestant Subjects," *Journal of the American Oriental Society* 3, no. 1 (1852): 218–20.

16. This phenomenon was described in the British-Indian context by Viswanathan, *Outside the Fold*; Peter Van der Veer, ed., *Conversion to Modernities: The Globalization of Christianity* (New York: Routledge, 1996); and Peter Van der Veer, *Imperial Encounters: Religion and Modernity in India and Britain* (Princeton: Princeton University Press, 2001).

17. Nadya Danova, "Les étudiants bulgares a l'Université d'Athènes" (paper presented at the Colloque International: Université, Idéologie et Culture, Athens, 1989); Nadya Danova, "Bulgarski studenti na Ostrov Andros," *Istoricheski pregled* 1 (1996): 32–69; Paschalis M. Kitromilides, " 'Imagined Communities' and the Origins of the National Question in the Balkans," *European History Quarterly* 19, no. 2 (1989): 149–92.

18. A voluminous literature exists in Bulgarian on this movement, which, in Bulgarian historiography, is considered to be part of the final phase of the Bulgarian National Revival (*Vuzrazhdane*). For syntheses, see Roumen Daskalov, *Kak se misli bulgarskoto Vuzrazhdane* (Sofia: Izdatelstvo Lik, 2002); and Nikolay Genchev, *Bulgarskoto Vuzrazhdane*, 4th ed. (Sofia: Ivan Vazov, 1995). On urban and economic development, see Michael Palairet, *The Balkan Economies c. 1800–1914: Evolution without Development* (Cambridge: Cambridge University Press, 1997). On developments in Bulgarian education, see Angel Dimitrov, *Uchilishteto, progresut i natsionalnata revolyutsiya: Bulgarskoto uchilishte prez Vuzrazhdaneto* (Sofia: Bulgarska akademiya na naukite, 1987).

19. For an analysis of the social changes wrought by an emerging merchant middle class in the Ottoman Empire that emphasizes Greek communities, see Fatma Müge Göçek, *Rise of the Bourgeoisie, Demise of Empire: Ottoman Westernization and Social Change* (New York: Oxford University Press, 1996). For the concept of imagined communities and an analysis that does not factor in religion or gender, see Benedict Anderson, *Imagined Communities: Reflections on the Origin and Spread of Nationalism*, rev. ed. (London: Verso, 1991).

20. "Journal of Mr. Dwight," *Missionary Herald*, October 1841, 415–16; "Letter from Messrs. Adger and Dwight, dated 20th May, 1841," *Missionary Herald*, November 1841, 462–63; "Letter from Mr. Van Lennep, Sept. 1st, 1842," *Missionary Herald*, February 1843, 76–77. On the distribution of the first edition of the modern Bulgarian version of the New Testament, published by the British and Foreign Bible Society in 1840, see James F. Clarke, *Bible Societies, American Missionaries, and the National Revival of Bulgaria* (New York: Arno Press, 1971), 269–90.

21. Elias Riggs to the Board, February 23, 1842, ABC:16.7.1.6, item 117; Elias Riggs to Rufus Anderson, January 30, 1843, and November 16, 1843, ABC:16.7.1.6, items 124 and 128, ABCFM.

22. On the importance of translation, see Lamin Sanneh, *Translating the Message: The Missionary Impact on Culture* (Maryknoll, N.Y.: Orbis, 1989).

23. "Letter from Mr. Hamlin, May 18, 1857," *Missionary Herald*, September 1857, 293–99; "European Turkey as a Field of Christian Missions," *Missionary Herald*, October 1858, 322–24.

24. Khadzhi Gospodin Slavov, "Khronologichno opisanie na po-vazhnite i zabelezhitelni subitiya v gr. Stara Zagora, v cherkovno, uchilishtno i obshtenarodno otnoshenie v XIX vek," unpublished, undated manuscript in the archive of the City Historical Museum, Stara Zagora, 118.

25. On the subsequent efforts of French Jews to bring education to their co-religionists in the Ottoman Empire, see Aron Rodrigue, *French Jews, Turkish Jews: The Alliance Israélite Universelle and the Politics of Jewish Schooling in Turkey, 1860–1925* (Bloomington: Indiana University Press, 1990).

26. On the Public Education Law of 1869 see chapter 3, note 99.

27. Rayna Popgeorgieva, *Avtobiografiya* (Sofia: Otechestven front, 1986); Suba Vazova, *Spomeni* (Sofia: Lyubomudrie, 1993); Elif Ekin Aksit, "Girls' Education and the Paradoxes of Modernity and Nationalism in the Late Ottoman Empire and the Early Turkish Republic" (Ph.D. diss., State University of New York, Binghamton, 2004); Elizabeth Brown Frierson, "Unimagined Communities: State, Press, and Gender in the Hamidian Era" (Ph.D. diss., Princeton University, 1996).

28. On poor pay in the textile industry, see Donald Quataert, "Ottoman Women, Households, and Textile Manufacturing, 1800–1914," in *Women in Middle Eastern History: Shifting Boundaries in Sex and Gender,* ed. Nikki R. Keddie and Beth Baron (New Haven: Yale University Press, 1991), 161–76.

29. See a letter by Vassil Aprilov, a prominent merchant and educational reformer, in which he explains the importance of an educated wife for his nephew, who was in the Ottoman administrative service: Vassil Aprilov to Kera Aprilova, April 10, 1846, in *V. E. Aprilov: Izbrani suchineniya,* ed. Petko Totev (Sofia: Bulgarski pisatel, 1968), 360–62.

30. On the infiltration of new ideas, see Rumyana Radkova, *Inteligentsiyata i nravstvenostta prez Vuzrazhdaneto, XVIII-purvata polovina na XIX vek* (Sofia: Prof. Marin Drinov, 1995). On the development of Bulgarian education, see Krassimira Daskalova, "Obrazovanie na zhenite i zhenite v obrazovanieto na vuzrozhdenska Bulgaria," *Godishnik na Sofiyskiya universitet "Sv. Kliment Okhridski"* 85 (1992): 5–18; Dimitrov, *Uchilishteto;* Peter John Georgeoff, "The Education of Women during the Bulgarian Reawakening," *Balkanistica*

9 (1996): 64–73; Virzhiniya Paskaleva, *Bulgarkata prez Vuzrazhdaneto* (Sofia: Otechest-ven front, 1984). On literacy, see Krassimira Daskalova, *Gramotnost, knizhnina, chitateli, chetene* (Sofia: Lik, 1999).

31. Papers of Alexander Ekzarkh, II.A.5189, Bulgarian Historical Archive, National Library, Sofia; Julietta Velitchkova Borin, "Les projets d'éducation bulgares au XIXe siècle: Affir-mation nationale et transferts culturels" (Ph.D. diss., École des Hautes Études en Sciences Sociales, 1998); Pierre Voillery, "La renaissance bulgare et l'occident: La France et les Bul-gares, 1762–1856" (Ph.D. diss., École des Hautes Études en Sciences Sociales, 1980).

32. Anastasiya Tosheva, *Avtobiografiya* (Stara Zagora: Svetlina, 1911), 4–5.

33. Neycho Kunev et al., *150 godini Obshtina Stara Zagora: Dokumentalen letopis, 1849–1999* (Stara Zagora: Trakiyski svyat, 1999), 17–18.

34. "Nyakolko dumi po obrazovanieto na devoykite," *Tsarigradski vestnik,* November 16, 1857.

35. "Nyakolko slova za obrazovanieto na momichetata," *Tsarigradski vestnik,* November 16, 1857; "Obshto umolyavane za prosveshtenieto," *Tsarigradski vestnik,* November 22, 1858; "Ot edna Eski-zagranka za sichkite," *Tsarigradski vestnik,* December 20, 1858.

36. James F. Clarke to Rufus Anderson, March 7, 1860, William Merriam to Rufus Anderson, July 18, 1860, Theodore Byington to Rufus Anderson, July 15, 1861, and Charles Morse to Rufus Anderson, July 31, 1861, ABC:16.9.4, items 156, 270, 122, 279, ABCFM.

37. Report of Committee on Bulgarian Schools, Constantinople, June 20, 1862; and Six-point plan of the Female Boarding School at Eski Zagra, ABC:16.9.4, items 45 and 46, ABCFM. An earlier and more detailed analysis of the mission school in Stara Zagora was published in Barbara Reeves-Ellington, "A Vision of Mount Holyoke in the Ottoman Bal-kans: American Cultural Transfer, Bulgarian Nation-Building and Women's Educational Reform, 1858–1870," *Gender & History* 16, no. 1 (2004): 146–71.

38. American Board of Commissioners for Foreign Missions, *The Female Boarding School in Foreign Missions* (Boston: Missionary House, 1866), 1.

39. Slavov, "Khronologichno opisanie," 133.

40. Sarah D. Locke Stowe, *History of Mount Holyoke Seminary, South Hadley, Mass., during Its First Half Century, 1837–1887* (South Hadley: Mount Holyoke Female Seminary, 1887), 210.

41. Annual report from Stara Zagora, 1863, ABC:16.9.4, item 17, ABCFM.

42. Atanas Iliev, *Spomeni* (Sofia: Bulgarska akademiya na naukite, 1926), 33, 42; Slavov, "Khronologichno opisanie," 119; Tosheva, *Avtobiografiya,* 11–12.

43. Annual report from Stara Zagora, 1863.

44. Slavov, "Khronologichno opisanie," 226, 122–29.

45. Ibid., 134.

46. Tosheva, *Avtobiografiya,* 13.

47. Annual report from Stara Zagora, 1865, ABC:16.9.4, item 19, ABCFM; "Spomeni ot Starozagorskoto devichesko uchilishte ot Anastasiya Tosheva," Papers of the Stara Zagora Girls' High School, F98K, inventory 3, folder 1, p. 13, State Archive, Stara Zagora.

48. Annual Report from Stara Zagora, 1866, ABC:16.9.4, item 20, ABCFM.

49. Theodore Byington to Dr. Wood and Dr. Clark, October 24, 1865, and June 6, 1866, ABC:16.9.4, items 133 and 135, ABCFM.

50. Charles Morse to the Board, August 28, 1865, ABC:16.9.4, item 289, ABCFM.

51. Annual Report from Stara Zagora, 1866.

52. Petrana Petrova Chirpanlieva, "Avtobiografiya," in *Kazanluk v minaloto i dnes* (Sofia: Pridvorna pechatnitsa, 1923), 192–95.

53. Annual report from Stara Zagora, 1868.

54. Ibid.

55. John Blunt to Sir Henry Elliott, November 24, 1867, FO/195/877, no. 67, British Foreign Office Correspondence, National Archives, Kew, U.K. (hereafter cited as BFOC). The correspondence does not mention the names of the Ottoman governor-general at Edirne or the governor at Plovdiv.

56. Henry Elliot to Edward Joy Morris, December 2, 1867, U.S. Department of State, *Despatches from United States Ministers to Turkey, 1818–1906,* microfilm ed. no. 757, reel 21 (hereafter cited as *DDT*); John Blunt to Henry Elliott, December 5, 1867, FO/195/877, no. 69, BFOC.

57. John Blunt to Henry Elliot, January 10, 1868. FO/195/901, no. 3, BFOC; John Blunt to E. J. Morris, January 6, 1868, *DDT.*

58. Slavov, "Khronologichno opisanie," 219–25.

59. "Zheleznik, 18 okt. 1867, ot cherkovnata obshtina," *Makedoniya,* October 28, 1867.

60. Chirpanlieva, "Avtobiografiya," 192–95.

61. M. G. Popruzhenko, *Arkhiv na Nayden Gerov,* vol. 1 (Sofia: Bulgarska akademiya na naukite, 1911), reports dated September 2, 1869, and December 15, 1869.

62. Nikolay Genchev, "Bulgarskata natsionalna prosveta i Russiya sled Krimskata voyna," *Godishnik na Sofiyskiya universitet* 66 (1975): 334–49.

63. "Devichesko uchilishte v Moskva," *Otechestvo,* July 17, 1871.

64. Annual report from Stara Zagora, 1868.

65. Foreign Accounts Current, 1858–1871, vol. 8, E1/2/2/8, British and Foreign Bible Society Papers, Cambridge University Library.

66. Manyo Stoyanov, "Petko R. Slaveykov i protestantskata propaganda v Bulgaria," *Rodina* 3, no. 3 (1941): 90–98.

67. "Bulgarskite vestnitsi," *Gayda,* August 23, 1864; "Za obrazovanieto na naroda," *Makedoniya,* March 2 and 9, 1868.

68. "Ot redaktora," *Makedoniya,* November 25, 1867.

69. Andrey Tsanoff, "Da vurvim napred," *Makedoniya,* February 24, 1868.

70. On Rakovski, see Mari Firkatian, *The Forest Traveler: Georgi Stoikov Rakovski and Bulgarian Nationalism* (New York: Peter Lang, 1996).

71. British Vice Consul John Blunt's discussions with Bulgarian Georgi Stoyanovich in Plovdiv suggest that some Bulgarians believed the Secret Central Committee was set up by Greeks and Russians to create the impression that the Bulgarians were "disaffected" and considering violence. Report of Blunt to Lyons, May 6, 1867, FO 195/877, no. 23, BFOC.

72. Petitions, with translations, among reports of British Vice Consul John Blunt, FO 195/901, nos. 64, 71, 72, BFOC.

73. "Kum chitatelite na 'Makedoniya,'" *Makedoniya,* November 25, 1868.

74. Charles Morse to N. G. Clark, February 13, 1869, ABC:16.9.4, item 309, ABCFM.

75. Charles Morse to N. G. Clark, November 27, 1869, ABC:16.9.4, item 311, ABCFM.

76. Debates about evangelizing or teaching (Christ or culture) created regular tensions among missionaries. See William R. Hutchison, *Errand to the World: American Protestant Thought and Foreign Missions* (Chicago: University of Chicago Press, 1987). On similar tensions in other mission fields that provoked the 1856 report, see Paul William Harris, *Nothing but Christ: Rufus Anderson and the Ideology of Protestant Foreign Missions* (New York: Oxford University Press, 1999), 133–52; and Dana Robert, *American Women in Mission: A Social History of Their Thought and Practice* (Macon, Ga.: Mercer University Press, 1997), 116–24.

77. Roseltha Norcross to the Board, December 27, 1869, ABC:16.9.4, item 336, ABCFM.

78. Lewis Bond to N. G. Clark, December 5, 1870, ABC:16.9.4, item 115, ABCFM.

79. Report of the Trustees of the Mission School, June 23, 1871, ABC:16.9. 4, item 47, ABCFM.

80. "Turkey. A Missionary Tour. School at Eski Zagra," *Life and Light for Heathen Women,* March 1872, 204.

81. Slavov, "Khronologichno opisanie," 134.

82. "Marika's Letter," *Life and Light for Heathen Women,* March 1872, 207–9.

83. Nevena Ganeva, "Tri vuzrozhdenski prevodachki," *Bibliotekar* 1 (1987): 25–28.

84. Diana Mishkova, "Literacy and Nation-Building in Bulgaria, 1878–1912," *East European Quarterly* 29, no. 1 (1994), 63–93.

85. Maria Tsanova, *Yakov Knyazheski, ili okayanstvoto na edno domochadie* (Vienna: Yanko C. Kovachev, 1874).

86. Boris Kozhukharov, *Purvata evangelska tsurkva v Bulgaria: Deynostta na amerikanskite missioneri* (Sofia: Nov chovek, 1998); Khristo Kulichev, *Vestiteli na istinata: Istoriya na evangelskite tsurkvi v Bulgaria* (Sofia: Bulgarsko bibleysko obshtestvo, 1994).

3. The Mission Press and Bulgarian Domestic Reform

1. *51st Annual Report of the Missionary Society of the Methodist Episcopal Church* (New York: Missionary Society of the Methodist Episcopal Church, 1870), 131–36, Missionary Files, United Methodist Church Archives–GCAH, Madison, N.J. (hereafter cited as UMCA-GCAH).

2. James F. Clarke, "Konstantin Fotinov, *Liuboslovie,* and the Smyrna Bulgarian Press," in Clarke, *The Pen and the Sword: Studies in Bulgarian History,* ed. Dennis P. Hupchick (Boulder, Colo.: East European Monographs, 1988), 321–27; Nadya Danova, *Konstantin Georgiev Fotinov v kulturnoto i ideyno-politicheskoto razvitie na Balkanite prez XIX vek* (Sofia: Bulgarska akademiya na naukite, 1994), 102.

3. Elias Riggs to Rufus Anderson, June 5, 1844, ABC:16.7.1.6, item 134, Papers of the American Board of Commissioners for Foreign Missions, Houghton Library, Harvard University (hereafter cited as ABCFM).

4. Elias Riggs to the Board, February 23, 1842, ABC:16.7.1.6, item 117; Elias Riggs to

Rufus Anderson, January 24, 1843 ("reading Christians will ever be the soundest Christians"), and November 16, 1843, ABC:16.7.1.6, items 123 and 128, ABCFM.

5. Albert Long to John P. Durbin, December 8, 1857, Missionary Files (microfilm edition), UMCA-GCAH. On the importance of the development of modern vernaculars in the Ottoman Empire, see Johann Strauss, "Who Read What in the Ottoman Empire (19th–20th Centuries)?," *Arabic Middle Eastern Literatures* 6, no. 1 (2003): 39–76; and Maria Todorova, "Language as Cultural Unifier in a Multilingual Setting: The Bulgarian Case during the Nineteenth Century," *East European Politics and Societies* 4, no. 3 (1990): 439–50.

6. Albert Long to John P. Durbin, October 10, 1862, Missionary Files (microfilm edition), UMCA-GCAH.

7. Ibid.; Pandeli Kissimov, *Istoricheski raboti: Moite spomeni,* vol. 1 (Plovdiv: Edinstvo, 1897), 65.

8. Strauss, "Who Read What."

9. Clarke, "Konstantin Fotinov"; Serif Mardin, "Some Considerations on the Building of an Ottoman Public Identity in the Nineteenth Century," in *Converting Cultures: Religion, Ideology and Transformations of Modernity,* ed. Dennis Washburn and A. Kevin Reinhart (Leiden: Brill, 2007), 169–82.

10. On the evangelical press in the United States, see Candy Gunther Brown, *The Word in the World: Evangelical Writing, Publishing, and Reading in America, 1789–1880* (Chapel Hill: University of North Carolina Press, 2004); and David Paul Nord, *Faith in Reading: Religious Publishing and the Birth of Mass Media in America* (New York: Oxford University Press, 2004).

11. To appeal to the different nationalities in the Ottoman empire, the Minasian family also rendered their name in Turkish as Minasoglu and in Bulgarian as Minasov.

12. Thomas A. Meininger, *The Formation of a Nationalist Bulgarian Intelligentsia, 1835–1878* (New York: Garland, 1987), 292–301; Michael Pailaret, *The Balkan Economies c. 1800–1914: Evolution without Development* (Cambridge: Cambridge University Press, 1997), 58–84. For changes in urban centers in general, see Raina Gavrilova, *Bulgarian Urban Culture in the Eighteenth and Nineteenth Centuries* (Selinsgrove, Pa.: Susquehanna University Press, 1999).

13. Meininger, *Formation of a Nationalist Bulgarian Intelligentsia,* 292–301; Monika Skowronski, "Die Distribution bulgarischer Volksbücher im 19. und 20. Jahrhundert (bis 1944)," in *Südosteuropäische Popularliteratur im 19. und 20. Jahrhundert,* ed. Klaus Roth (Munich: Münchner Vereinigung für Volkskunde, 1993), 137–58.

14. On the Ottoman press for women, see Elif Ekin Aksit, "Girls' Education and the Paradoxes of Modernity and Nationalism in the Late Ottoman Empire and the Early Turkish Republic" (Ph.D. diss., State University of New York at Binghamton, 2004); and Elizabeth Brown Frierson, "Unimagined Communities: State, Press, and Gender in the Hamidian Era" (Ph.D. diss., Princeton University, 1996).

15. Albert Long to John P. Durbin, June 22, 1864, Missionary Files (microfilm edition), UMCA-GCAH.

16. "Tabular View of Printing at Istanbul, 1866," ABC:16.9.3.1, item 153; "Report of the

Publications Department for 1867," ABC:16.9.3.1, item 154; Elias Riggs to N. G. Clark, July 8, 1867, ABC:16.9.3.3, part 2, item 485, ABCFM; Papers of Petur Musevich-Borikov, Special Collection no. 605, folder 1, p. 2985, Bulgarian Historical Archive, National Library, Sofia (hereafter cited as BHA).

17. *49th Annual Report of the Missionary Society of the Methodist Episcopal Church* (New York: Missionary Society of the Methodist Episcopal Church, 1868), 113–17; *52nd Annual Report of the Missionary Society of the Methodist Episcopal Church* (New York: Missionary Society of the Methodist Episcopal Church, 1871), 105–7. Missionary Files, UMCA-GCAH.

18. Manyo Stoyanov, *Bulgarska vuzrozhdenska knizhnina* (Sofia: Nauka i izkustvo, 1957), 440, 443.

19. Milen V. Petrov, "Tanzimat for the Countryside: Midhat Paşa and the Vilayet of Danube, 1864–1868" (Ph.D. diss., Princeton University, 2006), 79–81.

20. Stoyanov, *Bulgarska vuzrozhdenska knizhnina*, 445–46; Sonya Baeva, "Dnevnikut na v. Makedoniya," in *Literaturen arkhiv*, vol. 1: *P. R. Slaveykov*, ed. Petur Dinekov, Georgi Dimo, and Sonya Baeva (Sofia: Bulgarska akademiya na naukite, 1959), 79–146 (subscriber information on 80).

21. On Bible publishing and distribution in the nineteenth century, see Leslie Howsam, *Cheap Bibles: Nineteenth-Century Publishing and the British and Foreign Bible Society* (Cambridge: Cambridge University Press, 1991); and Peter J. Wosh, *Spreading the Word: The Bible Business in Nineteenth-Century America* (Ithaca: Cornell University Press, 1994).

22. Stoyanov, *Bulgarska vuzrozhdenska knizhnina*, 441.

23. For selling prices of *Suvetnik, Gayda, Turtsiya, Vremya, Makedoniya*, and *Pravo* see Stoyanov, *Bulgarska vuzrozhdenska knizhnina*, 439–49.

24. See, for example, "Kum chitatelite," *Pravo*, August 23, 1869.

25. Iliya Bluskov, *Spomeni* (Sofia: Otechestven front, 1976), 137–43.

26. Ibid.

27. Petko Slaveykov to Irina, January 7, 1868, in Sonya Baeva, Docho Lekov, Stoyanka Mikhaylova et al., eds., *Petko R. Slaveykov: Suchineniya*, vol. 8: *Pisma* (Sofia: Bulgarski pisatel, 1982), 144; "Za obrazovanieto na naroda," *Makedoniya*, March 2 and 9, 1868.

28. Martha Jane Riggs, *Pisma za mayki, ili rukovodstvo za mayki v dobroto otkhranvanie na detsata im* (Tsarigrad: A. Minasian, 1870). The 1870 edition appears to have been the second; no copies of the first edition are extant. The third edition was published in 1880. In subsequent notes the individual letters are cited from *Zornitsa*.

29. Skowronski, "Distribution bulgarischer Volksbücher."

30. Atanas Iliev, *Spomeni* (Sofia: Bulgarska akademiya na naukite, 1926), 116.

31. Elias Riggs to Rufus Anderson, February 20, 1839, ABC:16.7.1.6, item 98, ABCFM.

32. *List of Books and Tracts Published by Protestant Missionaries in Malta, Corfu, Greece, Turkey, and Syria* (Smyrna: ABCFM, 1839); "United Journal of the Missionaries," *Missionary Herald* 37 (July 1841), 287.

33. *Encheiridion tes metros, etoi, Epistolai pros adelphen peri anatrophes teknon* (Smyrna: G. Griffith, 1842, 1844). The book is written in the *katharevousa* or purified dialect of modern Greek, which had been adopted as the national language by the new Greek state,

rather than the more informal *demotiki*. I am indebted to Sophie Papageorgiou at the Gennadius Library in Athens for information on the Greek publications and to Mary Bellino for locating copies in the United States.

34. Elias Riggs to Rufus Anderson, September 22, 1842, and January 24, 1843, ABC:16.7.1.6, items 119 and 123, ABCFM.

35. For the history of the Society of the Friends of Education (*Philekpaideutike Etaireia*), see http://archive.arsakeio.gr/allhistory.pdf (in Greek).

36. Dositej Obradovic, *Dva razkaza na prochuti zheni i Azya chelovekomrazetsa*, trans. Stanka Nikolitsa (Belgrade: Pravitelstvena pechatnitsa, 1853). The title of this work leads to some confusion, because it reads "Two Tales of Famous Women and Asem the Man-hater." They are two separate tales, yet in Bulgarian the title of Nikolitsa's translation is usually referred to as *Two Tales of Famous Women;* "Asem the Man-hater" is ignored. "Asem," the tale of a misanthrope's redemption (the title character is male), was written by the eighteenth-century British writer Oliver Goldsmith and first published in *The Royal Magazine* (London) in 1759. *Famous Women* can be identified by its content as an English original. Obradovic visited England in 1785, and there he made the acquaintance of a Mrs. Livie, whom he described as "my teacher and benefactress." It seems that Mrs. Livie or another of his acquaintances may have given him these reading materials, which he subsequently translated into Serbian. On Obradovic, see George Rapall Noyes, trans. and ed., *The Life and Adventures of Dimitrije Obradovic* (Berkeley: University of California Press, 1953), quote on 299. Obradovic received the name Dositej as a monk.

37. Aleksandra Mikhaylova, "Mayka koyato dava polezen urok na dushterya si," *Tsarigradski vestnik*, November 15, 1858.

38. For this and other examples of American gender models introduced into the Bulgarian press in the 1860s and 1870s (although, interestingly, not *Letters to Mothers*), see Betty Grinberg, "Gender Issues and American Source Materials in the Bulgarian National Revival Press," in *Essays in American Studies*, ed. Kornelia Slavova and Madeleine Danova (Sofia: Polis, 1999), 21–33.

39. On images of mothers in Bulgarian literature, which emphasize self-sacrifice but not moral influence, see Amelia Licheva, "Za 'velikite mayki' i tekhnite bulgarski literaturni sinove," *Literaturna misul* 3 (1993): 26–38.

40. Ann Braude, *Women and American Religion* (New York: Oxford University Press, 2000), 59–82.

41. See, for example the series of articles by Slavka Dinkova in *Makedoniya* from February through May 1868. Dinkova criticized the hellenization of Bulgarian culture and translated ideas about female education from French sources.

42. On the concept of literacy networks, see Sarah Robbins, *Managing Literacy, Mothering America: Women's Narratives on Reading and Writing in the Nineteenth Century* (Pittsburgh: University of Pittsburgh Press, 2004).

43. Earlier analyses of Riggs's writings appeared in Barbara Reeves-Ellington, "Gender, Conversion, and Social Transformation: The American Discourse of Domesticity and the Origins of the Bulgarian Women's Movement, 1864–1876," in *Converting Cultures: Religion, Ideology and Transformations of Modernity*, ed. Dennis Washburn and A. Kevin Reinhart (Leiden: E. J. Brill, 2007), 115–40; and Reeves-Ellington, "Women, Mission,

and Nation Building in Ottoman Europe, 1832–1872," in *Competing Kingdoms: Women, Mission, Nation, and the American Protestant Empire, 1812–1960*, ed. Barbara Reeves-Ellington, Kathryn Kish Sklar, and Connie Shemo (Durham, N.C.: Duke University Press, 2010), 270–92.

44. "Pisma za mayki, purvo pismo: Maychini chuvstva i maychini dluzhnosti," *Zornitsa*, January 1864, 3–5.

45. Horace Bushnell, *Views of Christian Nurture, and of Subjects Adjacent Thereto* (New York: Edwin Hunt, 1847).

46. "Pisma za mayki, vtoro pismo: Nuzhnite na maykite preimushtestva," *Zornitsa*, February 1864, 13–14. The phrase "parents' association" can also be found in the Greek original.

47. See, for example, "Practical Hints to Members of Maternal Associations and Christian Mothers. By a Mother," *The Mother's Magazine*, November 1836, 161–71.

48. Bonyu S. Angelov, *Suvremenitsi na Paissiy* (Sofia: Bulgarska akademiya na naukite, 1963), 66–69.

49. *Zornitsa*, June 1865 to November 1866.

50. "Pisma za mayki, pismo 14: Umstvenno razvitie," *Zornitsa*, December 1866, 90–92.

51. *Zornitsa*, January through June 1867.

52. "Pisma za mayki, pismo 19: Trudolyubie," *Zornitsa*, June 1867, 45–46; "Pisma za mayki, pismo 20: Bogatstvo.—Gordost.—Prostota," *Zornitsa*, July 1867, 54–55.

53. "Za zhenite: Vlyianieto na zhenskiya pol," *Zornitsa*, April 1866, 27–28.

54. "Za maykite: Otvetstvenostta na maykite," *Zornitsa*, December 1865, 91–92.

55. "Pisma za mayki, pismo III. Vliyanie na khristiyanstvoto v sustoyanieto na zhenite.—Primeri na maychinoto vliyanie," *Zornitsa*, March 1864, 21–23.

56. "Sustoyanieto na zhenite v Kitay," *Zornitsa*, May 1864, 33–34.

57. "Indiyska mayka," *Zornitsa*, June 1867, 42; repeated in June 1869, 46–47.

58. "Amerikanskite indiyantsi," *Zornitsa*, November 1869, 84–86.

59. "Pisma za mayki, pismo III"; L. H. Sigourney, *Letters to Mothers* (Hartford: Hudson & Skinner, 1838). Riggs's text is so close to Sigourney's that I have quoted from Sigourney to supply the translation, lightly modernizing the punctuation.

60. "Pisma za mayki, vtoro pismo."

61. "Pisma za mayki, purvo pismo."

62. See Caroline Winterer, *The Mirror of Antiquity: American Women and the Classical Tradition, 1750–1900* (Ithaca: Cornell University Press, 2007), 131–41.

63. Gavrilova, *Bulgarian Urban Culture*, 103.

64. "Pisma za mayki, pismo III."

65. For a discussion of the emerging middle classes in other Orthodox Christian communities, see Fatma Müge Göçek, *Rise of the Bourgeoisie, Demise of Empire: Ottoman Westernization and Social Change* (New York: Oxford University Press, 1996); and Haris Exertzoglou, "The Cultural Uses of Consumption: Negotiating Class, Gender, and Nation in the Ottoman Urban Centers during the 19th Century," *International Journal of Middle East Studies* 35 (2003): 77–101.

66. Donald Quataert, "Ottoman Women, Households, and Textile Manufacturing, 1800–1914," in *Women in Middle Eastern History: Shifting Boundaries in Sex and Gender*, ed. Nikki R. Keddie and Beth Baron (New Haven: Yale University Press, 1991), 161–76; Olga Todorova, "Bulgarkata-Khristiyanka ot XV do XVIII vek," *Istoricheski pregled* 4 (1992): 3–28.

67. Anna Ilieva, "Subscription Lists and the Development of Education for Girls in the 1840s and 1850s" (paper presented at the International University Seminar on Balkan Studies, Ninth International Round Table, Bansko, Bulgaria, February 27–29, 2000).

68. Margarita Cholakova, *Bulgarsko zhensko dvizhenie prez Vuzrazhdaneto, 1857–1878* (Sofia: Albo, 1994), 37–38.

69. Pamphlet of the Turnovo women's association, Papers of Evgeniya Kissimova, IIA6744, BHA; *Makedoniya*, October 18, 1869, 131–32.

70. "Dopisk ot Kazanluk," *Makedoniya*, May 31, 1869, 107.

71. Anastasiya Tosheva, *Avtobiografiya* (Stara Zagora: Svetlina, 1911), 16.

72. Ibid., 14–15.

73. Velichka Koycheva, *Vuzrozhdenki* (Stara Zagora: Obshtinski suvet na zhenite, 1989).

74. "Dopisk ot uchilishtnoto nastoyatelstvo, Zheleznik," *Makedoniya*, April 19, 1869, 87.

75. See, for example, Anastasiya Tosheva in *Makedoniya*, April 19, 1869, and *Pravo*, March 7, 1870; Rakhil Dushanova in *Makedoniya*, May 31, 1869; Evgeniya Kissimova in *Pravo*, September 27, 1869; Elizaveta Maneva in *Pravo*, August 17, 1870; and Elefteritsa Petkovich in *Chitalishte*, January 1870.

76. "Dopisk ot Kazanluk," *Makedoniya*, May 31, 1869.

77. Evgeniya Kissimova, "Mili moi ednorodki," *Pravo*, September 27, 1869.

78. David Morgan, *Protestants and Pictures: Religion, Visual Culture, and the Age of American Mass Production* (New York: Oxford University Press, 1999), 227.

79. Clarke, "Konstantin Fotinov"; Danova, *Konstantin Georgiev Fotinov*, 344–45; Iliya Konev, *Bulgarsko Vuzrazhdane i prosveshtenieto*, vol. 3, part 1 (Sofia: Prof. Marin Drinov, 1998), 371–72.

80. Antonina Zhelyaskova, ed., *Vruzki na suvmestimost i nesuvmestimost mezhdu khristiyani i myusulmani v Bulgaria* (Sofia: Mezhdunaroden tsentur po problemite na maltsinstvata i kulturnite vzaimodeystviya, 1993); Nikolay Aretov and Nikolay Chernokozhev, eds., *Balkanski identichnosti* (Sofia: Institut za izsledvane na integratsiyata, 2001).

81. "Turnovo. Zhenska obshtina," *Makedoniya*, November 8, 1869.

82. Ibid.; "Za maykite: Bulgarskite mayki," *Zornitsa*, January 1866, 4.

83. "Turnovo. Zhenska obshtina."

84. Pandeli Kissimov, *Istoricheski raboti: Moite spomeni*, vol. 1 (Plovdiv: Edinstvo, 1897).

85. Kissimova, "Mili moi ednorodki."

86. Frierson, "Unimagined Communities," 72–73.

87. On the concept of dual loyalty, see Mardin, "Some Considerations."

88. All quotations in this paragraph are from Anastasiya Tosheva, "Pooshtrenie na bulgarkite kum napreduka," *Pravo*, March 7, 1870, 7.

89. Rumyana Koneva, "Yubileyut—faktor na sotsialno, politichesko i kulturno sebeopredelyane," *Balkanistichen Forum* 7 (1998): 80–86.

90. Krassimira Daskalova, *Ot syankata na istoriyata: Zhenite v bulgarskoto obshtestvo i kultura* (Sofia: Bulgarskata grupa za istoricheskoto izsledvance na zhenite i pol, 1998), 11–41.

91. "Turnovo. Zhenska obshtina," *Pravo*, May 29, 1872, 2.

92. For example, *Uchilishte*, August 19, 1871, 197–98.

93. Cholakova, *Bulgarskoto zhensko dvizhenie*; Daskalova, *Ot syankata*; Virzhiniya Paskaleva, *Bulgarkata prez Vuzrazhdaneto* (Sofia: Otechestven front, 1984).

94. "Za zhenskite druzhestvo v bulgarsko," *Svoboda*, November 7, 1869, 2–3; "Nashite zheni," *Svoboda*, December 11, 1869, 43–44.

95. *Znanie*, January 1875 through March 1876.

96. *Gayda*, July 13, 1863, 19; August 10, 1863, 40; November 16, 1863, 94. On the development of Slaveykov's thinking about women and education, see Barbara Reeves-Ellington, "Petko Slaveykov, the Protestant Press, and the Gendered Language of Moral Reform in Bulgarian Nationalism," in *American Missionaries and the Middle East: Foundational Encounters*, ed. Mehmet Ali Doğan and Heather J. Sharkey (Salt Lake City: University of Utah Press, 2011), 211–36.

97. "Zhenite v otnoshenieto na narodstvoto," *Makedoniya*, December 2, 1867.

98. "Zhenskite druzhestva u nas," *Makedoniya*, August 23, 1869; for reports of the women's associations, see *Makedoniya*, February 22, 1869, and April 19, 1869.

99. For the text of the Public Education Law in a contemporary French translation, see Gregoire Aristarchi, "Loi sur l'Instruction Publique," in *Législation ottomane, ou recueil des lois, réglements, ordonnances, traités, capitulations et autres documents officiels de l'Empire Ottoman, Troisième partie: Droit administratif,* ed. Demetrius Nicolaides (Constantinople: Bureau du Journal Thraky, 1874), 277–315. The decree was translated and printed in the newspapers of the various language communities of the empire; a Bulgarian version was published in issues of *Pravo* from August to November 1869. On reforms in Ottoman education, see Aksit, "Girls' Education and the Paradoxes of Modernity"; Benjamin C. Fortna, *Imperial Classroom: Islam, the State, and Education in the Late Ottoman Empire* (Oxford: Oxford University Press, 2002); Elizabeth Brown Frierson, "Unimagined Communities: State, Press, and Gender in the Hamidian Era" (Ph.D. diss., Princeton University, 1996); and Selçuk Akşin Somel, *The Modernization of Public Education in the Ottoman Empire, 1839–1908: Islamization, Autocracy and Discipline* (Leiden: Brill, 2001).

100. "Obshtestvenoto obrazovanie," *Makedoniya*, May 20, 1867; and "Uchilishtniya vupros," *Makedoniya*, November 11, 1867.

101. "Zhenata: Vazhnostta i v krugut na obshtestvoto i neynoto vuzpitanie v Bulgaria," *Makedoniya*, July 26, 1869.

102. "Raboti za predstaviteli," *Makedoniya*, July 31, 1870.

103. "V zashtita na zhenite," *Makedoniya*, November 9, 1871.

104. "Za obrazovanieto na zhenskiya pol," *Pravo*, December 20, 1869, and March 28 to April 27, 1870; "Za obrazovanieto na detsata," *Pravo*, July 20, 1870; "Za obrazovanieto na zhenata," *Pravo*, March 6, 1872. The byline for this series of articles was "Maria R." The historian Manyo Stoyanov attributed this series of articles to Martha Jane Riggs. I have been unable to substantiate this claim, but the content of the series is certainly consistent with the ideas she expressed in *Letters to Mothers*.

105. *Pravo*, September 11, 1872.

106. For the term "subject position," see Mrinalini Sinha, "Mapping the Imperial Social Formation: A Modest Proposal for Feminist History," *Signs: Journal of Women in Culture and Society* 25, no. 4 (2000): 623–44.

4. Unconventional Couples—Gender, Race, and Power in Mission Politics

1. Esther Maltbie to N. G. Clark, January 3, 1877, ABC:16.9.6, item 238, Papers of the American Board of Commissioners for Foreign Missions, Houghton Library, Harvard University (hereafter cited as ABCFM).

2. J. A. Tonjoroff to "Dear Brother in Christ" [N. G. Clark], July 3, 1877, ABC:16.9.6, item 415, ABCFM.

3. Ann Laura Stoler, "Sexual Affronts and Racial Frontiers: European Identities and the Cultural Politics of Exclusion in Colonial Southeast Asia," in *Tensions of Empire: Colonial Cultures in a Bourgeois World,* ed. Frederick Cooper and Ann Laura Stoler (Berkeley: University of California Press, 1997), 198–237.

4. Reginald Horsman, *Race and Manifest Destiny: The Origins of American Racial Anglo-Saxonism* (Cambridge, Mass.: Harvard University Press, 1981); Paul A. Kramer, "Empires, Exceptions, and Anglo-Saxons: Race and Rule between the British and United States Empires, 1880–1910," *Journal of American History* 88, no. 4 (2002): 1315–53.

5. Stoler, "Sexual Affronts and Racial Frontiers."

6. Peggy Pascoe, *What Comes Naturally: Miscegenation Law and the Making of Race in America* (New York: Oxford University Press, 2010).

7. On the whiteness spectrum, see Matthew Frye Jacobson, *Whiteness of a Different Color: European Immigrants and the Alchemy of Race* (Cambridge: Harvard University Press, 1998), 41–43.

8. On "not quite/not white," see Homi Bhabha, "Of Mimicry and Man: The Ambivalence of Colonial Discourse," in Cooper and Stoler, *Tensions of Empire,* 152–60.

9. For the repercussions for an American woman missionary who adopted Chinese children and invited the foreign into her home, see Connie Shemo, " 'So Thoroughly American': Gertrude Howe, Kang Cheng, and Cultural Imperialism in the Woman's Foreign Missionary Society, 1872–1931," in *Competing Kingdoms: Women, Mission, Nation, and the American Protestant Empire, 1812–1960,* ed. Barbara Reeves-Ellington, Kathryn Kish Sklar, and Connie Shemo (Durham, N.C.: Duke University Press, 2010), 117–40. Intermarriage in missions is an unexplored theme, but one that raises many questions, as an extended exchange on the e-mail discussion group of the Yale-Edinburgh Mission Group (www.library.yale.edu/div/yale_edinburgh/) between 2009 and 2011 confirmed.

10. *European Turkey Missions: Information with Regard to the Protestant Missions in Bulgaria, Aided by the "Turkish Missions' Aid Society"* (London: W. J. Johnson, n.d.), 8.

11. Patricia R. Hill, *The World Their Household: The American Woman's Foreign Mission Movement and Cultural Transformation, 1870–1920* (Ann Arbor: University of Michigan Press, 1985).

12. Capsule summaries of Maltbie's and Mumford's missionary service may be found in the Vinton Books, vol. 3: The Near East (Armenia, Persia, Syria, and Turkey), bound typescript, Congregational Library, Congregational Christian Historical Society, Boston, available at www.archive.org/details/vintonbookarmeni03vint.

13. For the experiences of women at Oberlin before the Civil War, see Carol Lasser, "How Did Oberlin Women Students Draw on Their College Experience to Participate in Antebellum

Social Movements, 1831–1861? (2002), on the *Women and Social Movements in the United States, 1600–2000* website, http://womhist.alexanderstreet.com/oberlin/intro.htm.

14. The Vinton Books, vol. 3. For the suggestion that missionaries who worked among freedmen in the southern states of the United States after the Civil War were more likely to develop liberal attitudes toward race, see Heather Sharkey, "American Presbyterians, Freedmen's Missions, and the Nile Valley: Missionary History, Racial Orders, and Church Politics on the World Stage," *Journal of Religious History* 35, no. 1 (2011): 24–42.

15. Mrs. Asa Mahan, *The Bulgarian Faith Mission* (London: Morgan & Scott, n.d.; an article reprinted from *The Christian*).

16. James Clarke to N. G. Clark, August 31, 1868, ABC:16.9.4, item 170, ABCFM.

17. Margaret Haskell to N. G. Clark, September 4, 1868, ABC:16.9.4, item 231, ABCFM.

18. William Locke to N. G. Clark, March 5, 1873, ABC:16.9.6, item 108, ABCFM.

19. Esther Maltbie and Anna Mumford to N. G. Clark, April 18, 1873, ABC:16.9.6, item 226; and Maltbie and Mumford to Clark, July 29, 1873, ABC:16.9.6, item 227, ABCFM.

20. Clark to Maltbie and Mumford, November 24, 1873, ABC:2.1 (microfilm reel 25), item 197, ABCFM.

21. On Finney and Christian Perfection, see Charles E. Hambrick-Stowe, *Charles G. Finney and the Sprit of American Evangelicalism* (Grand Rapids, Mich.: William B. Eerdmans, 1996); and Keith J Hardman, *Charles Grandison Finney, 1792–1875: Revivalist and Reformer* (Syracuse: Syracuse University Press, 1987).

22. William Locke to N. G. Clark, June 21, 1873, ABC:16.9.6, item 112, ABCFM.

23. James Clarke to N. G. Clark, March 24, 1874, ABC:16.9.6, item 292, ABCFM.

24. Minnie Beach to N. G. Clark, March 7, 1874, ABC:16.9.5, item 239, ABCFM.

25. James Clarke to N. G. Clark, March 24, 1874.

26. Anna Mumford to N. G. Clark, April 12, 1874, ABC:16.9.6, item 335, ABCFM.

27. Ibid.

28. *Life and Light for Heathen Women*, September 1871, 134; December 1871, 184; March 1872, 231.

29. Minutes of the fourth annual general meeting of the European Turkey Mission, June 18, 1874, ABC:16.9.5, item 24, ABCFM.

30. Historians have explored the tensions between mission wives and single women. See, for example, Elizabeth E. Prevost, *The Communion of Women: Missions and Gender in Colonial Africa and the British Metropole* (New York: Oxford University Press, 2010).

31. Anna Mumford to N. G. Clark, April 8, 1876, ABC:16.9.6, item 339, ABCFM.

32. Ellen Stone, Report of the Girls' Boarding School at Samokov, April 17, 1879, ABC:16.9.6, item 406, ABCFM.

33. "European Turkey. Extracts from Miss Maltbie's Letters," *Life and Light for Woman*, September 1876, 280–83.

34. N. G. Clark to Esther Maltbie, June 28, 1876, and N. G. Clark to William Locke, July 10, 1876, ABC:2.1 (microfilm reel 27), items 589 and 657, ABCFM.

35. Clark to Maltbie and Mumford, August 12, 1876, ABC:16.9.6, item 235, ABCFM.

36. Clark to Maltbie, December 28, 1876, and February 20, 1877, ABC:2.1 (microfilm reel 28), ABCFM.

37. Edward Jenney to N. G. Clark, November 1876, ABC:16.9.6, item 51, ABCFM. Although

such attitudes differed among missionaries through time and space, gender was at the heart of many mission battles. As late as the 1950s, single women missionaries in a German mission in South Africa experienced similar efforts by male missionaries to control their work, relationships, and movement. See Lize Kriel, "A Space Too Vast and Silent? German Deaconesses and the Patriarchy of the Berlin Mission in Apartheid Transvaal," *Comparativ* 17, no. 5/6 (2007): 55–75.

38. William Locke to N. G. Clark, February 1, 1877, ABC:16.9.6, item 150, ABCFM.
39. Lewis Bond to N. G. Clark, October 21, 1876, ABC:16.9.6, item 91, ABCFM.
40. N. G. Clark to Esther Maltbie, December 28, 1876, ABC:2.1 (microfilm reel 28), item 223, ABCFM.
41. Locke to Clark, April 8, 1876; Jenney to Clark, November 1876 and March 1, 1877; J. W. Baird to Clark, January 10, 1877, March 26, 1877, June 25, 1877, ABC:16.9.6, items 51, 53, 138, 139, 141, 142, ABCFM.
42. Mumford, "the pastor," and "a Bible woman" had apparently been assaulted while traveling between Samokov and Bansko. See *European Turkey Missions,* 8.
43. Maltbie to Clark, January 3, 1877, ABC:16.9.6, item 238, ABCFM.
44. Mumford to Clark, March 12, 1877, ABC:16.9.6, item 343, ABCFM.
45. Mumford to Clark, July 10, 1877, ABC:16.9.6, item 344, ABCFM.
46. Records of meetings, box 2, vol. 6, Locke Family Papers, Archives and Special Collections, Mount Holyoke College, South Hadley, Mass. (hereafter cited as MHC).
47. Julietta Velitchkova Borin, "Les projets d'éducation bulgares au XIXe siècle: Affirmation nationale et transferts culturels" (Ph.D. diss., École des Hautes Études en Sciences Sociales, 1998); Pierre Voillery, "La renaissance bulgare et l'occident: La France et les Bulgares, 1762–1856" (Ph.D. diss., École des Hautes Études en Sciences Sociales, 1980).
48. Minnie Beach to N. G. Clark, March 7, 1874, ABC:16.9.5, item 239, ABCFM.
49. Maltbie to Clark, January 3, 1877, ABC:16.9.6, item 238, ABCFM.
50. Mumford to Clark, July 10, 1877, ABC:16.9.6, item 344, ABCFM.
51. Clark to Mumford, January 4, 1877, ABC:2.1 (microfilm reel 28), item 298, ABCFM; Mumford to Clark, July 10, 1877.
52. On the significance of the ancient Greek and Roman worlds in the early American Republic and the antebellum era, see Caroline Winterer, *The Culture of Classicism: Ancient Greece and Rome in American Intellectual Life, 1780–1910* (Baltimore: Johns Hopkins University Press, 2002); and Caroline Winterer, *The Mirror of Antiquity: American Women and the Classical Tradition, 1750–1900* (Ithaca: Cornell University Press, 2007).
53. "Constantinople: Extracts from the Journal of Mr. Dwight, in Roomelia," *Missionary Herald,* February 1835, 169–72; "Constantinople. Journal of Messrs. Dwight and Schauffler during a Tour in Macedonia and Thrace," *Missionary Herald,* July 1836, 245–49, and August 1836, 284–88.
54. William Jenks, *The Explanatory Bible Atlas and Scripture Gazetteer* (Boston: Charles Hickling, 1847), 93; Sylvester Bliss, *Analysis of Geography,* 4th ed. (Boston: John P. Jewett, 1850), 4.
55. *Missionary Manual: A Sketch of the History and Present State of Christian Missions to the Heathen* (Philadelphia: American Sunday School Union, 1834), 21.

56. Albert Long to John P. Durbin, December 8, 1857, Missionary Files (microfilm edition), United Methodist Church Archives–GCAH, Madison, N.J. (hereafter cited as UMCA-GCAH).

57. "Letter from Mr. Hamlin, May 18, 1857," Missionary Herald, September 1857, 293–99, quotation on 298.

58. "European Turkey as a Field of Christian Missions," Missionary Herald, October 1858, 322–34.

59. Wesley Prettyman to John Durbin, July 2, 1863, and Albert Long to John Durbin, April 27, 1863, Missionary Files (microfilm edition), UMCA-GCAH.

60. Annual report from Edirne, 1861, ABC:16.9.4, item 6, ABCFM.

61. Henry Haskell to N. G. Clark, January 8, 1869, ABC:16.9.4, item 233, ABCFM. The letter does not list the converts, but their names can be gathered from other sources.

62. Annual report from Plovdiv, 1868, ABC:16.9.4, item 33, ABCFM.

63. For a study of naming practices and job titles in a British mission in India, see Rhonda Semple, "Ruth, Miss Mackintosh, and Ada and Rose Marris: Biblewomen, Zenana Workers and Missionaries in Nineteenth-Century British Missions to North India," Women's History Review 17, no. 4 (2008): 561–74.

64. A facsimile is included in James F. Clarke, The Pen and the Sword: Studies in Bulgarian History, ed. Dennis P. Hupchick (Boulder, Colo.: East European Monographs, 1988), 536.

65. Lewis Bond to N. G. Clark, August 12, 1871, ABC:16.9.4, item 118, ABCFM.

66. Annual report from Stara Zagora, April 1860, ABC:16.9.4, item 14, ABCFM.

67. An unusual exception is the Woman's Board of Missions annual report for 1889, which lists the names of seven of the eight Bible women working in the European Turkey Mission: Gana Yankova, Tsanka Mehova, Minka Stoeva, Mareeka Raikova, Evanka Abrakova, Haloo Georgeva, and Katerinka Toddova.

68. Boris Kozhukharov, Purvata evangelska tsurkva v Bulgaria: Deynostta na amerikanskite misioneri (Sofia: Nov chovek, 1998); Khristo Kulichev, Vestiteli na istinata: Istoriya na evangelskite tsurkvi v Bulgaria (Sofia: Bulgarsko bibleysko obshtestvo, 1994).

69. Annual estimates of the European Turkey Mission, 1879, ABC:16.9.5, item 33, ABCFM.

70. For a discussion of the difficulties of comparing currencies and income distributions among Bulgarians in the 1860s and 1870s, see Thomas A. Meininger, The Formation of a Nationalist Bulgarian Intelligentsia, 1835–1878 (New York: Garland, 1987), 431–38.

71. Khadzhi Gospodin Slavov, letters of July 27, 1871, and August 16, 1872, IIA1784 and IIA1750, Bulgarian Historical Archive, National Library, Sofia.

72. Brian Stanley, The World Missionary Conference, Edinburgh 1910 (Grand Rapids, Mich.: William B. Eerdmans, 2009), 137.

73. J. A. Tonjoroff to "Dear Brother in Christ" [N. G. Clark], July 3, 1877.

74. Paul William Harris, Nothing but Christ: Rufus Anderson and the Ideology of Protestant Foreign Missions (New York: Oxford University Press, 1999), 113–114.

75. Stanley, World Missionary Conference, 91.

76. First Annual Meeting of the Mission to European Turkey, June 30, 1871, ABC:16.9.4, item 3, ABCFM.

77. Minutes of the Ninth Annual Meeting, April 26, 1880, ABC:16.9.5, item 28, ABCFM.

78. "Central Turkey Mission," *Missionary Herald,* August 1873, 248.

79. Edward W. Said, *Orientalism* (New York: Pantheon, 1978); Mrinalini Sinha, *Colonial Masculinity: The 'Manly Englishman" and the "Effeminate Bengali" in the Late Nineteenth Century* (Manchester: Manchester University Press, 1995).

80. William Locke to N. G. Clark, October 1, 1878, ABC:16.9.6, item 180, ABCFM.

81. Ellen Stone to N. G. Clark, January 26, 1888, ABC:16.9.9, item 411, ABCFM.

82. Kozhukharov, *Purvata evangelska tsurkva,* 53; Kulichev, *Vestiteli,* 146.

83. John House to N. G. Clark, June 9, 1877, ABC:16.9.6, item 28, ABCFM.

84. J. A. Tonjoroff to "Dear Brother in Christ" [N. G. Clark], July 3, 1877.

85. WBMI Ohio branch Jubilee year pamphlet, 1911, ABC Individual Biographies, box 39:40, Maltbie, Esther Tappan, ABCFM.

86. Mrs. Mumford, "Report for Two Years, from July, 1877, to July, 1879," in Mahan, *Bulgarian Faith Mission,* 1–14, quotation on 13.

87. Theodore Byington to N. G. Clark, May 15, 1897, ABC:16.9.5, item 272, ABCFM.

88. Kozhukharov, *Purvata evangelska tsurkva,* 23.

89. Diary of Zoe Noyes Locke, entry for August 26, 1890, Locke Family Papers, MHC; Mahan, *The Bulgarian Faith Mission.*

90. *The Christian,* March 23, 1882, 11; *The Missionary Review of the World,* July 1882, 263.

91. Personal communication (e-mail) from Rob Bevan, great-grandson of Elizabeth Bevan, January 21, 2010.

92. Frances Anne Budge, *Isaac Sharpe, an Apostle of the Nineteenth Century* (London: Headley Bros., 1898), 184.

93. The quotation is from the diary of Zoe Noyes Locke, entry for August 25, 1890, Locke Family Papers, MHC.

5. The Constantinople Home

1. "The Working Plan for the Constantinople Home as modified by the Com. of the Woman's Board," May 10, 1875, ABC:16.7.1 (microfilm reel 533), Papers of the American Board of Commissioners for Foreign Missions, Houghton Library, Harvard University (hereafter cited as ABCFM).

2. On settlement houses, see Kathryn Kish Sklar, "Hull House in the 1890s: A Community of Women Reformers," *Signs: Journal of Women in Culture and Society* 10, no. 4 (1985): 658–77.

3. For a study of the American College for Girls that uses a postcolonial feminist approach to analyze the rhetoric of the female faculty, see Carolyn Goffman, "Masking the Mission: Cultural Conversion at the American College for Girls," in *Altruism and Imperialism: Western Cultural and Religious Missions in the Middle East,* ed. Eleanor H. Tejirian and Reeva Spector Simon (New York: Middle East Institute, Columbia University, 2002), 88–109; Goffman, "From Religious to American Proselytism: Mary Mills Patrick and the 'Sanctification of the Intellect,'" in *American Missionaries and the Middle East: Foundational Encounters,* ed. Mehmet Ali Doğan and Heather J. Sharkey (Salt Lake City: University of Utah Press, 2011), 84–121; and Goffman, "'More Than the Conversion of

Souls': Rhetoric and Ideology at the American College for Girls in Istanbul, 1871–1923" (Ph.D. diss., Ball State University, 2002), 88–119. At the center of Goffman's analysis are three "rhetorical moments" of Mary Mills Patrick, showing her evolution "from evangelist to secularist." My focus is on the language of domesticity and the gendered tensions within the mission.

4. Patricia R. Hill, *The World Their Household: The American Woman's Foreign Mission Movement and Cultural Transformation, 1870–1920* (Ann Arbor: University of Michigan Press, 1985); Dana Robert, *American Women in Mission: A Social History of Their Thought and Practice* (Macon, Ga.: Mercer University Press, 1997).

5. For an example of this effect see Noriko Kawamura Ishii, *American Women Missionaries at Kobe College, 1873–1909* (New York: Routledge, 2004).

6. For a study of feminist internationalism that does not include religious groups, see Leila J. Rupp, *Worlds of Women: The Making of an International Women's Movement* (Princeton: Princeton University Press, 1997).

7. For a general overview of these changes, see M. Şükrü Hanioğlu, *A Brief History of the Late Ottoman Empire* (Princeton: Princeton University Press, 2008), 72–149. On consumption patterns, see Haris Exertzoglou, "The Cultural Uses of Consumption: Negotiating Class, Gender, and Nation in the Ottoman Urban Centers during the 19th Century," *International Journal of Middle East Studies* 35 (2003): 77–101; and Donald Quataert, ed., *Consumption Studies and the History of the Ottoman Empire, 1550–1922* (Albany: State University of New York Press, 2000).

8. Edhem Eldem, "Istanbul: From Imperial to Peripheralized Capital," in *The Ottoman City between East and West: Aleppo, Izmir, and Istanbul,* ed. Edhem Eldem, Daniel Goffman, and Bruce Masters (Cambridge: Cambridge University Press, 1999), 135–206, quotation on 205.

9. On the Public Education Law of 1869 see chapter 3, note 99.

10. On Anderson's closing of mission girls' schools in India and Ceylon at this time, see Robert, *American Women in Mission,* 116–24.

11. "To Christian Women, in Behalf of Their Sex in Heathen Lands," *Missionary Herald* April 1868, 39.

12. *Life and Light for Heathen Women* (hereafter cited as *Life and Light*), March 1869, 7, 8. The name of this publication changed in 1873 to *Life and Light for Woman.*

13. *Life and Light,* September 1869, 94.

14. Mrs. N. G. Clark, "The Home at Constantinople," *Life and Light,* December 1871, 156–59, quotations on 157.

15. N. G. Clark to Ira Pettibone, April 23, 1869, ABC:16.7.1 (microfilm reel 533), ABCFM.

16. Quoted in George Washburn, *Fifty Years in Constantinople and Recollections of Robert College* (Boston: Houghton Mifflin, 1911), 31.

17. N. G. Clark to Julia Rappleye and Mary Wadsworth, April 23, 1872, ABC:2.1 (microfilm reel 27), ABCFM.

18. N. G. Clark to Ira Pettibone, July 26, 1872, ABC:16.7.1 (microfilm reel 533), ABCFM.

19. N. G. Clark to George Wood, January 7, 1874, ABC:16.7.1 (microfilm reel 533), ABCFM.

20. N. G. Clark to Kate Pond Williams, April 21, 1876, ABC:2.1 (microfilm reel 27), ABCFM.

21. N. G. Clark to E. E. Bliss, February 16, 1880, ABC:16.7.1 (microfilm reel 533), ABCFM.

22. All quotations and material summarized in this and the following three paragraphs are from "The Constantinople Home," *Life and Light*, December 1872, 350.

23. "The Constantinople Home," *Life and Light*, April 1873, 105–6; "The Constantinople Home," *Life and Light*, July 1873, 196–988; "Turkey. The Constantinople Home. Letter from Miss Rappleye," *Life and Light*, December 1873, 353–55, quotations on 354; "Letter from Mrs. Bliss," *Life and Light*, December 1873, 355–57.

24. "The Constantinople Home," *Life and Light*, September 1874, 268–70, quotation on 269.

25. Eliza Anderson, Pauline Durant, Helen Gulliver, and Abigail Treat to Prudential Committee, May 10, 1875, Woman's Board of Missions, ABC:16.7.1 (microfilm reel 533), ABCFM.

26. Ibid.

27. Mary Mills Patrick, *A Bosporus Adventure: Istanbul (Constantinople) Woman's College, 1871–1924* (Stanford: Stanford University Press, 1934), 88.

28. "The Constantinople Home," *Life and Light*, March 1877, 68–69, and October 1877, 298–99.

29. "Constantinople Woman's College" (manuscript), ACG 5-5, MS, 23, American College for Girls Records (hereafter cited as ACG plus the item number), housed at the Executive Offices of Robert College, New York City. The archives have since been rehoused and recatalogued at Columbia University.

30. Mary Mills Patrick to Caroline Borden, October 4, 1889, ABC:16.7.1 (microfilm reel 533), ABCFM.

31. Albert Long and Henry Dwight to Abbie Child, September 13, 1889. ABC:16.7.1 (microfilm reel 533), ABCFM.

32. Carrie [Caroline] Borden, *Constantinople Home* (Boston: Frank Wood, Printer, 1890).

33. American College for Girls, *Act of Incorporation and Constitution and By-Laws* (Boston: Frank Wood, 1890).

34. American College for Girls, *Calendar, 1889–1890* (London: Sir Joseph Causton & Sons, 1890), 15.

35. Selim Deringil, "The Invention of Tradition as Public Image in the Late Ottoman Empire, 1808–1908," *Comparative Studies in Society and History* 35, no. 1 (1993): 3–29.

36. Halide Edib, *Memoirs of Halide Edib* (New York: Century, 1928), 148–49, 189–206.

37. Caroline Borden to George Plympton, November 6, 1909, ACG 8-62.

38. Meeting of the Corporation of the American College for Girls, Boston, April 30, 1891, ABC:16.7.1 (microfilm reel 533), ABCFM. The members of the corporation discussed a draft of Judson Smith's subsequent letter to Dwight.

39. Judson Smith to H. O. Dwight, May 1, 1891, ABC:2.1 (microfilm reel 62), ABCFM.

40. Meeting of the Corporation of the American College for Girls, Boston, April 30, 1891, ABC:16.7.1 (microfilm reel 533), ABCFM.

41. Faculty of the American College for Girls to the Trustees of the American College for Girls, March 12, 1892. ABC:16.7.1 (microfilm reel 533), ABCFM.

42. Mary Mills Patrick to Caroline Borden, May 26 and 31, 1892, ACG 5.

43. Henry Barnum, W. W. Peet, and Ira Pettibone to Caroline Borden, September 5, 1892, ABC:16.7.1 (microfilm reel 533), ABCFM.

44. A. C. Thompson to Abbie Child, March 2, 1893, ACG 2.

45. Abbie Child to Ira Pettibone, March 31, 1893, and Meeting of the Trustees, March 27, 1893, both ABC:16.7.1 (microfilm reel 533), ABCFM.

46. Mary Mills Patrick to Abbie Child, October 20, 1892; Patrick to the Trustees of the American College for Girls, June 27, 1893, ACG 2-6.

47. Caroline Borden to "The President and the Corporation," July 25, 1893. ACG 2-3.

48. For example, Isabel Dodd to Abbie Child, January 6, 1894, ACG 2-5; Carrie Borden, "The American College for Girls in Constantinople," *Life and Light,* November 1894, 507–11; Gwen Griffiths, "Turkey. The Religious Work of the American College for Girls at Constantinople," *Life and Light,* July 1901, 296–301; quotation in Griffiths, 301.

49. Patrick, *A Bosporus Adventure,* 89.

50. Manuscript, ACG 5-5, p. 16.

51. W. W. Peet to Abbie Child, April 5, 1895. ACG 2-5.

52. Patrick, *Under Five Sultans,* 185. The subject of the Armenian massacres remains a controversial one. See Jeremy Salt, *Imperialism, Evangelism, and the Ottoman Armenians, 1878–1896* (London: Frank Cass, 1993); and Taner Akcam, *A Shameful Act: The Armenian Genocide and the Question of Turkish Responsibility* (New York: Metropolitan Books, 2006).

53. "Appropriations for 1901," *Annual Report of the Woman's Board of Missions, 1900* (Boston: G. C. Rand & Avery, 1901), 176.

54. Mary Mills Patrick to Harriet Stanwood, April 2, 1896, ACG 2-8.

55. Henry Barnum to Judson Smith, January 27, 1899, ACG 2-11.

56. Mary Mills Patrick to Abbie Child, May 5, 1899, ACG 2-11.

57. "Items in the life of Mary Mills Patrick, Ph.D., President of the American College for Girls at Constantinople," undated manuscript, ACG 8-68.

58. See, for example, Emma Paddock Telford, "The American College for Girls at Constantinople," *New England Magazine,* March 1898, 10–20; "Girls' College in Turkey: It Is in Constantinople and the Only One in the Orient," *New York Times,* March 12, 1899; Mary Mills Patrick, "The American College for Women at Constantinople," *Leslie's Weekly,* January 16, 1902.

59. *Report of the Centenary Conference on the Protestant Missions of the World,* vol. 2 (London: James Nisbet, 1889), 185–92, 160–67.

60. *Ecumenical Missionary Conference, New York, 1900,* vol. 1 (New York: American Tract Society, 1990), 455.

61. Mary Mills Patrick to Harriet Stanwood, October 20, 1899, ACG 2-11.

62. C. O. Tracy to Harriet Stanwood, April 16, 1901, ACG 2-13; W. W. Peet to Stanwood, November 18, 1901, ACG 2-13.

63. See president's annual reports, ACG 19-8 to 19-11. Other major donors included Mrs. Henry Durant, Mrs. Henry Villard, Mrs. William E. Dodge, Miss Grace Dodge, Miss Helen Gould, Miss Elizabeth Houghton, and John Converse.

64. Caroline Borden, untitled handwritten manuscript of notes for a history of the college from 1875 to 1906, n.p. The two quotations in the following paragraph are also from this document, ACG 8-62 and 8-68.

65. On this, see Emily Clark, *Masterless Mistresses: The New Orleans Ursulines and the Development of a New World Society, 1727–1834* (Chapel Hill: University of North Carolina Press, 2007).

66. Patrick, *Under Five Sultans*, 234–35.

67. Patrick, *A Bosporus Adventure*, 133.

68. *Constantinople College for Women: A Fortress of Americanism in This Oriental City* (New York: Constantinople College, 1919), ACG 33.

Conclusion

1. "Letter from Mrs. Dwight to Mrs. H.," *The Mother's Magazine*, January 1836, 15.

2. "Pisma za mayki, vtoro pismo: Nuzhnite na maykite preimushtestva," *Zornitsa*, February 1864, 13–14.

3. Esther Maltbie to N. G. Clark, January 3, 1877, ABC:16.9.6, item 238, Papers of the American Board of Commissioners for Foreign Missions, Houghton Library, Harvard University (hereafter cited as ABCFM); "The Working Plan for the Constantinople Home as modified by the Com. of the Woman's Board," May 10, 1875, ABC:16.7.1 (microfilm reel 533), ABCFM.

4. Woman's Board to Prudential Committee, May 10, 1875, ABC:16.7.1 (microfilm reel 533), ABCFM.

5. Mary Mills Patrick, *A Bosporus Adventure: Istanbul (Constantinople) Woman's College, 1871–1924* (Stanford: Stanford University Press, 1934), 120.

Index

Abbott, John, 85
Abdülaziz, Sultan, 100
Abdülhamid II, Sultan, 142, 154
Abrakova, Evanka, 198n67
advice manuals, 31
Albania, xvi
American Board of Commissioners for Foreign
    Missions, 1–2, 7–9; absorption of the
    Woman's Board of Missions by, 173;
    appointments of single women missionar-
    ies by, 48, 111–15; archives of, 7; childbirth
    policies of, 25–26; conflict over Mumford
    in, 136–37; contested versions of the Chris-
    tian home of, 26–38, 48–49; expanded
    educational program of, 151–52; place
    names used by, xv–xvi; policies on mis-
    sionary homes of, 19–28, 48–49, 179n17;
    publishing projects of, 80; screening of
    missionary candidates by, 38–40. See also
    mission work
American College for Girls in Constantinople,
    15–16, 137, 151–58, 173; corporate
    board of, 152–53, 157, 163; educational
    program of, 151–52, 159, 163–64;
    evangelizing activities of, 154–57, 164;
    feminist internationalism in, 153–55,
    158–65, 173; financial patrons of,
    159–64; independence of, 141–42,
    158–64, 173; male advisory board of,

152–53, 156–58, 162, 164; students at,
    153–54, 161, 164–65
Anderson, Eliza, 143
Anderson, Rufus, 8; on missionary wives,
    23–25, 27–28, 39, 48; mission school poli-
    cies of, 143; on self-supporting churches,
    133–35; on single women missionaries,
    111; travels of, 180n22, 225
Antim I, Exarch of Bulgaria, 106
Aprilov, Vassil, 185n29
Armenian population, 81, 158–59, 189n11,
    202n52
Arms, Emily Meekins, 35, 39
Arms, William, 35
Asiatic Turkey, xv–xvi

Balkan Mission, xvi
the Balkans, 3–5; arrival of American mis-
    sionaries in, 8–9; emigration to the U.S.
    from, 123–24; nationalist movements in,
    3, 4–5, 10–11, 51–57, 99–100, 166–67;
    political reform in, 4, 52–57, 100–101,
    167, 175n5; publishing in, 80; as term,
    xvi; wars against the Ottomans in, 53–54,
    124. See also Bulgaria/Bulgarians
Ball, Jasper, 35
Bansko (Bulgaria), 72, 74–75, 134
Beach, Minnie, 118
Beecher, Catharine, 18, 21–22, 114

Bevan, Elizabeth Tonjoroff. See Tonjoroff, Elizabeth

Bible translation, 56–57, 68, 79, 81f, 129–30, 170, 185n20

Bible women, 43, 71–76, 130–33, 147, 170; exclusion from mission affairs of, 133; Gencheva's work as, 73–75; reporting of names of, 128–29, 198n67; salaries of, 132; supervision of, 119, 122

Bliss, Annie, 150

Blunt, John, 66, 187n71

Bluskov, Iliya, 83

boarding schools, 33–34, 49, 116, 181n47

Bond, Fannie, 38, 41–47, 49, 130, 168

Bond, Lewis, 45f, 130; preaching on perfectionism by, 117–18; support of Mumford and Maltbie by, 122–23, 125; support of wife by, 43–44, 49, 168

Borden, Caroline, 152, 154, 157–65, 173

Bowker, Sarah Lamson, 144

Boyadjieff, Nikola, 128, 134

Boycheva, Tonka, 96, 102–3

Brainerd, David, 20

Brewer, David, 163

Britain: imperial power of, 5; involvement in mission affairs of, 51, 66, 68

British and Foreign Bible Society, 68

Bulgaria/Bulgarians, xvi, 7–12; conversions to Protestantism in, 11, 12, 14, 63–70, 127–33, 135; education of girls in, 52, 57–64, 78–79, 95–96, 170; emigration to the U.S. of, 123–24; first Protestant church in, 72–75; folk tales of, 88–89; Greek assimilation efforts of, 55–56, 100; independence from Ottoman rule of, 74–75, 136, 142, 171; independence of Orthodox church of, 72, 105, 106; literacy in, 74, 77, 79, 95, 106; nation-building efforts of, 4–5, 10–11, 14–15, 51–57, 69–70, 99–100, 104–7, 166–67, 170–72; participation in mission work by, 12–13; Protestant millet in, 53–57; Protestant racial ranking of, 126–28; rearticulations of domesticity in, 94–103, 170–71; revolutionary movement in, 69, 99–100, 120–21, 124, 170, 171, 187n71; urban middle-class culture in, 56, 58, 81–82,

94–95, 127–28, 132, 142, 170–71, 184n18, 195n29; women's associations in, 94–103. See also names of specific towns

Bulgarian Bible, 56–57, 68, 79, 81f, 129–30, 170, 185n20

Bulgarian Evangelical Association, 134

Bulgarian Secret Central Committee, 69, 187n71

Bulgarian transliteration, xvi

Bulgarski knizhitsi journal, 86

Bushnell, Horace, 88

Byington, Margaret Hallock, 39, 42f, 57, 60–64, 96

Byington, Theodore, 57, 65, 80, 130, 169–70; mission school of, 60–64, 96; on single female missionaries, 137

Byzantine Greeks, xvi

Calvinism, 21

Carruth, Ellen, 152

Catholic Church, 55, 62

Centenary Mission Conference, 160

Chalakov, Atanas Mikhaylov, 106

Chalakova, Baba Gena, 106

Child, Abbie, 152, 160

children: Christian nurture and maternal associations for, 30–31, 43; contamination by outside influences of, 29, 32–33; conversion of, 21–22, 29; deaths during childbirth of, 25–26. See also education

Chirpanlieva, Petrana, 64–65, 67

Chopin, Mary, 39

Christian home, 17–49, 61, 167–68, 170–71; Christian nurture in, 31; ideal construct of family in, 20; as models of social change, 23–24; New England visions of, 18–19, 48–49; racial purity in, 110; women's roles in, 20–23, 38, 49, 167–68. See also domesticity

Christian missionary home, 47–48, 167–68; American Board's policies on, 19–26, 48–49, 179n17; childbearing in, 25–26, 44; contamination by outside influences of, 29, 32–33; female moral authority in, 47–49; gender equality in, 41–44, 49; Hawaiian experiences of, 23; hosting and boarding obligations of, 34–35, 108, 115,

118; male absences from, 36–37; porous borders of, 26–38, 49, 181n44, 181n47; schools and educational programs in, 32–34, 168, 181n47; servants in, 42; spousal death and remarriage in, 35–37; supports for wives in, 27–32, 88. See also male missionaries; single female missionaries

Christian nurture, 30–31, 43

Christian Perfection, 117–18

civilizing mission of women. See domesticity

Civil War, 112–13, 114, 168, 196n14

Clark, Elizabeth, 73, 130, 144–45

Clark, Nathaniel G., 1, 73, 108–9, 128; on appointment of single women missionaries, 111, 125; on autonomy of single women missionaries, 117–21; on the Constantinople Home, 143–46, 160; on domestic arrangements of single women missionaries, 116–17; on Ivan Tonjoroff, 134–35

Clarke, Isabella, 36, 37f, 38, 46, 120

Clarke, James, 37f, 115, 121–22, 128

class, 15

Cleopatra, 92

colonial society. See imperialism

colporteurs, 84

commercial intervention, 15–16

Constantine the Great, 93

Constantinople, 3. See also Istanbul

Constantinople Home, 1–2, 68, 140–51, 163–65, 172–73; Borden's history of, 152; construction of, 148–50; educational program of, 145–48, 150–51; evangelizing activities of, 147, 148; female management of, 116, 144, 145, 148, 149, 164, 168; feminist internationalism in, 10, 15–16, 150–55, 177n24; funding and ownership of, 144–45, 148, 149; goals of, 140, 148–49; male missionary trustees of, 147–52, 168; opening of, 144–45; renaming of, 141, 151–53; student fees for, 146–47; students of, 150–51; teachers of, 150. See also American College for Girls in Constantinople

conversion/converts, 3–4, 10, 12, 75–77, 107; Bible women's work in, 71–76; coercion

in, 50–51, 55; domestic spheres of, 21–22, 29, 75–76; from Eastern Orthodoxy, 3–4, 51–52, 144; inferior social status in Protestantism of, 128–31, 133–35, 172; local contexts of, 51–57, 67; at mission schools, 63–72; mission wives' responsibilities for, 33, 34; of Muslims, 54, 144; national concerns over, 11, 14, 67–70, 96. See also Gencheva, Maria; native pastors

Cornelia (Roman matron), 92–93, 99

Crimean War, 8

cultural intervention. See domesticity; education

Saint Cyril, 101

damaskini (popular sermons), 89

Day, Moses, 39

Deringil, Selim, 11–12

Dinkova, Slavka, 191n41

domesticity, 1–16, 75–76, 170–71; appeal of, 3; Bulgarian rearticulations of, 94–103, 170–71; challenges to conventional hierarchies in, 16; educational programs on, 4; as frontier of cross-cultural encounters, 5–8, 12–13; link with nation-building of, 14–15, 104–7, 168; missionary uses of, 2–3, 8–9; New England visions of, 18–19, 48–49, 87–88; publications for Bulgarians on, 87–94; role of the Christian home in, 18–26, 179n17; in uncommon households, 15. See also Christian home; women

Doolittle, C. K., 137

Dushanova, Rakhil, 97

Dwight, Elizabeth, 28, 29–30, 36, 167

Dwight, Harrison, 26, 27, 56–57

Dwight, Henry, 126, 151–52, 154–55, 156

Eastern Orthodox Christians, 144; feast days of, 101; Greek patriarch of, 53–54, 55, 70; independent Bulgarian church of, 72, 105, 106; nationalist movements of, 3, 4–5, 51–57; New Englanders' views of, 126–27; Protestant mission of conversion of, 3–4, 51–52, 144; reforms of, 68; Uniate movement of, 62. See also Bulgaria/Bulgarians

Ecumenical Missionary Conference, 160–61